The Choices Program:

Cognitive-Behavioral Intervention
For Domestic Violence

William E. Adams, Ph.D.

For information about this book, please contact

William E. Adams, Ph.D.
1945 Palo Verde Avenue, Suite 204
Long Beach, CA 90815
(562) 799-1226
www.drwilliamadams.com or

Additional copies of this book can be purchased at
www.amazon.com

ISBN 13: 978-1535204521
ISBN 10: 1535204524

Printed in the United States of America

Introduction

The issue of partner abuse has always aroused ambivalence and controversy in American society. The ambivalence about partner abuse, and what to do about it, is evident in court decisions from the 19th century, which show great variance in their perception of domestic violence. In 1824, for example, the Supreme Court of Mississippi ruled that a husband had the traditional right to beat his wife with a rod no thicker than his thumb, and that the law allows a husband to use force *"to make the wife behave herself and know her place."* The North Carolina Supreme Court ruled in 1868 that, if the husband inflicted no permanent injury on the wife it was better to *"leave the parties to forget and forgive."*

In sharp contrast, the 1871 decision of the Supreme Court of Alabama stated, *"The privilege, ancient though it may be, to beat [one's wife] with a stick, to pull her hair, choke her, spit in her face or kick her about the floor ... is not now acknowledged by our law."* In 1881, Delaware courts began sentencing partner abusers to the whipping post. *"It is stiffly contended by Delaware magistrates,"* wrote an author of the era, *"that as a restraint over wife beaters and other cruel and vicious criminals, the whipping post is a distinct success and of marked benefit in its influence in the community (Earle, 1896, p. 84)."*

In many ways, partner abuse is as controversial and emotionally charged an issue in the 21st century as it was in the 19th. More has been asserted about partner violence than has ever been demonstrated. After thirty years of research, the interested clinician finds little consensus in the partner abuse literature about basic questions such as, "What are the rates of partner violence in America?" In nationally representative samples of 8,145 families, Straus (1990) reported that partner violence occurred in about 16% of the households in the year of the study, and that among those households severe abuse occurred about 3% of the time. However, incidence rates vary widely in the literature, depending upon the population studied and the way researchers operationally define and measure partner violence.

Related issues, such as the frequency and severity of female on male violence (Do women get violent too?), the efficacy of court-mandated counseling (Does it work?), and the wisdom of aggressive arrest policies (Do they really lower recidivism?) continue to spark heated polemics among academics and activists. Yet the literature provides little in the way of practical help for the mental health practitioner who wants to help his or her clients put an end to family violence.

The Choices Program is a small step toward addressing that problem. As the director of a program dedicated to domestic violence intervention, I have had many opportunities to speak to counselors about applied assessment and treatment strategies they use in their work. Those who attend my seminars expecting a lengthy review of the literature on partner abuse must have been disappointed, as that is not the purpose or focus of my presentations. On the other hand, the response from counselors looking for specific assessment and intervention strategies to apply in their practice has been overwhelmingly positive. While the ongoing research and political debates in the field are vitally important (I fear I have often bored my friends and colleagues to tears with unsolicited dissertations about new developments in the literature, and I apologize for that), this is a book in applied psychology. If you're wondering how to get your clients to stop hitting their partners, this book is for you.

The pages to come present skills and concepts developed over decades of work with men and women who endeavored to stop their abusive behavior and maintain violence-free relationships. It is my hope that you will find them helpful in your work with clients whose relationships have suffered the devastating effects of partner abuse.

Table of Contents

Assessment and Detection

The following vignette comes from a police report of a domestic violence incident. Carol was watching television with her boyfriend, Greg, when Carol's cell phone rang. Carol answered it. A soft woman's voice asked, "Is Greg there?" Carol passed the phone to a flustered Greg, who mumbled to the woman on the phone that he would have to call her back and hung up. Carol asked Greg why girls were calling him on her cell phone, and an argument ensued. The argument grew heated, and Carol told Greg to leave her apartment. Greg stood up and towered over Carol. "Bitch," shouted Greg, "say something so I can hit you!" When Carol told Greg to leave, he punched Carol in the face with his fist and stormed out of the apartment. When Greg arrived home, he called Carol and left a series of angry messages on her answering machine.

Eventually, Carol called the police and reported the incident. In a victim statement given to investigators, Carol said that she felt that Greg was wrong for what he did, but also told investigators what really bothered her about Greg's behavior. "It was OK when he hit me," Carol said, "but leaving the messages was what did it."

The point I want to make is this: a counselor must see domestic violence as a serious issue, because your clients often will not. In my practice, clients experiencing partner abuse rarely identify it as the problem that initially brought them to counseling, even when partner violence has reached high levels of frequency and severity. Clients typically see partner abuse as a relatively unimportant problem - a side issue of poor communication, substance abuse, depression, or stress. Counselors sometimes unwittingly collude with their client's perception that abusive behavior is unworthy of inclusion in the treatment plan by failing to assess for it.

Both counselors and their clients use the intake interview to get information. Counselors ask questions to get information about what matters to his or her clients. Clients listen to the questions asked to get information about what matters to the counselor. For example, responsible clinicians routinely assess for suicidal ideation and substance abuse. By proactively asking about these issues, we not only obtain information relevant to the care of our clients.

We also reveal to our clients that we perceive these problems as important treatment issues. While it may not be our intent to do so, failure to take the time to ask about partner abuse may convey to our clients that it's not important to us, and that it's not relevant to their care. The old saying, "If you want to know what matters to people, watch how they spend their time," applies to the intake interview. Clients watch how we spend our time in a session, and which issues seem to matter to us.

In an even worse scenario, the victim of abuse may be justifiably concerned about violent retaliation from the partner after the session, and afraid to volunteer information to the counselor about past assaults. The clinician who fails to assess for partner abuse, yet pushes clients to be open and honest during counseling sessions, unwittingly places clients who are victims of abuse in an untenable position and exposes them to the danger of further assaults. After all, the relative safety of the clinician's office ends when the session is over.

To illustrate my point, let me introduce you to Mary and Jim. At the intake interview, Jim was friendly, confident, and talkative. Mary was visibly anxious, said nothing unless spoken to, and avoided eye contact. The imbalance in power between Mary and Jim was obvious. When I asked to speak to Mary alone, her anxiety rose so quickly that I feared she would have a panic attack. After assuring both Mary and Jim that this was my standard intake protocol, Mary reluctantly agreed to talk with me privately.

Once in my private office, Mary's eyes darted from the door to the windows and back to the door. At her request I locked the door, assured her that her husband couldn't see through the windows, and that she was safe. In her anxiety, Mary started to stutter to the point that she couldn't speak and her hands shook visibly. In time, Mary calmed down enough to tell me that Jim beat her every day. She had once called the police, but he beat her severely the day he returned from jail, and threatened to kill her two children, who were from a prior marriage, if she ever called the police again. He also assured her that he would find her and kill her if she tried to leave him.

Mary had no family in the area and felt trapped. I asked Mary to talk with a representative of a woman's shelter on my office phone, but she refused, fearing that Jim would find out. I asked her to take a list of community resources for victims of partner abuse, but she refused, saying that Jim was sure to search her on the way home. Mary finally accepted the list of resources, but folded the page into a small square and hid it inside her clothing, much as a prisoner might hide contraband from a brutal guard. Never have I seen a woman so terrorized by her husband as Mary was of Jim.

As it turned out, Mary was a success story. She is living happily with her children in another state, free of Jim's threats and brutality. Suppose I had completed the intake interview without raising the question of partner abuse, or inquired about it in a way that Mary could not answer honestly. What might have happened to her and her children had I pushed her to reveal thoughts and feelings that angered Jim?

People like Jim and Mary walk into counselors' offices every day. We may never know the number of clients exposed to violence by counselors who fail to evaluate the risk of partner abuse. I'm sure, however, that the number can be reduced through skillful and thoughtful assessment. The following bullet points will provide you with suggestions to organize the assessment procedure.

Primary considerations in assessment and detection

Assessment and detection starts by evaluating your own attitudes about partner abuse. Do you think partner abuse should be a primary treatment issue? How highly do you place it in your treatment plan? Your attitude will affect the way your clients perceive the problem, and influence their willingness to disclose or talk about the issue.

- *Observe the balance of power between the partners.* Does one partner seem to dominate the other? Is one partner able to intimidate the other through looks, gestures, or body language? Do both partners express themselves to you freely and in a relaxed manner? If not, consider taking time to speak with each partner individually and assess the situation further. Don't jump to conclusions: an imbalance in power is not necessarily indicative of partner abuse. Further investigation, however, is justified and recommended.

- *Be mindful that partner abuse comes in many forms.* The emphasis of this book is on physical abuse. I'm sure you know, however, that partner abuse comes in other forms: verbal, sexual, economic, and emotional. Be alert and mindful of these abusive behaviors as well as physical abuse. The concepts and strategies discussed here will be helpful in addressing these forms of abuse as well.

- *When clients disclose abusive behavior, evaluate the frequency and severity of the behavior.* Is the abuse limited to verbal threats, or is the victim experiencing physical assaults? Are assaults increasing in frequency and severity? If so, how does that information affect your treatment plan? The Conflict Tactics Scale (Straus & Gelles, 1999) can be helpful in your assessment. The Conflict Tactics Scale (CTS) has a good

Coefficient of Reliability in research settings (alpha for couples = .88), and provides the counselor with a structured way to evaluate the frequency and severity of partner abuse. The individual items that comprise the CTS follow. Ask clients how often each item has occurred in their relationship.

Conflict Tactics Scale Items (Straus & Gelles, 1999)

Tell me how many times in the past 12 months you . . .

a.   Discussed an issue calmly

b.   Got information to back up your/his/her side of things

c.   Brought in, or tried to bring in, someone to help settle things

d.   Insulted or swore at him/her/you

e.   Sulked or refused to talk about an issue

f.   Stomped out of the room or house or yard

g.   Cried

h.   Did or said something to spite him/her/you

i.   Threatened to hit or throw something at him/her/you

j.   Threw or smashed or hit or kicked something

k.   Threw something at him/her/you

l.   Pushed, grabbed, or shoved him/her/you

m.   Slapped him/her/you

n.   Kicked, bit, or hit him/her/you with a fist

o.   Hit or tried to hit him/her/you with something

p.   Beat him/her/you up

q.   Choked him/her/you

r.   Threatened him/her/you with a knife or gun

s.   Used a knife or fired a gun

- **Evaluate risk factors.** When clinicians detect suicidal ideation among clients, they routinely evaluate lethality and risk factors (the presence of a plan, means, prior attempts, etc.). In the same way, take the time to evaluate potential lethality and risk factors once you detect partner abuse. To help you with this, I've presented below the lethality/risk factors proposed by the Los Angeles County Probation Department Specialized Domestic Violence Monitoring Unit. Some of the items are obvious risk factors, while others are less so. Use common sense and sound clinical judgment in evaluating risk factors, and be aware of the possibility of false positives. On the other hand, while the presence of one or more risk factors does not always mean that the victim is in imminent danger of potentially lethal assaults, you should be aware of the possibility and take common sense steps to enhance victim safety. For example, the development of a victim safety plan, written behavioral contracts, and inclusion of community resources in the treatment plan may be appropriate.

Potential Lethality/Risk Factors:

a.   Attempt/threat/plan of homicide or suicide

b.   Homicidal or suicidal ideation

c.   Alcohol/substance abuse

d.   Depression

e.   Prior threats or use of a knife or gun

f.   Obsessions about the partner

g.   History of rage

h.   Pet abuse

i.   Stranger (generalized) violence

j.   Antisocial traits

k.   Violence against multiple partners

l.   Increasing cycle of violence

m.   Social isolation of the victim

n.   Lack of remorse for past abuse

o.   Violence in the family of origin

p.   Sexual abuse/ rape of spouse

q.   Severe injuries inflicted on victim in previous assaults

r.   Access to victim

(Based on my clinical experience, to this list I would add the presence of child custody issues. In every domestic homicide in which my clients have been involved (fortunately, there have been few), the partners were engaged in a vicious custody battle.

Another useful instrument in evaluation of risk is the *Partner Assault Risk Assessment Guide* (SARA). The SARA is a 20-item structured interview designed to screen for risk factors of partner or family related assault. The SARA insures that the risk factors deemed to be of crucial predictive importance are measured in individuals suspected of, or who are being treated for, domestic violence. The SARA is a useful instrument for determining the extent to which an individual poses a future threat to his or her domestic partner, children, or other family members. It should be noted that the SARA is not the instrument of choice for determining the frequency or severity of past domestic assaults. Rather, it is a useful tool to evaluate the risk of *future* assaults. As such, the SARA is particularly helpful when addressing safety issues and making treatment recommendations.

- Avoid passive collusion with the aggressor. By passive collusion, I mean failing to confront abusive behaviors or blaming the victim. This is not a time to be nonjudgmental. At a minimum, make your own values about partner abuse clear to your clients and adopt a directive approach to the issue. Be supportive of both partners, but make it clear that you are supporting them in their efforts to make meaningful changes, not to maintain the status quo. Confront minimizing, blame, or denial when you hear it. Consider making the cessation of partner violence a condition of treatment, or the use of written behavioral contracts that prohibit future assaults, much as you would use written no-suicide contracts. While such measures may have limited effect, they may enhance the safety of family members. (When children are the object of violence, the obligation to report is clear.)

- Victim safety should be the first consideration in any treatment plan involving partner abuse. Review the frequency, severity, and potential risk factors in the case, and consider the need for a victim safety plan. The basic components of a safety plan are:

A Basic Victim Safety Plan:

a.   Keep some money on you for an emergency.

b.   Keep emergency numbers in a place you can get to them quickly.

c.   If possible, obtain a cell phone and keep it with you.

d.   Keep an extra set of car keys on you.

e.   Confer with a friend, family member, or counselor about how to handle an emergency call from you for help. Create a code word to use when you need someone to call police for emergency assistance.

f.   Consider obtaining a domestic violence protective order.

g.   Keep a change of clothes for you and the children in the car.

h.   Decide ahead of time at what point you should leave or call 911. If possible, discuss the issue with your counselor.

i.   Memorize the National Domestic Violence Hotline (800) 799-SAFE, or the numbers of other agencies in your community that can provide you with a list of community resources.

j.   If possible, have all firearms removed from the home.

Community Resources

Educate yourself about community resources for partner abuse, and incorporate them into your treatment plan as appropriate. Most communities have resources available for your clients. The following are potential adjuncts to treatment:

a. Educate the victim about his or her legal rights, and inform the aggressor about potential legal and economic consequences should the criminal justice system become involved. Whatever your feelings are on the issue, since the early 1980's, the criminal justice system has become more directly involved with the problem of partner abuse in communities across the nation. The criminalization of domestic violence, mandatory arrest policies that leave little discretion to the victim or the police in the matter of arrest, legislation requiring physicians to report domestic abuse to the police, and aggressive enforcement of protective orders are examples of the active role of the criminal justice system in matters of partner abuse.

b. Educate the victim about the pros and cons of domestic violence protective orders, and provide information about how to obtain one in your state. Consider the use of protective shelters. Most communities have domestic violence shelters that can provide victims of partner abuse and their children a safe haven and specialized counseling that may be appropriate for your client.

c. Remember that specialized counseling programs for the aggressors are becoming more available in communities across the nation.

d. Inform yourself and your clients about specific resources in your community by contacting local shelters or calling agencies such as the National Domestic Violence Hotline (800) 799-SAFE, or the numbers of other agencies in your community.

Cultural issues

Be aware of cultural influences that may affect the client's willingness to acknowledge abuse behavior in the relationship, or even consider it an issue worthy of treatment. Faced with culture-specific issues, a wise counselor will look for training and guidance from professionals and community leaders familiar with the client's primary culture. Far from an exhaustive list, the items below will familiarize you with some of the cultural issues that may be a factor in the treatment of partner abuse:

a. Male privilege and gender roles: male privilege is the idea that men are inherently superior to women, and what a man decides, wants, needs, and believes is more important than what a woman decides, wants, needs, or believes. I assure you, one doesn't have to travel outside of this country to find examples of male privilege (bear in mind some of the court decisions mentioned in the introduction to this book). However, male privilege is more pronounced in some cultures than in others. Such clients may perceive the counselor's efforts to stop partner violence as an intrusion into a man's "right" to absolute control of the family unit. (When faced with this problem, I've found it helpful to talk about stopping the violence as an essential adjustment to American culture that is necessary for survival in this country.)

b. Guilt due to a betrayal of trust: The notion of an "all sacrificing wife and mother" is very strong in some cultures. The victim may feel a duty to sacrifice any insult or indignity rather than expose the husband (and indirectly the family) to ridicule. The desire for help and assistance is in conflict with the need to avoid bringing shame to the family.

c. Geographical isolation: Immigrants, especially first generation immigrants, may find themselves isolated from the support and counsel of family and friends that were left behind. Due to geographical isolation and financial constraints, the victim may in effect be trapped in the home, as there is nowhere to turn.

d. Lack of knowledge: Victims and aggressors alike may lack knowledge about legal rights, potential criminal consequences, and community resources for partner abuse.

e. Language barriers: Even when knowledgeable about the issues above, a language barrier may prevent the victim from seeking assistance that is available in the community.

f. Fear of deportation: In some jurisdictions, criminal conviction for an act of partner abuse carries with it a very real possibility of deportation. Fear of deportation may dissuade many from using what protection from assault the criminal justice system can offer, or even acknowledging the problem to mental health or medical professionals.

Abuse in same gender relationships

Partner abuse is a human phenomenon. It is not a peculiar characteristic of one ethnic, socioeconomic, or educational group, nor is partner abuse idiosyncratic of one sexual orientation. The varieties of abusive behaviors encountered in heterosexual relationships (physical, verbal, sexual, emotional) are also found in gay and lesbian relationships, and their effects are no less destructive. It doesn't hurt any less to be abused by your partner because you're in a same gender relationship. On the other hand, there are some important differences that the therapist should be mindful of when counseling gay or lesbian clients. Some of the important issues regarding abuse in same gender relationships are:

a.   People sometimes assume men and women in same gender relationships are "on an equal playing field," and that the abuse cannot, therefore, be as serious as that found in heterosexual relationships. The truth is, domestic assaults in same gender relationships can be every bit as violent and as dangerous as those in heterosexual relationships.

b.   People in gay and lesbian relationships may have more difficulty securing assistance from community resources such as shelters and specialized counseling programs. On the other hand, they may underutilize the community resources that are available, fearing that they will face discrimination because of their sexual orientation.

c.   Concerns about the consequences of "coming out" may prevent victims and perpetrators form seeking help. Revealing one's sexual orientation is a major life decision. There are legitimate fears about losing custody of one's children, rejection by the family of origin, potential adverse effects on one's career, and a lifetime of exposure to prejudice in its many forms. For a number of my clients, the involvement of the criminal justice system in a domestic violence incident had the effect of an involuntary "outing." This was the case whether my client was the victim or the aggressor. As with cultural issues, the counselor must be aware of and prepared to address a wide range of concerns heightened by the presence of partner abuse.

Additional Considerations in a Treatment Plan

Develop a reasoned policy about disclosing and receiving information from the abused partner, and discuss your policy with your client. The freedom to talk openly with the abused partner is important, as situations often arise in which client confidentiality is at issue. Further, clients may not be forthcoming about continued abusive

9

behavior. I suggest that you obtain a release of information that allows you to talk to the abused partner about the progress made by the abuser, answer questions, provide safety recommendations based on information disclosed in treatment sessions, and to receive reports from the victim about new episodes of abusive behavior.

In my own practice, I may refuse to treat an abusive client who refuses to allow limited communications with his or her partner unless there are legitimate and overriding reasons that make them inappropriate. On the other hand, some of my experienced colleagues, whom I greatly respect, argue that such intrusions upon the confidentiality of the therapeutic hour are unnecessary and unjustified. Put some thought into where you stand on the matter, and explain your policy carefully to your clients.

Differences of opinion also arise on the issue of behavioral contracting. I require that all abusive clients contract to stop physical violence towards their partner as a condition of treatment, much as one may require a client to avoid suicidal behaviors or gestures. Clients understand that violation of the contract may result in their discharge from counseling. "I'm going to work as hard as I can to help you maintain a non-abusive relationship," I tell my clients, "but I need to know that you are as committed to this goal as I am. If not, I need to know now." I want my clients to know that meaningful behavioral change is their part of the counseling contract I am making with them.

This approach has served my clients and their families well over the years. Conversely, some clinicians believe that such contracts are ineffective and only increase their clients' reluctance to disclose continuing assaults upon their partner. Whatever your position on the issue, be aware that behavioral contracting is an option available to you.

Initial Intervention Strategy

The first step in intervention for domestic violence is to define the primary goal of counseling as stopping the abuse. Getting your clients on board, helping them identify ending abusive behavior as a worthy goal, can be a time consuming chore in itself, but it is vitally important. Meaningful progress will be difficult unless your clients accept and understand its importance.

Second, provide clients with a nonviolent strategy to address relational conflict. The strategy should enhance self-monitoring and appropriate problem solving, and provide behavioral strategies that disengage clients from conflict when abusive behavior is imminent. The strategy provided here, referred to as "Staying in the Box" by clients, often becomes a way of life for many of them. "The Box" model, discussed in detail, also provides the framework within which more advanced skills and concepts (such as self-talk and evaluation of core beliefs) are eventually applied.

Third, improve self-monitoring skills by making clients aware of their personal warning signs. Warning signs, as used here, are cognitive, behavioral, and physiological precursors to abusive behavior. Clients learn to use affective tension as a cue to look for their warning signs. The process enhances self-monitoring and helps clients identify the point at which temporary disengagement from the conflict is necessary.

Fourth, teach clients effective time-out strategies. While most clients think they know all about time-out, there are usually misunderstandings about it. Time-out is not a panacea, and when misused it can actually intensify the conflict. In fact, many acts of domestic abuse occur just as one partner is trying to walk out the door. There are rules that apply to the time-out procedure. Further, clients must understand the difference between "just leaving" or "storming out," which usually make things worse, and time-out, which has a calming effect.

These four steps will not resolve all of the problems faced by your clients. However, they accomplish two important objectives: (1) they decrease the likelihood of injury in the heat of family conflict, and (2) they foster an environment in which partners can begin to resolve their problems rather than fight about them.

As mentioned earlier, be prepared to explain the importance of these objectives to abusive clients, as they often want to talk about other problems in the relationship early in the counseling process. More specifically, they want to talk about how their partner angers them, and they want you to do something about it. The strategy presented thus far directs clients in the early stages of counseling away from daily problems in the relationship and toward an evaluation of the strategy used to handle the problems.

In the interest of victim safety, address specific problems only after a non-abusive strategy for dealing with them is in place. Redirect clients toward the larger problem: they react to conflict in an abusive manner. Start there. Develop non-abusive strategies for addressing conflict first - then address specific concerns within the framework of those strategies.

Staying in "The Box"

"The Box" model took form over many years of experimentation in a dedicated counseling program for partner abuse. Known by our clients as "Staying in The Box," they consistently rated it as one of the most important components of their program in post-treatment questionnaires. As an aside, colleagues and I have also found the model a useful starting point in counseling for anger management, borderline personality disorders, and in couples' counseling for partners whose hostility for each other has risen to the point that they consistently attack each other rather than their problems.

When presenting "The Box" model to your clients, it's helpful to begin with visual illustrations of the concepts such as the one below:

THE BOX

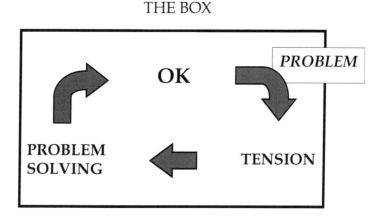

The Box model starts with the area marked "OK." The "OK Zone" represents a period of calm, in which there are no serious problems to resolve. Things may not be perfect in the OK Zone, but the client and his or her partner are generally satisfied with the way things are going. I advise clients to enjoy this period of calm while it lasts, because it never lasts for long. It ends when a significant problem comes up.

The Problem

Following the arrows in the box, you see that the OK zone ends when a problem arises. Relational problems, of course, are an inevitable part of living with another person. No two people are exactly alike. Each partner has their own expectations and attitudes about issues like how to spend money, how much time to spend with friends, and how to use leisure time. Differences may exist about the division of household chores, the proper roles of men and women, sex, work, children, the desire to stay close to the extended family, future goals, or anything under the sun. If one partner is abusive, they almost certainly disagree about the proper way to resolve their problems and express anger towards each other.

Tension: Things Are Not OK

Problems inevitably cause tension between the partners. Things were OK before the problem came up, but they are definitely not OK now. They know things are not OK because there is a feeling of "tension" between the partners that was not there before. The word tension, as used here, is a generic word that refers to feelings of anger, frustration, resentment, jealousy, or any other feeling associated with anger. Emotions such as those listed below are associated with the "Tension Zone" of The Box.

Forms of Tension:

Frustration	Insecurity	Indignation
Annoyance	Anger	Jealousy
Defensiveness	Resentment	Rage
Bitterness	Infuriation	Spite
Rivalry	Exasperation	Aggravation

The sequence of events suggested by The Box is critically important to abusive clients: the calm of the OK Zone - disrupted by a problem - creates tension. The Box model attributes the abuser's tension to a problem, rather than to his or her partner. It follows that resolving tension requires that the problem be attacked, not the partner.

Problem Solving

"What you do now," clients are told, "is extremely important. How you choose to behave when tension arises determines the type of relationship you have. The important thing to understand is that you cannot get rid of feelings like anger by venting, lashing out, or hurting your partner. The only way to get rid of anger is to solve the problem causing it - by problem solving."

Tension builds until clients solve the problem behind it in a way that both partners find acceptable. Tension levels may go up and down over time, but the tension never goes completely away until they solve the problem and return to the OK Zone. If one partner walks away and refuses to talk, or if one partner gets his or her way by bullying the other partner, tension remains because the problem is still there.

Once clients understand the relationship between tension and problems, tension becomes an affective cue to begin the problem solving process, rather than a prompt for verbal or physical aggression. This link between negative affect and problem solving is an essential element in meaningful change, and the therapist must be sure that the client thoroughly understands it. In addition, the concept that problem solving is the only way to eliminate tension (the negative affective state) cannot be overemphasized. There is no alternative route back to the "OK Zone" (emotional equilibrium).

What Happens When You Don't Solve Your Problems

"When a problem comes up," I tell clients, "tension starts to build and disconnects you from your partner. When this happens, the goal is to reconnect with your partner (get back to the OK Zone) by solving the problem. If you do that, the tension between the two of you will go away, but let me make this point once more - tension never goes away until the problem behind it is solved. Problem solving is the only way to make things really OK again. When you feel tension (or anger, frustration, jealousy, etc.) between you and your partner, it means there is a problem that needs to be solved."

The way abusive clients choose to handle problems and tension can define their relationships. Successful couples understand that the feeling of tension is a signal telling them that they need to work together as a team to resolve a problem. It is not a signal to vent anger or abuse each other. Effective problem solving strategy does NOT include yelling, throwing tantrums, or acting like a spoiled child. Instead, successful couples are respectful and work together as a team. They attack the problem, not each other. They know that things will be OK again once the problem is solved. Actually, things will be better than they were before. Confidence in their relationship and their trust in each other is confirmed from the experience of working through a problem successfully. After all, they've demonstrated their ability to work together and successfully resolve a problem, and they know that they can do it again if they have to.

Clients must understand that whether their relationship flourishes or fails does not depend on the quantity or nature of their problems. Rather, success depends on how they handle the problems that come up. Couples who enjoy long-term, satisfying, (and non-abusive) relationships have their share of problems just like everyone else. Their relationships work because they tend to be good problem solvers. They know that communication, respect, compromise, and negotiation get good results, while venting, yelling, and controlling tactics do not. Unfortunately, many people in relationships have yet to figure this out.

Clients must understand that when they respond to problems in an abusive manner, they put themselves on opposite sides of the fence from their partner. They become an adversary instead of a teammate. The problem becomes a wedge driving the two partners apart, making problem solving impossible. This is why some couples never really solve their problems - they only argue and fight about them. They never really get back to the OK Zone. Tension from unresolved problems builds up over months and years and bleeds over into new problems. Partners blow up over relatively minor issues and they fight constantly. Over time the softer feelings of love, support, and caring are covered with a heavy blanket of anger, mistrust, and resentment. Communication becomes increasingly hostile and abusive; each new abusive act and hostile word further erodes the relationship. Finally, as a beach washed away in a storm, there is nothing left to save. Their relationship damaged beyond repair, the couple can never get back to the OK Zone.

The Argument Phase

When the solution to a problem is not readily apparent to both partners, an argument often begins, as shown by the dark arrows in the illustration below.

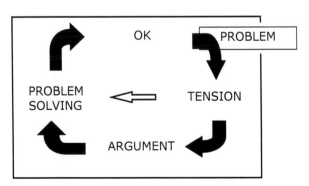

The word "Argument" for this area of The Box was chosen carefully. Many abusive clients minimize their behaviors by using the word "argument" to describe them. Clients must understand the difference between an argument and abuse. Clients often need help with this concept, and some clients call anything an argument. There can be abusive incidents that have babies crying, dogs barking, police helicopters circling, and frightened neighbors calling the police. Asked, "What's going on?" some clients will say, "We're having an argument." The "Argument Zone" of The Box is included in an effort to address this issue. Notice that the "Argument Phase" lies inside the box, indicating that arguing is acceptable behavior during conflict, as long as one understands where an argument stops and a fight (or abuse) begins. An argument, as discussed here, does not involve verbal abuse or violence.

Helen is a good example of a client who needed help with the "argument" concept. One day Helen drove to the apartment of her boyfriend, Tom. When Helen arrived, she saw Tom talking to a voluptuous young girl on the sidewalk by the apartment. Helen, in a jealous rage, stomped on the gas and drove her car straight for Tom. He saw her coming and, as Tom is no dummy, he jumped onto one of the cars parked nearby. Helen slammed into the car Tom was perched on and threw her car into reverse for another try. Tom nimbly jumped from car to car as Helen repeatedly tried to turn him into road-kill. This went on until the police arrived. After her release from jail the court sent Helen to me for counseling. When I asked her what happened on the day of her arrest, she said meekly, "I had an argument with my boyfriend."

In an argument there is no attempt to abuse (or as in Helen's case, to kill) your partner. Anger expressed during an argument is free of threats, name-calling, or physical violence. You can tell someone you're angry without telling them off, and that's the difference between an argument and a fight. Clients respect their partners during an argument, but disrespect their partners during a fight. When clients engage in abusive, hostile, or disrespectful behavior, they are not arguing. They are fighting. The chart below shows the difference between behaviors that are "in the box" (arguing), and those that are "out of the box" (abusing).

In "The Box":

- Keep your tone of voice down
- Show respect in the words you choose
- See yourselves as teammates
- Constructive focus: Attack the problem, not your partner

Out of "The Box":

- Yell and shout
- Swear, insult your partner, call your partner names

- See your partner as your adversary
- Destructive focus: Attack your partner and forget the problem

Clients cannot always avoid arguments and appropriate expressions of anger. Nor should they always try. When clients assume personal responsibility for expressing anger in a non-abusive way, positive change can occur in their relationships. When people assume responsibility for expressing their anger in a non-abusive way, their partners do not feel personally attacked or threatened. They listen to one another without getting defensive. They come to trust each other well enough to express themselves and their feelings openly. A better understanding of the each other's needs and expectations is the result. The better clients understand each other, the more effective they will be at problem solving.

In abusive relationships, the focus is not on solving the problem. Rather, one person (the abuser) vents anger towards his or her partner. The abuser is not interested in resolving problems or working as a team. Instead, he or she is motivated to control, harm, humiliate, and intimidate. The abusive person attacks his or her partner rather than the problem, as shown in the following illustration of The Box.

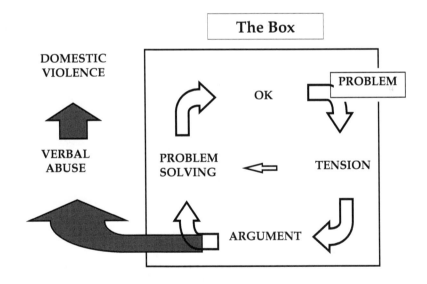

Getting Out of "The Box": Verbal Abuse

The dark arrows in The Box show the road that leads to abuse and violence. Tension starts to build when a problem comes up. An argument follows. When tension reaches a certain point, the problem is forgotten and the abuser gets "out of the box." In other words, the abuser starts to attack his or her partner. In most instances, the attack starts with verbal abuse, which is usually the first sign that the client is out of the box. The verbal abuse further escalates the tension between the couple. Verbal abuse is like throwing a match into a pool of gasoline – it's just as explosive. It is often helpful to provide clients a list of behaviors identified as "verbal abuse," such as the one below.

Forms of Verbal Abuse

yell	humiliate	sarcasm
offend	insult	bully
swear	rant	put down
threaten	belittle	call names
chew out	condescend	scold

After listening to so many people relate the chain of events that led to violence against their partner, I am convinced that in the vast majority of cases, verbal abuse "unlocked the door" for the physical violence that followed. One of the most beneficial and important resolutions that your client can make is to stop engaging in verbal abuse. When clients become angry during the argument phase, they have a choice to make. Take the road toward violence by engaging in verbal abuse, or take the high road toward problem solving and conflict resolution. Clients must understand that the choice is theirs alone, and they must take full responsibility for it.

As the model suggests, verbal and physical abuse usually occurs after a period of tension building and arguing, especially in the early stages of a relationship. But that is not always the case. In time, a person may begin to abuse the partner with little or no argument phase. Clients must understand that in any stage of a relationship, every person who abuses does so because he or she wants to, because he or she chooses to. In every case, without exception, the only person responsible for the violence is the one doing the hitting.

This concept is crucial, as it challenges two commonly held beliefs about abusive behavior: "I can't be held responsible for the way I act when my partner pushes my buttons," and (2) "Abusive behavior is justified when I am justifiably angry."

Establish the Goal of "Staying In the Box"

The goal of is to help clients stop abusive behavior by staying inside the boxed area on the chart. We call this "staying in The Box." As long as clients are in The Box, they won't engage in abusive behavior.

To accomplish this goal, they monitor and attend to their own words and behavior, especially words and behaviors that are abusive. Usually, the first warning that they are outside of The Box will be their own verbally abusive language. Explain that verbal abuse escalates anger, and unlocks the door for physical abuse to follow. It is an indication that the client is out of the box, and moving towards a violent incident. Develop a behavioral contract with clients stating that they will step back and cool off when they find themselves outside of The Box. In other words, use their head rather than your hands, and take a time-out to regain self-control. The details of the time-out procedure follow.

Time-Out

Imagine that you are the coach of a professional basketball team. The score is tied and there is a minute left to play. Suddenly, the other team scores two quick goals. As the coach, what are you likely to do? If you're a sports fan you know the answer: *call a time-out.*

Professional sports teams call a time-out when they're not playing well. A time-out gives them a chance to get organized, calm down, and plan the next play. Hopefully, they start working together as a team again. Time-out can also be used in our relationships, and for the same reasons. In this lesson we'll be talking about calling a time-out to stay in control of feelings and behavior. A time-out can help your client and his or her partner work together as a team and, more importantly, it can prevent future episodes of verbal or physical abuse.

Time-out seems like an easy tool to use. When your clients think they're going to lose it, they leave until they calm down. That's all there is to it, right? Wrong. Time-out is not a cure-all. It won't work for everyone, and it won't solve all of our clients' relational problems. Secondly, there's a lot to know about taking a time-out. If used incorrectly, a time-out actually makes things worse. Many people who come to me for counseling tell me that their domestic violence incident took place as they were trying to walk out the door. Lastly, a time-out is very different from just leaving or storming out. There are rules to the time-out procedure that your client should know about.

Before going over the time-out procedure in detail, let's be very clear about what a time-out *is not*. It is *not* the purpose of a time-out to avoid talking about problems. The purpose of a time-out is to give clients a chance to regain their composure and judgment so that they can discuss problems calmly and without verbal or physical abuse.

Occasionally, I hear of clients who call a time-out whenever their partner brings up something that they don't want to talk about. The wife of a client once called me to ask, *"What in the world are you teaching my husband in that group of yours?"* I could tell from her voice that she was frustrated. "What's wrong?" I asked. *"I'll tell you what's wrong!"* she shouted. *"Every time I try to talk to him he calls a time-out and leaves the house!"* Don't allow clients to use a time-out to dodge problems.

It's also wrong to use a time-out to control a partner. One client tried to use time-out to control his wife by placing her on time-out whenever she was angry. In a voice that a parent might use when sending a child to her room, he would point at her and say in his most official voice: "You're out of control! Go take a time-out!" (I can't tell you how badly that worked.) The time-out procedure is not a way for clients to punish their partner for expressing anger. Advise them against calling a time-out for anyone but himself or herself. Time-out is a way for clients to take responsibility for their anger, not a strategy to control the anger or behavior of others.

And then, there was Scott. Scott was a new client attending his first session. As it happened, we were talking about time-out. When he heard the words time-out Scott sat up and practically shouted to the group, "Listen to this, guys. This time-out stuff really works! Last time "my lady" and I got into it, I left and went to Vegas. I didn't come home for three days! Man, was she sorry." Explain that a time-out does not mean storming angrily out of the house, deliberately causing your partner to worry about what you're doing and whether you're ever coming home. Time-out is not an excuse to leave and have fun. It's certainly not a way to win a fight by making your partner feel "sorry."

Time-out Is Not Storming Out

During an argument, people sometimes *storm out* of the house. We all know what storming out is. When you yell in your loudest and most dramatic voice, *"I'm not listening to this s*** anymore,"* stomp through the door and slam it behind you, you've stormed out.

Help clients understand that storming out is unfair to their partners, and it only makes the situation worse by escalating tension. When you think about it, storming out is nothing more than an attempt to punish a partner by causing him or her worry about where you are, what you're doing, who you're with, and when you'll return. Your partner doesn't know whether you're leaving for now or for good. Storming out of the house also provokes feelings of disrespect and abandonment on the part of your partner. It suggests that you don't take your problems seriously enough to stay and work them out, and that you don't care anymore. It escalates anger and the risk of violence. When you storm out your partner may try to prevent you from leaving. As I noted earlier, many domestic violence incidents happen just this way.

Time-out is different. There are rules to follow during the time-out period, and it's important to follow them. In fact, clients should discuss the time-out rules with their partner before attempting to use it in the heat of conflict. If they discuss the purpose of a time-out and the guidelines that they will follow during the time-out period, the partner will be more likely to cooperate when a time-out is called.

The Time-out Rules

RULE 1: DON'T USE ALCOHOL OR DRUGS DURING THE TIME-OUT PERIOD

Abstinence from drugs and alcohol is important during the time-out period. Once warning signs are present, clients need their judgment intact. The whole purpose of a time-out is to recover one's judgment and emotional stability, and to apply the skills and concepts learned in counseling. Self-impairment with drugs or alcohol defeats that purpose.

RULE 2: SPEND THE TIME-OUT PERIOD ALONE

It is also important that clients spend the time-out period alone. When clients turn to their friends during a conflict with their spouse, friends usually side with the clients. Rather than calming the situation, friends can escalate it by reinforcing the notion that the partner is the sole cause of the conflict. There are exceptions of course, but friends and family usually take the client's side. After all, they are the client's friends and family. Statements like, "I always knew he wasn't the man for you," "I wouldn't take that s*** from my girlfriend!" or, "You've got to show her who's the boss!" are one-sided and do not help the client see their role in the conflict.

Advise your clients to spend the time-out period alone doing things that calm them down. Recommend that they listen to music, take a walk, shoot some baskets, jog, or choose some other solitary activity. Relaxation techniques such as deep breathing and progressive muscle relaxation also can help to reduce the tension level. Most importantly, clients must talk rationally to themselves about what's going on. To encourage rational thought, teach clients to ask themselves questions during the time-out period, such as those below:

- *Am I blowing this problem out of proportion?*
- *What are the consequences going to be if I get out of the box?*

- *Have I handled my anger in an appropriate way, or have I made the situation worse?*
- *Have I done or said anything for which I should apologize?*
- *Am I really interested in my partner's point of view?*
- *Am I coming across as hurtful, blaming, or controlling?*
- *Have I shown respect for my partner during this argument?*
- *Have I behaved like a loved one or an adversary?*
- *Can I compromise and negotiate, so we can both get part of what we want?*
- *Have I been trying to solve a problem, or just arguing about who's right and who's wrong?*
- *Have I been attacking the problem or my partner?*

RULE 3: IT'S NOT A TIME-OUT UNTIL YOU SAY THE WORDS: "TIME-OUT"

Remind your clients that their spouses can't read their minds. "If you want a time-out," I advise my clients, "you have to say so. When you use the words 'time-out,' you're telling your partner that you promise to abide by the rules during the time-out period. Unless you say, 'I need a time-out,' you're just leaving or storming out."

RULE 4: TELL YOUR PARTNER WHEN YOU'LL BE BACK

How long should a time-out last? In my program, a time-out lasts between 15 minutes to an hour. This is in sharp contrast to those who advise: "Don't come back until you calm down." If clients call a time-out as soon as they start to get out of The Box - and if they do what they are supposed to do during the time-out period - one hour is plenty of time to start thinking rationally and reduce anger to manageable levels. In addition, when partners know that clients will be back in a reasonable time they are more likely to cooperate with the time-out process. This is an important consideration, because everything tends to come unraveled when the partner refuses to allow the abusive client to take a time-out.

RULE 5: RETURN ON TIME

Suppose your client promises his or her partner to be back in 30 minutes, but comes home three days later. The client has created an entirely new conflict. Further, what happens the next time the client wants a time-out? Will the partner let your client leave again? The effectiveness of time-out depends upon the client's willingness to follow the rules. Breaking the rules reduces the chances that time-out will be successful in the future. There is no limit on the number of time-outs that can be called while working on a problem.

Monitor Warning Signs

When do clients call a time-out? Clients call a time-out when they see their own warning signs. Warning signs tell your client that they are about to express anger in an abusive and destructive way (get out of The Box). They are acting out of anger, rather than good judgment. Anger is running the show and they are not thinking rationally. Most likely, they aren't doing much thinking at all, and they've lost sight of the original problem. Problem solving has stopped, and they are about to attack their partner rather than the problem. When clients see their warning signs, teach them to stop and call a time-out.

The moment that tension starts to rise, clients should start to monitor themselves for warning signs. It is vital that they have a keen awareness of their personal warning signs. People who fail to monitor themselves or recognize their warning signs have difficulty using the time-out procedure, and they are much more likely to engage in new incidents of abuse because they will not call a time-out when needed. The time to pinpoint their personal warning signs is early in the counseling process. I have had many opportunities to interview clients who failed to stay in The Box and engaged in new incidents of partner abuse.

In most cases, their failure to stay in The Box was due to: (1) a lack of client commitment to end abusive behaviors, or (2) inadequate client awareness of their warning signs, which are the cues that prompt the request for a time-out. In most cases, addressing one or both of these issues with the client resulted in an increase of appropriate time-out calls by the client, and a corresponding reduction of abusive behavior toward their partner. When a client reports new abusive behavior, explore with the client why the warning signs were not seen, or if the client did see the warning signs, why they were ignored.

Clients need to develop an intimate and experiential understanding of three types of warning signs:

(1) **Behavioral Warning Signs:** Behavioral warning signs are aggressive words and hostile behaviors that clients may engage in as tension rises. I have listed examples of behavioral warning

signs below. This is not an exhaustive list. Take time to explore for behavioral warning signs that may be unique to each client.

Yell	*Break something*	*Throw something*
Curse	*Slam a door*	*Say hurtful things*
Threaten	*Invade personal space*	*Glare at someone*
Kick a chair	*Punch a wall*	*Call your partner names*

(2) **Cognitive Warning Signs:** Cognitive warning signs refer to the thoughts that run through your client's mind as the tension level rises. At higher tension levels, there are important changes in the way abusive clients think. Common examples of cognitive warning signs are:

- *"Awfulize": Blow things out of proportion by labeling a day to day annoyance as terrible and awful.*
- *Think, "You've got this coming, you asked for it!"*
- *Visualize yourself hurting you partner.*
- *Obsess about some perceived slight or injustice.*
- *Tell yourself someone is pushing your buttons.*
- *Selectively attend to your partner's negatives and ignore his or her positives.*

3) **Physiological Warning Signs:** Physiological warning signs refer to the changes that take place in the body of your clients when the tension level rises. Common examples include:

Tight stomach	*Flushed face*	*Clinched teeth*
Rapid heart rate	*Rapid breathing*	*Tension headache*
Sweating palms	*Muscle tightness*	*Trembling hands*

Teach clients to use tension as a cue to start looking for their warning signs, and to call a time-out as soon as they their warning signs appear, as illustrated below:

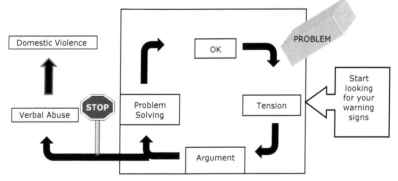

Warning signs vary greatly from person to person. With thought and practice, your clients will start to understand the warning signs that are meaningful to them. After giving it some thought, some of my clients have identified warning signs that are unique and distinctive to them alone:

- *John: "When I'm really mad I start to smile. This means I'm ready to hit someone."*
- *Kareem: "I get really quiet. I mean, I just stop talking. It's like I'm trying to hold the lid on and not explode."*
- *Lisa: "I start to bite my cheek and pinch myself."*
- *Andrea: "I think about the way I was abused by my ex, and now I'm going to hit first."*
- *Patricia: "I start to clean everything around me as hard and as loud as I can."*
- *Pedro: "I start to feel sorry for her, really sorry for her, because I know what I'm going to do to her."*

The following two examples illustrate how clients learn to apply their warning signs. The examples come from the homework of two clients in my counseling program, who I will call Paula and Darryl. Both clients are relatively new, and the homework illustrates their initial efforts to incorporate new skills and strategies to resolve conflict in a non-abusive manner.

Paula's Homework:

My daughter Michelle and I got into an argument. I had placed her on restrictions. I said to her that she is grounded for failed grades. I went off to work and she decided to step out of the house. She disobeyed the rules. When I came home, she was not in the house. I waited for her arrival. She walked in and said hello. I asked her of her whereabouts and she replied, 'I'm not staying home - I don't care what you say. I'm not staying home - I'm on vacation.'

My blood is boiling. I feel hot. My hands are perspiring, my voice cracking. I was MAD. Michelle was hostile. I recognized my warning signs. I decided to take a time out until I cooled off. I then asked her to come into the bedroom so we may have a discussion.

I could have behaved erratically and as hostile as she did. Because of the time out, I was able to gather my thoughts and calm myself down for problem solving. I reminded myself of the quote I read in class: "I am today what my choices were yesterday, I will be tomorrow what my choices are today."

Darryl's Homework:

On Wednesday night, after getting out of class, my girlfriend picked me up from the classes. So right then when everything was fresh on my mind I explained to her every little detail I was taught in class and explained to her if she could help me with my homework. Anyway, the topic was about taking time out and setting up an agreement about taking time out. So we did (talked about the time outs) and agreed to get out of each other's face when tensions flare up, and take a 20-minute time out. About a few days ago, we both got into an argument. (Hey, who would of knew that an argument would of come up!) A perfect time to practice my time outs. She noticed it first that me and her were going at it at each other. It started to build up (the argument). So right then she tells me, "I need a time out." (Why, I ask myself, didn't I notice it first?) But anyways, she tells me to leave the house and my first reaction was, "NO, I WANT TO FINISH THIS ARGUMENT." (As I said in my mind, and not out loud. Well really, thanks to Wednesday's classes for that practice.) Anyhow, as I left out of the house and took off with anger inside me.

I finally snapped and told myself, "F***!!!! I need a time out." So as I left the house I took a ride to McDonalds, all mad and aggressive, but at the same time calming down. So I was gone for about ... hmmmmmm, let's see, for about 15 to 20 minutes and she gave me a call on my cell phone and she asked me to come back home and talk about our argument. Right there and then I realized something. I'm the type of person (like my father) who has to finish the arguments right then and now!!! But I say thanks to those time outs, cause if this was, let's say 2 weeks ago, I'd probably be in more trouble than what I'm already in!

If your clients are having trouble identifying their warning signs, suggest that they ask people who know them well, "How do you know when I'm getting really angry?" They will be able to tell them what many of their warning signs are. Encourage clients to put vigorous effort into acquiring a perfect awareness of their warning signs. I tell clients that they should recognize their warning signs as easily as they recognize their own name or the faces of their own children. It's vital information.

Seagoing skippers keep a vigilant watch for reefs or rocks that may lie ahead. Once seen, they take decisive action to avoid them. To do otherwise would mean shipwreck and disaster. Warning signs are like reefs and rocks that are directly ahead. Failure to recognize them and avert them is reckless and foolish. Like the skipper of a sailing ship, clients have to watch for their own personal "warning signs" that signal the need for a time-out. Warning signs are like huge stop signs that say: *"STOP HERE! DANGER AHEAD! CHANGE COURSE NOW!* You are emotionally flooded. Do not proceed any further down the road you're on. It will only end in further abuse and trauma.

Whatever your clients' warning signs are, they need to recognize them as personal warnings that they are about to act in an abusive and destructive manner. As shown in the illustration above, tension becomes a cue to for self-monitoring. In time, clients habitually search for warning signs when they start to feel emotional tension. At the first appearance of one of their warning signs, they call a time-out and apply cognitive and behavioral strategies to reduce tension and increase rational thought before they become verbally or physically abusive.

Your Client Must Be His or Her Own Coach

Professional sports teams have coaches that call a time-out to help their players calm down, regroup, develop a game plan, and work together as a team. Unfortunately, there will be no coach on the sidelines when your clients need a time-out. They have to be their own coach. In other words, they have to call the time-out for themselves when they need it. Success requires knowledge obtained from the counselor, such as a thorough understanding of how the time-out procedure fits into The Box and insight into their personal warning signs, as well as the capacity for self-monitoring and the discipline to call a time-out "in the heat of battle," when part of the client would rather continue the fight. Clients acquire these skills through practice and perseverance, and they come easier to some clients than others.

I've found it helpful to warn clients that calling a time-out sounds simple and straightforward, but it may be difficult to do when tension is running high. It is often necessary to address problematic cognitions such as the belief that time-out is a sign of weakness, and the perception that the partner will take advantage of them if they don't respond to conflict aggressively. Defining the act of staying in The Box and calling a time-out as "showing leadership" has been helpful for many clients. Be sure, however, to clarify that leadership means leading by example, not controlling what others say and do.

The "I Don't Care" Lines

Sometimes clients fail in their efforts to call a time-out because they wait too long before calling it. Rather than calling a time-out at the first warning sign that their behavior was becoming destructive, they "run the stop sign." In other words, they saw their warning signs, but ignored them. As anger escalated they plowed on, swearing and yelling, running stop sign after stop sign. They knew they were out of The Box, but they didn't care anymore. Anger escalated to a point that they no longer thought or cared about the consequences of their behavior. As anger mounted, they crossed the "I don't care what I say" line. Then they crossed the "I don't care what I do" line.

The concept of the "I don't care what I say" and "I don't care what I do" lines has been very helpful to abusive clients. Many people avoid responsibility for their behavior my saying, "I lost control of myself." I tell clients that I don't believe they abuse people because they lose control of themselves. "That's nonsense," I argue. "We all know when we're saying and doing abusive things. We know exactly what we're saying and doing. We also know it's wrong. It's just that we allow our anger to grow to the point that WE DON'T CARE ANYMORE. That is very different from losing control. We do not lose control; rather, we get so mad that we "don't give a damn." When we stop caring about our partner or the consequences of our behavior, we allow ourselves to get abusive.

Abusive behavior is a choice that we must take full responsibility for." Depending upon your theoretical orientation, you may disagree with me on this issue. I strongly submit, however, that it is better for your abusive clients to think in these terms.

The first sign that people "no longer care" is when they choose to get verbally abusive. When we use idioms such as "flipping our lid," "going off," "blowing our stack," and "losing it," we mean that we have crossed the "I don't care what I say line." We're out of The Box at this point. Problem solving has stopped, and verbal abuse causes anger to build in a manner similar to the tornado below. Crossing the "I don't care what I say line" is like throwing a match into a pool of gasoline. Anger and tension escalate swiftly. As the verbal battle rages beyond the "I don't care what I say" line, clients move toward the "I don't care what I do line," which is even more hazardous. When clients reach that line, the hitting starts.

Skillful monitoring of warning signs and calling time-out will help keep clients in The Box and below the "I don't care" lines. On the other hand, clients ignore warning signs at their peril. Ignoring warning signs is like running stop signs on a busy street. They may run one or two without incident, but eventually they will find themselves in a wreck. The longer one stays beyond the "I don't care what I say" lines before calling the time-out (the more stop signs they run), the less chance there is that the time-out will be successful. Teach clients to call time-out at the FIRST appearance of their warning signs, while they still have the judgment and emotional stability needed to make wise choices.

When Time Out Is Over

A time-out is no substitute for problem solving. It only prevents clients from saying and doing things that make their relational problems worse. As discussed earlier, problems cause tension between clients and their partners, and the tension lingers until they solve the problem. Problem solving is the only passageway back to the OK Zone of The Box. When the time-out period is over, clients must resume their efforts to problem solve as a team, and stick to it until they are truly back in the OK Zone and the tension surrounding that problem is gone. To summarize, the steps that clients take in an appropriate time-out procedure are:

1. *Monitor your behavior by watching for your warning signs. Call a time-out as soon as you see them.*

2. *Acknowledge your anger to your partner and say you need a time-out. Say the words.*

3. *Tell your partner how long the time-out will last (15 minutes to an hour).*

4. *Agree to pursue the problem further when you return.*

5. *Spend the time-out period working to reduce your anger. Tools like relaxation exercises and physical exercise can help. Most importantly, self-talk (talk to yourself in a cool and rational manner).*

6. *Come back on time and continue problem solving inside The Box. Keep watching for your warning signs.*

7. *Call another time-out if you need to, but keep at it until you solve the problem and get back to the OK Zone of The Box.*

The Anger Inventory

The Anger Inventory reveals the effects of abuse, both in the lives of your clients and in the lives of their family members. Once aware of destructive patterns and behaviors, clients can more easily choose to avoid them in the future. However, clients must avoid denial, blame, and minimization of abusive behaviors to benefit from the exercise. An effective Anger Inventory helps clients to recognize denial, blame, and minimizing as adversaries to meaningful change, and to avoid them as they work to maintain violence-free relationships.

Jesse, a former client of mine, is a good example. After working on his Anger Inventory for several weeks, Jesse was surprised by what he discovered about himself. "I would never have believed it," he told the other men in his group. "The more I write about my life, the more I see that I've become just like my father. When I was a kid I hated the way he used to treat my mom, and I swore that I'd never, ever be like him. But now I see that I've done everything to my wife that my dad did to my mom. The put-downs, the yelling, the hitting, it's the same shit, and I've become just like him. I had no idea."

Martha, another client, also learned a lot from her Anger Inventory. She wrote, "I can't believe how abusive I've been. I can see how I used to 'go off' on others to get my way. I deliberately tried to intimidate people and make them afraid of me. You know, don't get her mad cause you don't know what she might do. I knew exactly what I was doing. It was all about getting my way."

What is An Anger Inventory?

Twelve-step programs such as Alcoholics Anonymous have helped countless people maintain their sobriety and regain their self-respect. Step four of twelve-step programs, making a searching and fearless moral inventory, is an important part of recovery. A personal inventory provides an understanding of the way alcohol has affected a person's life. It's a detailed account of a person's history, from childhood to the present day. Writing a personal inventory is no small undertaking. Particular attention is paid to the use and effects of alcohol, but as the inventory is written, a person gets an honest look at oneself and acknowledges problems and personal weaknesses openly. A person sees, perhaps for the first time, the way he or she really is. Writing an inventory is no small undertaking.

My clients also write an inventory, but the focus is on abuse and destructive anger rather than alcohol. We call it the Anger Inventory.

Anger Inventories help people understand the way abusive anger has affected them as children, adolescents, and adults. Clients come to see long-standing patterns in their lives that they were not aware of, and gain insight into how the same mistakes, repeated over and over, work havoc upon relationships. An honest, searching, and fearless Anger Inventory is a remarkable journey of self-discovery.

The questions below provide a starting point, but there is more to an Anger Inventory than simply answering this list of questions. An Anger Inventory looks into the people, relationships, and events that are unique to your clients' lives. They should feel free to write about people and events that are not on this list. Most importantly, they should be overtly encouraged to resist the temptation to write superficial answers. Superficiality, of course, profits them nothing. Help them find the courage to delve into their lives honestly, thoughtfully, and thoroughly.

Sometimes it is hard to for clients to remember the past, especially their childhood, accurately. Indeed, they may have worked hard to forget some things from their past. Looking at old family photos and talking to relatives often helps them recover the past. If possible, encourage them to visit places they have lived before, and take time to reflect. The insights and self-knowledge clients gain is worth the time and effort. Here are the questions that clients start with in my program. Remember, these questions are only a starting point.

Anger Inventory Questions:

1. How did your parents express anger towards each other?
2. How did they express anger toward you?
3. How did you know when your mother and father were angry? What were their warning signs?
4. Did they ever get out of the box?
5. Did you ever see your parents hit, push, or verbally abuse each other?
6. If so, how did it make you feel?
7. Were you abused as a child? If so, how did you cope with the abuse? Did you tell anyone?
8. As a teenager, how did you show anger to your family members?
9. Did you get out of the box as a teenager?
10. Did getting out of the box have anything to do with controlling others?
11. How did you express anger to your peers as a teenager?
12. In junior high school and high school, what did you learn from your peers about expressing anger?

13. By the time you were in high school, how did you think you were supposed to act when you were angry with someone?

14. How did you show anger to the people you were dating?

15. As an adult, how did you handle anger towards your partner when you were dating?

16. Did your behavior change after the honeymoon period ended?

17. How did the unspoken rules about anger and hostility change over the course of your relationship?

18. Have drugs or alcohol played a destructive role in your relationships?

19. What acts of verbal and physical abuse have you engaged in? (Be specific and give a full account!)

20. If you have children, has your angry behavior ever frightened them?

21. Has the way you express anger had negative consequences for you?

22. What negative consequences has your behavior had for your children and your partner(s)?

23. Have prior acts of abuse had anything to do with maintaining power and control over others?

24. Do you take full responsibility for acts of abuse in the past?

25. Do you owe anyone apologies for your behavior? If so, have you tried to make amends?

26. How has your behavior meaningfully changed your behavior for the better?

27. What concepts and skills from this book are most important and useful to you?

28. Give some specific examples of your ability to apply the concepts and skills you have learned to stay in the box.

29. What have you done to ensure that your relationships will be abuse and violence-free in the future?

30. Is this Anger Inventory totally free of denial, blame, and minimizing?

Denial, Blame, and Minimizing

Warn clients that they face three adversaries in their attempt to write a successful Anger Inventory - denial, blame, and minimization. They defeat the efforts of many to be truthful and honest with themselves. As impediments to change, they have the potential to thwart the attempts of your clients to make positive changes in their lives and maintain abuse-free relationships. Denial, blame, and minimizing undermine your clients' ability to learn from the past, and thereby block growth and meaningful change. They keep clients from doing what they need to do to stop abuse and violence in the future. To the degree that abusive clients avoid seeing things as they are and shirk full responsibility for their actions, no important changes will take place. They will be more likely to act abusively again.

When working with abusive clients, it is important that you confront denial, blaming, and minimizing whenever and wherever you find them. They are easy to recognize. If you listen, you will hear them in various forms in almost every counseling session. If you recognize them for what they are – impediments to meaningful change – and relentlessly bring them to the attention of your clients, you will greatly improve their chances for maintaining a violence-free relationship. Denial, blaming, and minimizing as they present themselves in partner abuse counseling, are easy to recognize. Let us look at denial first.

Denial

Abusive clients attending their first session of counseling are often big fans of denial. (Denial, as used here, more closely resembles the common language rather that the psychodynamic use of the term.) Consider Robert. In his first counseling session, he looks you in the eye and declares with heartfelt sincerity, "I don't belong in counseling! I didn't do anything wrong and I never abused anybody! This is all bullshit! My wife should be here, not me! She's the one with the problem!"

What do you do? If you are new to partner abuse counseling, you may be overly inclined to believe Robert. After all, he sounds like he is telling the truth. Denial of abusive behavior always places the clinician on the horns of a dilemma. No counselor wants to accuse a client of something he or she did not do. On the other hand, Robert, through his denial, may be telling you how he characteristically deals with his abusive behavior – he just denies it. If so, you do not want to collude with his strategy by failing to confront it.

Dilemmas like this are common, and they speak to the importance of a thorough assessment in the initial stages of counseling. Objective tools such as the Conflict Tactics Scale (CTS) and the utility of a release that allows you to speak with the partner can help clarify the issue for you. However, while the counselor needs to be confident in his or her facts, you will rarely have all of the information you would like to have. Take a moment to review all the information garnered in the initial assessment. If the evidence suggests that the client is denying his or her abusive behavior, confront the denial.

Unless abusive clients like Robert overcome their denial of the problem, it is doubtful that they will be able to make meaningful changes in their behavior. Refusing to collude with abusive clients is the responsibility of every counselor. In turn, clients must assume their responsibility for past abusive behaviors by acknowledging them. In my experience, this is the first step towards making meaningful behavioral change. Until clients take this first step, nothing meaningful happens in our time together. The counselor must be willing to confront Robert's denial, help him summon the courage within himself to face his problem, and provide support his efforts to change. The confrontation strategies below are consistently helpful when I find myself in this situation:

1. Ask Robert to clarify the discrepancy between his denial and the information at hand. Robert says, "I don't abuse anyone." The therapist responds, "How does that fit with what you told me on the CTS? It says here that you slapped your wife twice, swore at her six times, and pushed her three times in the past year."

2. Explore Robert's concerns about disclosure. Is he concerned about confidentiality issues or the possibility you will report disclosures to the police? Is there a child custody hearing or a criminal matter pending?

3. Try to develop an alliance with Robert, and assure him that he does not have to be alone in this. "Robert," says the counselor, "I think there is a lot more to this than what you are telling me. You need to let me be your friend in this. I really want to help you, but I can't unless you tell me what is going on."

4. Find out what Robert does care about, and link it to his partner abuse counseling. Robert may not care about the harm he is causing his wife, divorce, or even incarceration. He does not care about himself. Further, he may not like his wife much, and he may be unwilling to make the effort to change for her sake. However, Robert may care very much about his children, his medical license, or something else. Once you know what Robert cares about, suggest that ending abusive behavior can help him keep it. For example, I once had a client who cared about his son, but little else. He acknowledged that abusive behavior towards his son's mother also harmed the child, who often witnessed it. After a couple of sessions, he told me that he put his son's picture in a conspicuous place. When he needed to motivate himself to change (to stay in The Box), he looked at the picture. It worked.

5. Tell Robert what you want for him and his relationships. "Robert," says the counselor, "if your relationship is having problems like these, it's crying out for someone to step up and be a leader. That might as well be you. I want you to become a true leader in your home. I want you to have the skills and tools you need to handle problems in a way that makes you feel

proud, rather than ashamed. I want your family to be proud of you and not fear you." Please remember that use of the word "leader" is very powerful among this population of clients, but you must make it clear that you are talking about leading by example, rather than by making others do what you want them to do. For example, a leader is not a tyrant. Leaders stay in The Box, tyrants get out of The Box. Leaders spawn respect, not fear. Leaders control themselves, not others, etc.

6. Tell Robert what you need from him in order to continue. "Robert," the counselor says, "I want to help, but to do that I need you to be open and honest with me. I will always be truthful, and I need the same from you. If you are not willing to do that, it's hard to see how I can be helpful to you."

7. Wish Robert the best and tell him that the session is over. He can go home now. Known in some circles as "the bounce," the strategy is risky, but it often gets results where other strategies fail. Many of the most successful clients in my counseling program were "bounced" out of my office more than once before they provided sufficient disclosure to accept them as clients. It usually works best when there is significant external pressure on the client to participate in partner abuse counseling. External pressure may come from a partner threatening separation, a concerned counselor, or even a court order. The bounce goes like this:

Therapist: "Are you sure you don't need counseling?"

Robert: "That's right. I've never abused anyone."

Therapist: "Well, I guess our session is over. Thanks for coming in, Robert. It was nice talking to you."

Robert: "That's it? You don't want to see me anymore?"

Therapist: "I don't think so. I thought you wanted counseling for partner abuse, but it looks like there was some sort of mistake. Obviously, you don't want it. I don't think we need to meet again."

Robert: "But my wife (or partner, or counselor, or judge) said I have to come to counseling or else! She might even leave me."

Therapist: "Wow, that's really tough!"

Robert: "Well, will you give me a letter saying I don't need counseling?"

Therapist: "No, I can't do that. All I really know is that you don't think you need it. I'll be happy to give you a letter saying you don't think you have a problem with partner abuse and don't want counseling."

Robert" "That won't help."

Therapist: "Yeah ... I'm sorry about that. Why don't you take some time and think things over. You might remember things that you've done to your partner that you've forgotten about. My door isn't closed to you. If you decide that you do need partner abuse counseling after all, give me a call. Good luck, Robert."

A counselor may use one or several of these strategies in the same session to confront Robert's denial. As an aside, please understand that confrontation, as used here, does not include efforts to humiliate or degrade the client. Confrontation can be gentle or strong, as your clinical intuition and style indicate, but it is never hostile or demeaning.

Blame

Several years ago a newspaper published statements that people made in auto accident reports. One motorist wrote, "A pedestrian hit me and went under my car." Another wrote, "The telephone pole was approaching fast, I was attempting to swerve out of its path when it struck my front end." I could not help thinking of these statements as I listened to Hank, a new client describe his abusive behavior toward his spouse. When I asked Hank why he hurt his partner, he said, "Because I was mad!" When I asked him why he was angry he said, "Because of what she did!" According to Hank's line of reasoning, his own choices had nothing to do with his act of abuse; it's as if Hank wasn't even there. Hank thinks like an abuser, and that is why he acts like one.

The problem with Hank's way of thinking is that he blames his behavior on his anger, and he blames his anger on his spouse. What is Hank leaving out? He's leaving himself out. The goal of counseling is to put Hank back into the incident and help him understand the role his thoughts played in (1) the anger he felt, and (2) his choice to express that anger abusively.

Let us get back to Robert. Seeing that his old way of dealing with this problem (just deny it) is not effective, he changes gears: "I'm here because my wife is always pushing my buttons. Believe me, she knows just what buttons to push! She's the one who needs counseling, not me." Robert wants to convince you that he is the victim, so he tries to blame his wife for his actions. He points out her every flaw. He relates in detail every bad thing she ever did to him. In the hope of justifying his abuse, he tries to convince you that he had NO CHOICE other than violence.

When confronting blame, I tell clients like Robert that I understand why he gets angry, but anger does not justify his abuse. Every couple has legitimate problems, I tell him, but the only person responsible for violence is the one doing the hitting, and that was Robert. He does not always get to choose the situation he has to deal with (such as how his wife acts), but he always gets to choose how he reacts to the situation. Robert is responsible for how he responds to every situation and person in his life. If his reaction is verbally or physically abusive, he has to take responsibility for that. Finally, I tell him that, regardless of how angry he was, HE STILL HAD A CHOICE. Robert, not his wife, chose the violence.

So far, Robert is having an unpleasant session. His usual way of handling problems is not getting very far. Let us take a closer look at the subject of blame. Counselors must challenge their clients' attempts to blame others for their abusive behavior. Blame is an attempt to place responsibility for our choices on others. Blame is easy to recognize if you know what words to listen for. People who blame start sentences with words like you, he, she, and they. Blamers also like to say things like:

- *She wouldn't let me leave alone.*
- *He got me arrested.*
- *He had a message from his ex on his cell phone.*
- *She was seeing other guys.*
- *She hit me first; all I did was defend myself.*
- *She kept nagging until I blew up.*
- *He should be in these classes instead of me.*
- *She wouldn't do what I told her.*
- *It's his fault I have to take this counseling.*
- *She pushed my buttons.*

The easiest way to recognize a blaming statement is to listen to the first word used in the sentence. The first word used will often be "he" or "she". When you hear these words, you can be sure that the abuser is trying to take the spotlight away from him or her and place it on their partner. The blaming abuser wants to point out, in detail, all of their partner's shortcomings, and thereby avoid talking about their own behavior. The blamer wants to show that they were justifiably angry, jealous, or frustrated in the hope that it will excuse their abusive behavior. Playing the "blame game" is a waste of time because anger, however justified, is never an excuse for abusive conduct.

I remind clients like Robert that he does not get to choose how his partner behaves, but he always chooses his own behavior. While he does not get to choose the situation that he has to deal with, he always chooses how he reacts to it. If he chooses to react with abuse and violence, he must take full responsibility for that choice. Blaming does not make abusive behavior acceptable, or make violence against a family member any less hurtful. Robert alone is responsible for his actions, even when he is angry. Even when Robert is angry, he is still responsible for how he chooses to express his anger. If he expresses it in a destructive and harmful way, Robert alone is to blame. In short, justifiable anger is no excuse for partner violence.

Blaming is the adversary of change. Like denial, it prevents people from accepting responsibility for their choices. Focusing on others prevents clients from learning what they need to do differently the next time they are in a similar situation. Counselors must not allow their clients to spend large quantities of valuable session time addressing the victim's choices rather than their own choices. If clients spend a lot of time using the words "she" or "he," rather than the word "I", there is blaming going on. Encourage clients to focus on themselves, their choices, and on the change that they want to make in themselves.

Suppose Robert says, as clients often do, "If you only knew my wife, you would understand why I blow up!" The therapist may keep the focus on Robert by saying, "I'm not suggesting that your wife is perfect. At times, people behave in ways you cannot understand, or in ways that deliberately hurt and provoke you. Nevertheless, you are always responsible for how you choose to handle these situations. Let's face it - people are not always going to be nice to you. Sometimes people behave in ways that frustrate and infuriate. Still, if you respond to that behavior with abuse and violence, you are in the wrong, period, every time, no excuses.

Remember, explaining why you were angry does NOT explain why you chose to express your anger in a violent way. The reason you got angry is one issue. Your choice to express it abusively is a very different issue. What's the bottom line? One of the best things you can do for yourself and your family is to stop blaming others. Take full responsibility for everything you have ever said, and everything you have ever done. Do this, and you're well on your way to making positive changes in your life."

Abusive clients blame their partners, but they also blame their anger. Actually, they blame their partners for their anger, and their anger for their behavior. In a session, the blame sounds like the following exchange:

Therapist: "Why did you hit your wife?"

Client: "Because I was mad!"

Therapist: "Why were you mad?"

Client: "Because of the things she said and did!"

Therapist: "Well, why did she say and do those things?"

Client: "Because she's nuts! Like I said, Doc, she needs counseling more than I do."

Abusive clients attribute (blame) their abusive behavior to their emotional state, and their emotional state to their partner's behavior. They are, as they perceive it, victims of unavoidable anger caused by their partner's irrational behavior. When I listen to new clients describe their abuse, I often feel as though my clients and their partners were not even in the same room during the assaults. In some ways, partner abuse counseling involves putting the abusive client back in the room and keeping them there. Confronting blame is a decisive step towards this goal.

Minimizing

When we left Robert, he was having a hard time in his first session. You will remember that Robert tried denial and blame, but the counselor was not buying it. Frustrated, he changes gears once more. "OK," declares Robert, "maybe I was wrong! But I didn't hit her, I only slapped her!" Robert has entered the magical world of minimizing. People who minimize use certain words to magically make things appear smaller than they really are. At least, they try. Listening to a good "minimizer" is a little like having a front row seat to a Las Vegas magic show. When I hear minimizing words, I often sit back and enjoy the show. I know that I have to confront it eventually, but I can still admire the skill and talent of a good magic show.

Confront minimizing by teaching clients to avoid using minimizing words. "Robert," you say, "you just said 'I didn't hit her, I just slapped her.' Say that again, but this time leave out the word 'just.'" Robert says, "I slapped her." It sounds different without the minimizing word. Minimizing is an attempt to make abuse appear less severe, usually by using magic words like those in the box below. With a little practice, your clients will recognize them easily.

Magic Minimizing Words:

only	a little	merely	maybe
They said I . . .	I might have	at most	barely
just	only once	hardly	an argument

Abusive clients made the minimizing statements below. Can you identify the minimizing words? The information in parenthesis came out later.

Minimizing Statements:

- *It was only an argument. (Client was charged with assault with a deadly weapon.)*
- *I never really hurt her, she just bruises easily. (Client punched spouse repeatedly in the breasts and in her groin area where bruises were not likely to show.)*
- *I never hit her, I just slapped her. (You already met Robert.)*
- *I only pushed her away. I don't know how she hurt her head. Maybe she tripped. (Client pushed his girlfriend so hard that her head slammed against the wall, causing severe bleeding.)*
- *Maybe I had my hands around her throat, but I wasn't squeezing hard, so I never really choked her. (What can I add? This is a classic as it is.)*

When clients use words like these to describe acts of abuse, know that they are minimizing. Like denial and blame, minimization keeps clients from looking at their behavior honestly, learning about themselves, and making meaningful changes. To summarize, denial, blame, and minimizing sound like this:

Denial: "I didn't do anything wrong."

Blame: "I did something wrong, but it's his/her fault."

Minimizing: "I did something wrong, but only a little bit."

Abusive clients often use these behaviors to avoid making meaningful changes in their behavior, or just to talk themselves out of doing something that they know they should do, but would rather not. Martin, for example, came to recognize his tendency to use denial, blame and minimizing (he called these behaviors "B.S.") to avoid looking at himself honestly. He knew that they would keep him from making positive changes in his life, and reaching his goal of a violence-free relationship. One day after a session, he wrote this note to himself:

"As I was leaving group, I realized that I can BS (deny, blame and minimize) my way through my homework and my group and never change a thing. I can beat my next mate, go to jail, and return to this group, then repeat it all over again. It's up to me and me alone to take change to heart. I want to be different. I've got to take a more positive and active role in this group. I need to take responsibility for my life (no woman to blame everything on).

As I see it, the stronger I am the better my chances are to learn how to make the right choices now and in the future."

Aaron, another member of the group, worked courageously to keep denial, minimizing, and blame out of his Anger Inventory, even though he had to deal with painful memories and some unpleasant truths about himself. Aaron struggled in the beginning of his counseling the way most people do, but in the end, he was successful in his goal to remove violence from his relationship. Here are some excerpts from his Anger Inventory:

Aaron's Anger Inventory

If a person were to look at me, he would see evidence of intelligence and high achievement. He would see undergraduate and graduate degrees, and one year of law school. He would also see a number of academic and professional honors. What he would not see is the profile of an abuser: a physically violent and verbally abusive and assaultive man. Until a year ago, I never considered the possibility that I was abusive or physically violent, but now I know that I am and that I have been for a long, long time. I am aware of the violent and abusive potential within me.

As I agonized in jail for four days, I began my metamorphosis. My thinking evolved from "How could she!" to "What have I done?" Even so, a lot of my concern about what I had done was over the social ramifications and personal embarrassment of my awful behavior rather than on the horrible things I had said and done to my wife. My focus now is on my behavior and how to stay in "the box" and how I can make amends to my family. I never want to lose my vivid mental picture of the forgiving face of my wife through the glass of the visitor's section of the jail. I thank her for filing her complaint against me. In the process of exerting my "male privilege", I physically and emotionally damaged my wife and caused my children inestimable pain and distress. I have seen fear in their eyes as they recognize my rage. I have noticed their avoidance of me at times and their timid demeanor with me. I will forever try to rectify the damage I have done to all my loved ones. I can now empathize with them from the perspective of the scared, bewildered, and angry child that I was.

As I attended my weekly meetings that were mandated by Judge Andrews, I recognized myself in every element that the course covered. I recognized profound denial, blame, and minimizing in my behaviors that eventually necessitated my arrest. I recognized my exercise of male privilege, verbal abuse, and hurtful statements. Ultimately, I recognized that I was a violent man. I also realized that I had considered myself the "victim" while I was victimizing others. My experiences this past year as a result of my arrest for domestic violence have been the most profound of my life. I have learned more about myself than at any other time in my life. I sincerely appreciate the system that is in place to stop domestic violence and to compel me to take a long look at myself. I would not "reform" a single aspect of the unpleasantness that I experienced in jail. It should NOT be a pleasant experience!

Furthermore, the domestic violence classes have helped me recognize the awful potential within me and honestly begin to make real changes in my life. I now have tools and lessons to rely on to help me avoid abusive encounters of any kind in the future. Should I fail to heed them, I will have no one but myself to blame.

But what happened to Robert? Robert was an actual client, and he made the statements attributed to him in this chapter. In time, he became a leader in his group. He was successful in his counseling. His success was largely due to his willingness to look at himself honestly. When abusive clients evaluate their behavior and choices honestly, truthfully, and without reservation they open the door for great things to happen. Encourage clients to write their own Anger Inventory by answering the Anger Inventory Questions from this chapter, or similar questions of your own. After answering the questions, have your clients set the answers aside. After a day or two, have your clients read them again and ask themselves:

- *Was I able to identify and eliminate all denial, blame, and minimizing from my answers?*
- *Was I able to accept full responsibility for my choices and behaviors?*
- *What did I learn from the exercise?*

If you are a counselor working with a group, ask clients to share their answers to the Anger Inventory with other group members and get their feedback. If you are working individually, encourage your clients ask people that they trust and respect to read their Anger Inventory and solicit their suggestions and advice. Do not allow clients to cheat themselves. As Robert, Martin, and Aaron found, clients have to keep denial, blame, and minimizing out of the Anger Inventory if they are going to benefit from it.

A Last Word about Denial, Blame, and Minimization

Experience has accentuated the importance of confronting denial, blame, and minimization. They distort the client's perception of the problem and impede meaningful behavioral change. However, over the years I have come to see denial, blame, and minimization as a positive prognostic indicator as well. I feel more optimistic about a client who says, "I only slapped her, and that was only because she pushed me so far that I lost control," than a client who says calmly and with a smile, "Sure, I punched her. In fact, I beat the hell out of her. I'd do it again in a New York minute."

For many abusive clients, denial, blame, and minimization appear to suggest that their abusive behavior is ego-dystonic, rather than ego-syntonic. If ego-dystonic, abusive behavior is viewed by the self as unacceptable and inconsistent with the total personality. Hence, the client experiences a need to distort the behavior (to deny and minimize) and to avoid responsibility for it (to blame others).

If ego-syntonic, abusive behavior is acceptable and fully integrated into the personality. Through the act of blaming, for example, the client communicates that a part of his (or her) self, and rejects abusive behavior as unacceptable. That makes my job easier, and I feel more optimistic about helping the client rid himself (or herself) of the behavior. On the other hand, when clients present with no attempt to defend the self through denial, blame, or minimization, I feel less optimistic about change. Ego-syntonic clients may lack important internal motivation to make meaningful and difficult changes in their behavior.

Early Cognitive Interventions

The strategies presented thus far emphasize a behavioral framework that minimizes abusive behavior and ensures victim safety as quickly as possible. As counseling progresses, cognitive strategies play an increasingly important role. It is important to understand the "cognitive set" of the abusive client.

Understanding the "Cognitive Set" of the Abusive Client

Over the years, I have had the opportunity to interview thousands of men and women and listen to them talk about their abusive behavior. Some clients grew up in a home where witnessing violence between their parents was a way of life. Others never witnessed violence as a child. Some had been the object of violence themselves, while others had not. Some had tolerated abuse by their partner for many years before participating in the abuse themselves, while others were the sole abusers in the relationship. Among some clients, the violence was widely generalized. Among others, they had never engaged in a single violent act before the single instance of partner abuse.

While the circumstances surrounding the abusive behavior varied from client to client, there was one striking similarity among them. At the instant that clients became abusive, they shared a similar cognitive set consisting of three components. Whenever the cognitive set was fully active, they abused. Whenever the set was not active, or only partially active, they did not abuse. The clients' cognitive set at the time, rather than the situation they found themselves in (what their partners were saying or doing), seemed to regulate abusive behavior. I consistently found that when my clients think like an abuser, they act like one.

How do abusers think? When presenting this information at a live seminar, I ask the mental health professionals in the audience to think of a time when they verbally abused their own partners. This causes some shuffling around in seats, as none of us like to admit that we have ever done such a thing. Nevertheless, if we apply the operational definition of verbal abuse used in The Box model (yelling, swearing, name-calling, insults, etc.) most people acknowledge that they have verbally abused a partner at some time in their relationships.

Suppose that we have your incident of verbal abuse on videotape. Rewind the videotape to the moment just before you verbally abuse your partner (yell, swear, insult, etc.). At that moment, just as you are about to abuse, who are you blaming for what you are about to say? The answer is, you blame the person you are about to yell at. How did you convince yourself that it was OK to yell at your partner? The answer is, you either minimized the yelling, called it something else, or both (e.g., Damn it all, I'm only trying to make her understand!). At the instant before the yelling, did you think you had a right to take control? The answer is, yes. You believed, at that moment in time, if only for an instant, that you had the right to control another person by either making your partner do something against his or her will, or punish your partner for doing something you disagree with.

Every abusive act requires transfer of personal responsibility away from the self and to the person we are about to abuse, justification to the self of the imminent abuse, and assumption of power over the abused. At the moment of abuse, the cognitive set looks something like this:

1. *"I'm not responsible for what I'm about to do to you – you are."*

2. *"What I'm about to do is OK because it's only (minimize and call it something acceptable)."*

3. *"I'm the boss, and I have a right to make you do what I want and punish you if you do something I don't like."*

Some people abuse a lot. Others seldom or almost never abuse. The frequency with which the abusive set occurs seems to vary, depending upon the core beliefs and values of the individual. Similarly, the level and duration of relational conflict required before the set manifests itself vary according to one's own core beliefs and values regarding responsibility, overt hostility, and equality. The point that I want to emphasize is this – to the degree a person thinks like an abuser, he or she will abuse. I believe this to be true for you and for me, as well as for the clients with whom we work (and label "abusers"), for whenever you or I behave in a verbally (or physically) abusive manner towards another individual, we share, at least for an instant, the same cognitive set as the abusive clients with whom we work.

As counseling progresses, attention turns toward increasing the client's awareness of the cognitive set associated with partner abuse, and to confronting core beliefs and attitudes about personal responsibility, overt hostility during conflict, and control over others.

Responsibility

The first component of the cognitive set is a denial of personal responsibility for one's own imminent actions. Clients believe, if only for an instant, that they are not responsible for what they are about to do to their partner. If you could stop them just before an abusive act and ask them, "Who's to blame for what you are about to do to your partner?" they would answer, "He is!" or "She is!" Thoughts such as, "You're driving me to it," "You're pushing my buttons," and "You asked for it and now you're going to get it!" are characteristic of this part of the abusive set. The belief is, "I'm not responsible for what I'm about to do to you – you are!"

Typical cognitions associated with avoidance of responsibility

She's driven me to this!

It's her fault!

She pushed my buttons!

He's gone too far!

She's asking for it!

I can't take it anymore!

I warned him, and now he deserves what he gets!

She brought this on herself!

She didn't leave me any other choice!

The clinician should take every opportunity to challenge the cognitive set associated with abusive behavior, starting with the avoidance of responsibility. The challenges made by the therapist, in time, become the basis for "self-talk" that the client will use to avoid the abusive set. "I," the client comes to accept, "am fully responsible for my own words and behaviors. I can't always choose the situation I'm faced with, but I always choose how I react to it. If I react in an abusive manner, I have to take responsibility for it without blaming others."

Comfort with Violence (It's OK)

The second component of the abusive set is the belief that one's impending abusive behavior is OK – it is neither wrong nor abusive. Clients usually accomplish this by minimizing the abusive behavior, or by calling it something else such as self-defense, problem solving, being strong, or standing up for one's rights. In one case, a client established his comfort with extreme levels of abuse towards his ex-girlfriend by calling it an act of fatherly love. In his mind, it was not abuse he was about to engage in, but an act of love for his son, of whom the client wanted custody.

The client, whom we will call Isaac, was having a custody battle over his son with his ex-girlfriend, Alicia. Dan figured that the way to solve the problem and stand up for his rights as a father was to kill Alicia's new boyfriend in front of her. She would be frightened into giving up custody. Dan took a gun over to Alicia's apartment and barged in, waiving the gun. He called for Alicia, but to Dan's chagrin, Alicia was not home. The new boyfriend was there, but Dan wanted Alicia to see the killing in person. She would be intimidated by the killing and let Dan have the children. Frustrated, Dan pistol-whipped Alicia's boyfriend and left, disappointed that his plan did not work out. When I interviewed Dan several years after the incident, he told me that he was surprised when he was arrested a few hours after leaving Alicia's home. "After all," he said, "I didn't even shoot anyone! What's the big deal? I didn't even think her boyfriend would call the police over a little thing like that!"

Look into Dan's mind at the time of the incident, and you will see the cognitive set of the abuser come together. Imagine we could film the entire incident from start to finish, and that we could stop the film just before Dan broke through the door. At that moment, who does Dan blame for what he is about to do in Alicia's home? How does he convince himself that what he is about to do is OK? Dan's "set" at the time was as follows:

Dan's Denial of Responsibility: "Alicia's forcing me to do this by being so unreasonable about the children. She's pushing my buttons by taking them away from me. Alicia is bringing this on herself, and she's leaving me no other choice. She has it coming. I can't count on the courts anymore, so I have to take things into my own hands. They've all forced me into this."

Dan's Efforts to Minimize and/or Call the Abuse Something Else: "I'm just being a good father to my kid because he will be better off living with me than with his mother. I'm not a violent guy; hell no, I'm a good father who puts his son first and stands up for his welfare. My actions aren't abusive. This is just an act of love to give my son a better life." (Too bad about the trauma the kids went through when they witnessed Dan's loving act.)

Help clients avoid this component of the set by teaching them to identify and avoid minimizing language, and to avoid the tendency to call abuse something other than what it is. As you recall, examples of minimizing language often associated with partner abuse include:

48

| Only | Sort of | Maybe | At most |
| Just | A little | Barely | An argument |

Clients also label abusive behavior something more acceptable. For example, a client may say, "I am not abusing my wife, I am ..."

Having an argument	Acting in self-defense
Standing up for myself	Problem solving
Controlling the situation	Not being pushed around
Teaching him/her a lesson	Defending myself

Clients often label abuse "self-defense." Abusive men claim self-defense as often as abusive women do. In my experience, clients who assert that they hit their partner in self-defense are usually calling abuse something else. To clarify the issue, ask them, "What is the main thing a person feels when they act in true self-defense?" The answer, of course, is fear. "Now ask yourself," you continue, "what was the main thing you felt when you got out of The Box?" The client's answer is usually "anger." "If you were feeling anger rather than fear, I don't think you weren't acting in self-defense. I think you were mad about something and wanted to strike back. That's not self-defense."

Power and Control

The third part of the set involves convincing oneself that one has the right to secure power and control over the partner. Most often, it involves a belief that one has a right to make the partner do something against his or her will, or that one has a right to punish the partner for misbehavior.

The counselor must look for every opportunity to challenge the notion that the client ever has the moral or legal right to force or punish his or her partner. The basis for self-talk during conflict becomes, "My partner and I are two equals who voluntarily decided to build a home together. I'm not her (or his) boss, and she (or he) is not my boss. There are no bosses in our relationship."

Counselors see significant changes in the cognitive set of their clients as they proceed through counseling. When a new client enters a counseling group, he or she usually holds the following set of beliefs:

Belief System: New Client

Responsibility: New clients deny personal responsibility for their behavior. They believe their partner (and everyone else) is responsible for their actions. When asked who is responsible for the abuse, they will usually say, "He is!" or "She is!"

Comfort with Violence: New clients believe hostile and abusive behaviors are legitimate problem solving tools and minimize their abusive behaviors. Often, they think they were not abusive at all, and show a high comfort level with such behaviors. When asked whether their behavior was abusive, they will usually reply, "No way!"

Power and Control: New clients see themselves as the boss in their relationship, and want to control and dominate their partner. When asked, "Who is the boss in their relationship?" they usually say, "I am!"

Belief System: Intermediate Stages

In the intermediate stages of the counseling process, the cognitive set begins to change. Their set begins to look like this:

Responsibility: Clients who are starting to make progress accept some personal responsibility for their own behavior, but still believe their partner is at least partly responsible for their behavior. When asked who is responsible for the abuse or their arrest, they will usually say, "We BOTH were!"

Comfort with Violence: Intermediate clients see hostile and abusive behaviors as wrong, but still want to focus on their partners' problem behaviors rather than their own. They still minimize their abusive behaviors, but their minimizing is more subtle and less obvious (Ex: These groups are great, but I think she (or he) should be here too.). Their comfort level with abusive behaviors is lower, and the clients are experimenting with the new skills they are learning. When asked whether their behavior was acceptable, they reply, "No, I admit it was wrong to do that, BUT my partner shouldn't have ..."

Power and Control: Intermediate clients are willing to share some of their power as the boss, but not all. When asked, "Who is the boss in their relationship?" they usually say, "We BOTH are!"
Clients in advanced stages of counseling evidence significant changes in their belief system, as shown below.

Belief System: Seasoned Clients

Responsibility: Seasoned clients accept responsibility for their behavior without blaming others for their own choices. When asked who is responsible for the abuse or their arrest, the reply is, "I am." Quickly recognize blaming comments made by others, and willing to confront less experienced clients on the issue of responsibility.

Comfort with Violence: Seasoned clients see hostile and abusive behaviors as wrong, period. They are willing to focus on their own behaviors and goals, rather than the behavior of their partner. They do not engage in minimizing. Their comfort level with abusive behaviors is very low, and they show a high level of proficiency in the use of the skills they have learned. If asked whether their past behavior was acceptable, they reply "No," in a tone of voice that makes you feel stupid for having asked such a dumb question. They are willing to take a leadership role in the counseling group, and confront minimizing statements by others. Their comments are so "on target" that the counselor often feels useless and unneeded. (Very often, these feelings are accurate.)

Power and Control: Seasoned clients are willing to share power in their relationship, and they see their partner as an equal. If asked, "Who is the boss in their relationship?" they reply, "There are no bosses in my relationship."

To summarize, seasoned clients demonstrate the ability to maintain the following "set" during relational conflict:

Responsibility: "I am totally and solely responsible for everything I ever do and say."

Comfort with Violence (It is NOT OK): Verbal and physical abuse is always wrong. It is irresponsible, hurtful, and never justified.

Power and Control: My partner is my equal in every way. I never have the right to force my will on my partner.

Meaningful change requires that clients avoid the cognitive set associated with partner abuse. Specifically, clients must make changes in the way they think about responsibility, violence, and control issues. Early estimates of client progress are usually determined by his or her ability to stay in The Box, recognize warning signs, and use time-out appropriately. Yet, as important as these strategies are, the abuse and violence will not end unless there are accompanying changes in the cognitive set and the associated core beliefs that make abuse possible.

The Box in Advanced Stages of Counseling

Nevertheless, the early efforts to stay in The Box bear fruit in the later stages of counseling. The client and counselor have addressed issues of responsibility, blame, and minimizing. In addition, the self-monitoring skill developed by watching for warning signs is of particular value to the client during the shift from a behavioral to a cognitive focus in treatment. As the counselor and client address cognitive issues such as the abusive set and core beliefs, the client continues self-monitoring - he or she just looks for different things. Many years ago, a client asked, "Dr. Adams, is it normal for my warning signs to change?" She related how her warning signs changed over the course of counseling, from overt behavioral warning signs (yelling, cursing, throwing things, etc.) to more subtle, cognitive warning signs. "I don't ever yell at my husband or kids anymore," she reported. "Now I notice when I THINK about yelling, and I call a time-out then. Is that normal?"

Notice her implied acceptance of responsibility for her actions and her refusal to minimize or re-label verbally abusive behavior (components one and two of the cognitive set). Further, she reports a shift from the monitoring of large, overt behaviors to a monitoring of the more subtle, less overt cognitions associated with the abusive set.

Over the course of counseling, most clients experience a natural and stepwise shift in what they are able to monitor during times of interpersonal tension and conflict. Most clients are able to recognize large, loud, overt behaviors as indicators of imminent abusive conduct. As clients refine self-monitoring skills through experience and practice with behavioral indicators, they acquire a growing capacity to monitor their cognitions, particularly those associated with abusive behavior. In other words, clients learn to self-monitor in the early stages of counseling, and become increasingly skillful and knowledgeable about what to monitor in the latter stages.

For example, Darryl and Paula, two clients of mine, were discussed earlier in this book. Both applied the recognized warning signs, but with varying degrees of skill. Darryl wrote:

"About a few days ago we both got into an argument. A perfect time to practice my time-outs. She noticed it first that me and her were going at it at each other. It started to build up (the argument). So right then she tells me, 'I need a time out.' 'Why,' I ask myself, 'didn't I notice it first?'" Paula, who had much more experience with her warning signs, wrote, *"My blood is boiling. I feel hot. My hands are perspiring, my voice cracking. I was MAD. Michelle (Paula's daughter) was hostile. I recognized my warning signs. I decided to take a time out until I cooled off."*

Notice that Darryl failed to notice his warning signs even though he and his partner were out of The Box, or "going at each other." Paula, on the other hand, recognized more subtle warning signs and took a time-out well before she engaged in overt acts of hostility.

Clients continue to become more skillful over time. As clients shift from behavioral to cognitive warning signs, a sharp drop in the frequency of "out of The Box" incidents is experienced, often to the pleasant surprise of both clients and their partners. "My wife looked at me the other day," said a proud client recently, "and she said, 'Wow, have you changed!'"

Automatic Thoughts, Core Beliefs, and Self-Talk

As counseling progresses, they delve further into their beliefs and attitudes about responsibility, violence, and control. Clients also explore other relevant beliefs such as interpersonal trust, their expectations of others if they show vulnerability, their ideas about strength, and their ideals regarding manhood.

A cognitive-behavioral approach serves this purpose well, but requires that the clinician provide clients with more information about cognitive-behavioral terms and theory. Of course, the approach shown below is not the only way to address these important issues with clients. It may not even be the best of all possible ways. It is, however, a way that has been highly successful in my work with this population over the years.

Dave was a "rocket." Some people are "volcanoes" – their anger builds slowly over time until they explode violently – but Dave was a classic rocket. His anger could soar to explosive and abusive levels in a heartbeat. Right now, he had a puzzled expression on his face. "Dr. Adams," he said, "I understand everything you're saying. You're saying that abuse is caused by the way we think about responsibility, violence, and control. We abuse when we think like an abuser. That makes sense to me. But sometimes I get mad really fast, before I've had time to think anything at all. Like, my wife says something and 'BOOM!'... I'm mad.

How can I get mad when I don't have time to think anything?" The other clients in the group looked at me and nodded. They were thinking the same thing as Dave. Sometimes Dave's anger surfaced quickly, so quickly that there was not time for him to think anything at all. His anger and aggressive behavior came so fast that they had the appearance of a knee-jerk reaction, the way Dave's foot might jerk if a doctor tapped his knee with a hammer. Do Dave's thoughts cause anger in situations like these? If the way we think causes anger, how can we get angry before we have time to think?

When Dave asked his question, I thought of Brenda's story. While her case did not involve partner abuse, her belief system was characteristic of the abusive client. Indeed, Brenda had asked the same question in her group a couple of days earlier. Like Dave, Brenda was a rocket, and she told the following story.

One day, Brenda was leaving a department store when she heard her sister shout an insult to a man walking behind them. Brenda did not see what the altercation was about, but the man must have thought Brenda had insulted him because he grabbed her by the arm. Brenda reacted instantly. Although she was holding her infant daughter, she turned and punched the man in the face.

Brenda told us it was self-defense, and I might have believed her if she hadn't stopped "defending herself," handed her baby to her sister, and continued punching the man in the face. When a security guard tried to pull Brenda away, she went after him too. If Brenda were really acting in self-defense, as she claimed, she would have been looking for the security guard for help, rather than beating the crap out of him. Both the guard and the man who grabbed her were in ragged shape by the time the police arrived, and they arrested Brenda.

Brenda told us that she did not remember thinking anything at all when the man grabbed her arm. She was enraged instantly, before she had time to think. The person grabbed her by the arm and "BOOM!"... Brenda was mad. Did Brenda's thoughts play a role in this situation, or was her aggression an unthinking reaction?

To answer this question for clients, I explain the theoretical concepts of core beliefs and automatic thoughts. Core beliefs refer to the basic attitudes, beliefs, and values that we develop over the course of our lives. Most core beliefs are formed early in life, in our childhood and adolescence. They take form over the years, shaped by the experiences we have growing up, the things we are taught by others, and the way we see other people act in certain situations.

Later in life, as adults, the core beliefs we develop early in life continue to influence the way we think about ourselves, others, and the world we live in. Am I good or bad? Can I trust people, or will they hurt me if given the chance? Is the world a safe or a threatening place? Is it good to get angry? What types of things should I get angry about? Is it OK to get violent when I'm mad? If I'm slow to get angry and aggressive will my partner take advantage of me? Is violence a good way to solve problems and make my partner do what I want? Clients answer these questions in a manner that is consistent with their core beliefs.

Let us return to Brenda. To understand her emotional and behavioral reaction to the man grabbing her arm, we need to understand her core beliefs. There was a time, as a little girl, when Brenda would not have known how to act when a stranger grabbed her arm. As a young girl she would have wondered, should I be scared and cry and call for help? Should I ask the man what he wants? Should I tell him to let go? Should I run away or fight? She would not have known what to do. She would have had to think about it first. As she grew older, however, Brenda started to build a set of core beliefs or rules to live by. She watched the way others handled certain situations, and listened to the advice of people who seemed to know more than she did. She experimented with different behaviors in a variety of situations to see what worked best for her. She made assumptions about life based on her own experiences, and as the years passed, her core beliefs took shape. Brenda explored her core beliefs in her counseling sessions. Some of her most relevant core beliefs were:

Brenda's Core Beliefs:

- *The world is a dangerous place, people can't be trusted.*
- *People will take advantage and hurt me if they have the chance.*
- *Anger makes me strong, fear makes me weak. It's better to be angry and strong.*
- *When in doubt about a person's intent, assume the worst and get mad.*
- *People usually leave me alone when they see I'll "go off" on them.*
- *If someone makes me feel threatened and I hurt them, it's self-defense.*
- *It's better to hurt others before they can hurt me.*
- *I should apply these rules widely to almost every situation I get into.*

Brenda did not have to think all this when the man grabbed her arm. She had already done her thinking. She did her thinking years ago when she formed her core beliefs, before she ever met the man who now held her by the arm. Now, Brenda's core beliefs told her how she should feel, and what to do. Her thoughts were "automatic thoughts." That is, they were thoughts based on core beliefs formed long ago, rather than on an objective analysis of the current situation.

Automatic thoughts come instantly. They can generate instant anger and aggression. In contrast, thoughts based on analysis of a situation (analytic thoughts) take much longer. Analytic thoughts require clients to gather the facts about a situation and draw some conclusions about them, and that takes time. Whenever clients find themselves instantly angry and aggressive, core beliefs and automatic thoughts are at work. The definitions below help clients grasp the concepts and apply them.

Core Beliefs: Core beliefs refer to basic beliefs about self, others, and our future. Core beliefs are the rules we live by, and everyone has them. They begin to evolve in the early years of our lives. They are based on our thoughts about our early experiences - the things we see others do, and the advice others give us while growing up. Because core beliefs are formed early in life, they are often steeped in childlike and adolescent thinking.

Adolescent Thinking: Adolescent thinking refers to the type of thinking that lacks the insight and understanding that comes with greater life experience. For example, adolescent thinking usually ignores consequences, favors immediate gratification over long-term goals, perceives anger as strong, and overvalues aggression as a way to solve problems. When clients make choices based on adolescent thinking, they make decisions based on their personal wants and needs, rather than the greater needs of the family and the community.

Automatic Thoughts: The term refers to thoughts that flow automatically and without effort from one's basic core beliefs. Automatic thoughts come instantly when core beliefs are activated. For example, suppose a person developed a core belief in his childhood that spiders are extremely dangerous. One day, as an adult, the person sees a spider on his arm. Instantly, he feels fear, jumps around, shouts, and tries frantically to brush the spider off. He did not stop to think about what to do. He already did his thinking about situations like this as a child. When he saw the spider, the core belief about spiders was activated. Automatic thoughts told him what to feel (fear), and what to do (jump, yell, and brush it off fast!).

Analytic Thoughts: Analytic thoughts are the opposite of automatic thoughts. Analytic thoughts involve taking time to consider the facts about the current situation, and think about the best way to handle it. Analytic thoughts consider the long-term consequences of choices, for oneself, others, and the relationship.

Irrational Core Beliefs Can Cause Problems

Unfortunately, Brenda's core beliefs got her into a lot of trouble. There was a time when her core beliefs, and the automatic thoughts that flowed from them, made sense to her as a young woman on the street. She grew up in a gang-infested neighborhood where violence was commonplace. Her tendency to mistrust and assume the worst of others had some basis in reality. Painful experience taught her that it was foolish to trust easily, and danger was everywhere. Anger and violence are still survival strategies to many young people growing up on those streets. However, the same core beliefs that made sense to Brenda as a teenager got her into serious trouble as an adult. Acting on the core beliefs she developed as a child, Brenda now faced charges of battery, resisting arrest, and worst of all, child endangerment, which meant that her child could be taken from her and placed in a foster home.

That is the potential problem with core beliefs. The beliefs that we developed with juvenile minds and limited life experience continue to guide our feelings and behavior after we become adults. Core beliefs are formed early in life when we are young, before we have the capacity to think and reason like an adult, before we had the ability to consider the long-term consequences of our behavior. Many of our core beliefs about anger and physical aggression developed in adolescence, and beliefs based in adolescent thinking lead to adolescent-like behavior. That's why you often see a grown man acting like a child when he's cut off on the freeway, or a grown woman throw a childish tantrum over some perceived insult. Think like an adolescent, like a kid on the schoolyard, and you will act like one. That is how Brenda got in trouble.

Understanding Your Core Beliefs

If you want to live an abuse-free lifestyle, you have to understand your core beliefs and automatic thoughts. Your core beliefs about anger and violence will change over time as you rethink these issues as an adult. By applying adult reasoning, your beliefs will become less adolescent-like and more mature, and as your beliefs mature so will the automatic thoughts that flow from them. Clients notice this change when they find themselves staying surprisingly calm in situations that they used to get angry and aggressive about. They find it easier to stay in The Box, and to keep anger levels below the "I don't care what I say" line. Their core beliefs are changing, and their automatic thoughts no longer invoke anger, aggression, and abusive behavior as the desired response.

Making meaningful changes in core beliefs take time. Clients start by watching their warning signs. Warning signs tell clients when they are getting out of The Box, but they also indicate that adolescent core beliefs are activated. In other words, clients are starting to think and act like an adolescent. As clients have learned, the presence of warning signs is a signal to call a time-out. Now, during the time-out period, clients begin to ask themselves what they were thinking when they got out of The Box. What adolescent beliefs were active? What core beliefs and automatic thoughts were stimulated by the situation? Now is the time to challenge and change them, while they are fresh and available to clients for inspection.

To change your core beliefs, clients need to be aware of them, and the time-out period is a perfect opportunity to educate themselves about their core beliefs. Clients use the opportunity afforded by the time-out period to expose their core beliefs to the light of adult reasoning, something that they were not able to do when they formed them in childhood or the teenage years.

Take Time to Think

Whenever clients feel themselves getting angry (the Tension phase of The Box), it helps to stop and think before they say or do anything. By taking time to think before they react, they minimize the power of core beliefs and automatic thoughts, and increase their chances of staying in The Box. It is also a good idea to put their hands in their pockets until they calm down. (When abusive clients are angry they should always put their hands in their pockets. If they cannot do what they want to do with their hands in their pockets, it is probably a bad idea anyway. Clients must solve relationship problems with their heads, not their hands.)

By taking time to think, clients put automatic thoughts on hold and give analytic thinking a chance to start. For Marcus, a professional athlete who was in counseling several years ago, this was an extremely important concept. Marcus was a defensive back in professional football for many years. One day he made the following observation.

"All my life," said Marcus, *"I've been trained NOT to think. All through football in high school, college, and the pro's, I've been told not to think. You do your thinking during practice. But when the game starts, you've got to react without thinking. By the time you stop to think about what's happening, the play's over. The better I could react to a situation on the field and make a hit, the more I could do that without thinking, the better player I was and the more years I had in the pros.*

"That worked great in football, but it didn't work at home with my family. One day my wife said something and I hit her without thinking. I feel awful and ashamed about it. If I'd just taken a few seconds to think I never would have done it. I have talked to other guys who've played in the pros and they say they've experienced the same thing. The most important thing I've learned in this class is to STOP AND THINK BEFORE I REACT. It's made a big difference in my life."

The diagram below illustrates what Marcus was saying. Let us say that "S" stands for the situation you are in (something that someone says or does) and "R" represents your reaction to it. Marcus' football goals required that he get "R" (his reaction) as close to "S" (the situation on the field) as close to each other as possible, as shown by Figure 1. His goals for his family were different. He wanted to increase the time between the situation he faced and his reaction to it, as shown in Figure 2.

Figure 1:
Little time between the situation
and the response

Figure 2:
There is time to think between the
situation and the response

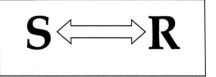

By giving himself time to think before he reacted, Marcus was actually taking steps to reduce the impact of his automatic thoughts and increase the role of analytic thoughts in his decision-making.

Self-Talk

Self-talk is the principal tool that clients in our counseling groups draw on to stay in The Box. Clients consistently rate self-talk as one of the most important skills they take from their counseling experience. Exit questionnaires indicate that self-talk is used more frequently than any other skill to stay in The Box and maintain violence-free relationships. Self-talk is also the main tool used to challenge core beliefs, and keep tension below the "I don't care what I say" and the "I don't care what I do" lines. Clients rely on self-talk to lower anger levels during time-out periods, give themselves time to think before reacting, and increase analytic thinking when deciding how to react to relational conflict.

Self-talk, as used by our clients, is the act of taking charge of one's thoughts. Rather than allowing automatic thoughts to run through their mind unchecked and unchallenged, they "self-talk" to think sensibly and rationally about the situation they are in, and to thoughtfully consider the best way to react. It is a type of analytic thinking. Self-talk is a skill, like riding a bicycle or hitting a curve ball, which takes time and practice to develop. It is an essential skill for abusive clients. The more effective clients become at self-talk, the more control they report over their behavior and emotional life.

Of course, some clients argue that they cannot help the way they feel or the way they think. This most often occurs early in the counseling process. They point to the selfish, unfair, or provoking behavior of their partners and say they cannot help being angry and aggressive. They believe that their anger and abuse is beyond their control. "If you believe that," I often say, "you're fooling yourself. While it is true that many things influence your feelings, they are never totally beyond your control. As long as you have the power to choose one thought over another thought, you have tremendous control over feelings like anger. In fact, your greatest freedom, a freedom that no one can ever take away from you, is the freedom to choose your thoughts, and hence your attitude, in any situation."

As clients become skillful at self-talk, they develop greater direction over their anger and behavior. Maintaining a cognitive-behavioral approach, I encourage clients to self-talk when tension starts to rise. "Let me remind you," I tell them, "that anger (or other feelings such as jealousy, frustration, and resentment) is caused by what goes on between your ears, not what goes on around you. Stop trying to control what is going on around you, and start controlling what is going on in your own head! When automatic thoughts start to invoke anger, use self-talk to regain your composure, reduce anger to manageable levels, and stay in The Box."

Before going any further, let me clear up some common misconceptions that newer clients have about anger and self-talk. First, it is not the goal of counseling to teach clients how to avoid the feeling of anger. Anger is not a "bad" thing – it is just a feeling. Even unpleasant feelings like sadness and anger add color and richness to our existence, and they are often an important source of information about our relationships. "You will always experience anger," I remind clients, "and that's OK. When you have been unfairly treated, when your partner takes advantage or disrespects you, when people deliberately try to hurt you and the people you love – when these things happen you are going to get angry. There are times when you SHOULD get angry. The goal is not to stuff or avoid anger, but to handle it appropriately - to handle your anger in a way that makes the situation better rather than worse." Self-talk is not a magic incantation that will shield them from anger, but it will help them manage your anger appropriately, and express it non-abusively.

Clients also confuse self-talk with happy thoughts (Gee, isn't it a pretty day?), self-affirmations (every day in every way, I'm better and better), and positive thinking (Gosh it hurts being shot, but at least the bullet missed my other vital organs!), or some other nonsense. Personally, I have nothing against this stuff, but it is not self-talk as applied by our clients. Self-talk is rational, logical, and most of all, honest. Self-talk is only effective if clients BELIEVE the things they say to themselves. In other words, self-talk will not help clients who tell themselves that they are not mad, jealous, or frustrated when they really are. If it's not honest you won't believe it, and if you don't believe it, it won't help. When clients self-talk, they think things like the following:

"I'm angry, but I don't want to make things worse. Yelling and shouting will definitely make things worse. Watch for my warning signs. I'll call a time-out if I see them. Stay in the box and try to solve the problem. I love my partner; keep that in mind. Don't 'awfulize' it (blow an ordinary problem out of proportion and make it more horrible, terrible, and awful than it really is). Just focus on the problem and use the skills I have learned. Remember to stop and think before I react. I am not trying to win a fight, and my partner is not my adversary. I want to solve this problem and get back to the OK zone of The Box. Keep my hands in my pockets and my voice down. Stay calm!"

That is how self-talk works. It will not make the tension disappear, but it will help keep clients you in The Box. "Self-talk," I advise clients, "is your line of defense against verbal or physical abuse. It keeps your anger in check. Although there is nothing inherently wrong with anger, anger should never run the show. Anger, unrestrained by self-talk, can grow into blind rage. At that point, reason stops and anger takes over, and anger only cares about immediate gratification. Anger does not care about consequences or who gets hurt. That is why you should never stop reasoning with yourself (using self-talk) when you are angry. Self-talk keeps anger at manageable levels." The story below is an example of what can happen when reason stops and rage takes over.

Rage Visits the Elderly Gentleman

An elderly man entered our counseling group after spending many years in prison. As a condition of his parole, he was required to participate in domestic violence counseling. In his first counseling session, the group asked him to tell his story, as is the custom in our program. The man began the story by describing a verbal argument he had with his son, who was about 25-years-old at the time. As the argument grew louder, the son became more and more disrespectful to the father. In turn, the father's words to his son became more cutting.

The father ordered his son to leave the house, but the son only grew more belligerent. Soon, the father and the son were swearing and physically threatening each other. Enraged by his son's behavior, the father went to his bedroom and got a handgun. Storming back to confront his son, the father brandished the pistol and ordered his son out of the home. He threatened to shoot the boy if he did not get out. Rather than leave, the son took a step towards his father - and the father shot him in the heart. The paramedics arrived a short time later, but his son was dead when they arrived.

The old man wept openly as he told his story, and the other men in the group were silent. He stopped to compose himself, and then continued. He said that his life would never be the same, and he often wished that it would end. He wished that he were dead. A day never went by, he said, that he did not remember his son, and he felt only contempt for himself. Many years had passed since the murder, but even now, he could scarcely believe that he had taken the life of his only son. He relived the nightmare every day of his life. He wept again, haunted by the memory of that night.

After a long pause, he spoke again. When his wife looks at him, he sees in her eyes only loathing for him - the murderer – the man who shot her boy. She lives with him, yes, but the marriage is over. He used to attend church regularly, but not now. He cannot look the priest in the eye. The son was married at the time of his death, and the boy's young wife was pregnant. The man had never had more than a passing glimpse of his grandson. The daughter-in-law has not spoken to the old man since the shooting, and she does not allow the grandson to visit him. After all, he will always be the man who killed the young boy's father. The elderly man sobbed and asked, "What kind of man am I? What kind of man can kill his own son?" The men in the group looked away.

This story is true. It is sad, but it is not unique. Similar things happen every day. How does a man kill his own son? It happened because reason stopped and blind rage took over. It started with the father's core beliefs and automatic thoughts. He came from a very traditional country where the father held absolute authority. His father and his grandfather were very strict. His core belief was that a real man demands unquestioning respect and obedience from his wife and children. When the son fought with him and disobeyed his order to leave the house, his core belief was activated and automatic thoughts relentlessly followed. He would not be a man, he told himself, if he allowed his son to disrespect him in his own home. His son did not respect him as a man. He had to stop his son or lose his self-respect! The man had these thoughts throughout the fight. Anger swelled past the "I don't care what I say line," beyond the "I don't care what I do line," and continued to grow. Riding a wave of anger, he did not think about the possible consequences of his behavior. He was so full of blind rage that he was past rational thinking when he pulled the trigger. The sound of the gunshot, he said, brought his reason back. He said he came to his senses then, and to the awful realization of what he had done. His son was dead.

When anger becomes so strong that clients act without the constraint of reason, they enter very dangerous territory. "How different would this story would be," I ask clients, "if the man had used self-talk to manage his anger?" What if he had stopped on the way to the bedroom and said to himself:

"Stop and think! What am I about to do? My son has spoken disrespectfully to me, but he hasn't done anything bad enough to die for! My son is young and, in some ways, very immature. I need to be patient with him. He is a good son. Someday he will be embarrassed by the way he is acting here tonight. And what might happen if I threaten him with a gun? Remember, he is my son and I love him. I won't be less of a man because he says things that are disrespectful. I only become less of a man by disrespecting others or myself. My manhood does not depend upon what other people say or do, but upon what I do. Consider the consequences of my actions. Self-respect comes from self-control and making wise decisions, not from harming those who do not treat me the way I like to be treated. Self-respect can never come from threatening my son's life."

If he had used self-talk like this, his life and the lives of his family would have been very different. He could have stopped to think, but he did not. When he stopped reasoning with himself, he allowed anger, rage, and adolescent thinking to take over. He never dreamed that he was capable of doing such a thing, but he was wrong. There is a lesson here for all of us, a lesson that his son will never get a chance to learn. "Self-control," clients are told, "comes from our dogged determination to keep reasoning with ourselves. Never stop using self-talk when you're angry."

Clients use a three-column technique to develop your self-talk skills and gain insight into their core beliefs. To start the assignment, have clients take a piece of paper and write situation, automatic thoughts, and self-talk in three columns, as in the example below.

SITUATION	Automatic Thoughts	SELF-TALK

Every day for a week or more, their job is to find situations in which they feel anger or some variation of tension (frustration, irritation, jealousy, etc.) towards their partner. By the end of the week, they should have at least seven situations on the list. Clients do not have to feel intense anger in these situations, but they must find one or more situations per day in which they feel some anger or tension.

Whenever they feel angry, they describe the situation they were in, the automatic thoughts that were behind the anger, and the self-talk they used to reduce their anger. This exercise may be difficult at first, but it gets easier with practice. Describing the situation will be easy. It may be harder to identify the thoughts behind their anger, and the counselor may have to help clients identify them. The recorded automatic thoughts are the key to understanding the core beliefs that drive them.

Recording self-talk is also important. It is important for clients to experience the manner in which their self-talk reduces their anger and promotes analytic thought. I have included homework assignments from my clients as examples. The first example is from Elliot. Notice how he describes the situation, his automatic thoughts, and the self-talk that was effective in reducing his anger:

SITUATION	Automatic Thoughts	SELF-TALK
Another driver cut me off on the freeway, causing me to slam on my brakes.	He did that deliberately! He doesn't care if he kills me! He's taking advantage of me! I'm not going to let that jerk get away with that! I'll teach him!	Calm down. This isn't a big deal. It wasn't personal, so don't take it personally. He just didn't see me. Everyone makes mistakes. I've done things like that before. No one was hurt, so let it go.

Here is an excerpt from Rebecca's homework. Rebecca and her boyfriend had a high comfort level with verbal abuse before she started counseling, and she was trying to change that. She was willing to take a leadership role in stopping the verbal abuse (lead by example). Rebecca was proud of the way she handled this incident.

Because of her determination to apply the concepts she had learned, she and her boyfriend were able to solve the problem rather than just fight about it. First, Rebecca did a good job of recognizing her warning signs and using self-talk. Although self-talk did not eliminate the anger she felt (it rarely does), it did reduce her anger below the "I don't care what I say line" and kept her in The Box.

Second, by lowering her anger, Rebecca was able to stay focused on problem solving, which is the only path back to the OK Zone. Third, she did a good job of getting out of the "YOU" mode. (A person is in the YOU mode when they point their finger at their partner, jab their finger in their partner's face, and start every sentence with YOU ... YOU ... YOU!) Rebecca knew that her relational problems could not be solved in the YOU mode.

SITUATION	Automatic Thoughts	SELF-TALK
We didn't have enough money to pay the rent, and my boyfriend was blaming me for our financial problems. I got mad and saw my warning signs.	This isn't fair! Who the hell are you to criticize me? You're the one who can't get a decent job! You're nothing but an asshole! You don't appreciate anything I do. You're asking for it! You're pushing my	I see my warning signs – I'm "in his face." I'm starting to yell, and I want to hit him. Calm down. In group they say the best way to deal with criticism is to find something in the criticism to agree

	buttons! This whole thing is *your* fault!	with. Is there some truth to what he's saying? I'm not the only one to blame, but I'm partly to blame for this problem and I'll take responsibility for that. I don't want to win a fight. I want to solve this problem. He's scared because we're in trouble and he doesn't know what to do. I'm scared too. I'll tell him how I fell, but don't yell or say hurtful stuff. What can I do to show leadership – to help solve the problem?

Elliot and Rebecca's homework assignments also gave them insight into their core beliefs about anger and aggression. When he looked over his homework assignment, Elliot discovered that his core beliefs were - "When something bad happens it's deliberate and directed at me personally. People are always trying to take advantage of me. I have to get angry and aggressive to stop people from walking all over me." These core beliefs were not very realistic, and they got him into a lot of trouble over his lifetime.

Elliot worked to modify his core beliefs and make them more realistic - "When something bad happens, it doesn't always mean that someone did it deliberately or that it was directed at me personally. Sometimes it is just an accident, and it doesn't always mean that someone is trying to take advantage of me. Not everyone is a threat to me, or trying to take advantage of me, and I don't have to get angry and aggressive every time something goes wrong."

Rebecca identified her core beliefs as – "It's awful and terrible when someone criticizes me. No one should ever criticize me! When they do, I have to get angry and aggressive and blame them back. Accepting criticism is a sign of weakness, and people will take advantage of it. If they push my buttons, I should hurt them to teach them a lesson and make them leave me alone."

Like Elliot, she worked to make her core beliefs less adolescent-like and more realistic – "It's uncomfortable to be criticized, but it's not awful. There is usually some truth behind criticism. Accepting criticism is not a sign of weakness. If handled the right way it can be an opportunity to show leadership, grow as a person, and solve a problem that threatens my relationship. A strong person can even invite constructive criticism. I do not have to get angry and abusive, and hurting my boyfriend only makes things worse. If I set an example by accepting criticism, my boyfriend will be more likely to do the same."

Learning the skill of self-talk, identifying core beliefs associated with anger and aggression, and modifying your beliefs to make them more realistic are important steps in maintaining an abuse-free lifestyle. When people identify adolescent core beliefs and modify them in a way that makes them more realistic, they experience significant changes in their feelings and behavior. Most importantly, significant progress is made toward the vital goal of stopping abusive behavior.

Expanding the Treatment Plan

Once clients demonstrate mastery of the basic cognitive and behavioral skills presented in this book, the therapist can add complementary skills and concepts to the treatment plan to enhance the client's ability to stay in The Box (avoid verbal and physical abuse). Changing unspoken relational rules regarding overt expressions of hostility, refining cognitive strategies that promote affective regulation, keeping sight of "The Big Picture," restructuring fundamental concepts about manhood, and appreciating the difference between fear and respect have demonstrated their efficacy with our clients.

Closing Thoughts

Over the years, I have had the opportunity to teach counseling strategies for partner abuse to many professionals at conferences and seminars. I enjoy these opportunities. However, I get the impression that most of my colleagues would do a lot to avoid working with abusive clients themselves. "Sounds like you're doing a fine job," they seem to say. "Keep it up and good luck!" Many participants report that, while they enjoyed the seminar, they doubt that they will be able to use the strategies they learned; after all, their clients have nothing in common with the men and women that I portrayed in the seminar. Others seem surprised (and unconvinced) that abusive spouses can possibly become non-abusive spouses.

You may have feelings similar to my colleagues. If so, there are two points that I should stress. First, the assumption that our clients maintain abuse-free lifestyles is, in my opinion, a dangerous one. Given the incidence rates for partner assault (Straus & Gelles, 1990; Rennison & Welchans, 2000; Tjaden & Thoennes, 2000), it is probable that the clientele of most counselors includes people who abuse, are abused, or both. Maybe they have not told us about it; maybe we have not bothered to ask. Either way, it is difficult to believe that the incidence rates reported in the average American household do not apply to the men and women who seek us out for counseling.

Straus (1990) found that about 10% of the men and women in his survey reported some victimization by their partner in a 12-month period. Approximately 3% of the respondents suffered severe partner abuse, such as punching with a fist, kicking, biting, and beatings. Either our clients are somehow able to avoid the abuse that other Americans experience, or there is a lot of hitting going on among our clients. Do we even know about it?

Secondly, many clinicians question the possibility of meaningful change among abusive clients. Certainly, not all clients make the same amount of progress, but when men and women do make meaningful changes, the changes profoundly affect their lives, the lives of their partners, and the lives of their children.

Indeed, the positive and meaningful change made by abusive clients is often profound. There is no area of my professional life that brings more satisfaction than my work with these clients. Carlos comes to mind. Carlos, an immigrant to this country, battered his wife on more than one occasion. He came to counseling following his criminal conviction for domestic violence. He was a hard man who had lived a hard life. With little formal education, he wrestled with cultural differences and struggled with many of the skills and concepts discussed in his group. Carlos persevered. Several weeks after his successful completion of The Choices Program, I received the following carefully typed letter from Carlos.

Dr William E. Adams,

Thanks very much to you and to your professional team that works very hard to help our society change our thoughts and behaviour, thoughts and attitudes, thoughts and anger, and to take responsibility and not minimizing, denying or blaming. I really appreciate the tools that you share with me to make my life easy, happy, and phenomenal. Thanks to these tools it make me feel that I am important in this society and it make me feel that I am not miserable. People like you our society needs to make better way to live. From the very deep of my heart thank you very, very much.

Many of my once-abusive clients are more learned, but few are more eloquent than Carlos.

References from this chapter

Adams, W. E. (2003). *The Choices Program: How to Stop Hurting the People Who Love You*. Treatment manual of the American Family Alliance Domestic Violence Counseling Program, 1945 Palo Verde Avenue, Suite 204, Long Beach, CA 90815. (562) 799-1226.

Buzawa, E. S., & Buzawa, C. G. (2003). *Domestic violence: The criminal justice response* (3rd Ed.). Thousand Oaks: Sage. An excellent review of important historical markers, legislative responses to partner abuse, and landmark judicial decisions such as those discussed in the introduction to this program.

Earle, A. M. (1896). *Curious punishments of bygone days*. Port Townsend, WA: Loompanics Unlimited.

Rennison, C. M., & Welchans, S. (2000). *Intimate partner violence* (Publication No. NCJ178247). Washington, DC: Bureau of Justice Statistics.

Straus, M. A. (1990). The National Family Violence Surveys. In M.A. Straus and R. J. Gelles (Eds.). *Physical violence in American Families: Risk factors and adaptations to violence in 8,145 families*. New Brunswick, NJ: Transaction.

Straus, M. A. & Gelles, R. J. (1990). How violent are American families: Estimates from the National Family Violence Resurvey and other studies. In M. Straus & R. Gelles (Eds.), *Physical violence in American families: Risk Factors and adaptations in 8,145 families*. New Brunswick, NJ: Transaction

Tjaden, P., & Thoennes, N. (2000). *Extent, nature, and consequences of violence against women: Findings from the National Violence Against Women Survey*. Washington, DC: National Institute of Justice.

It's Not Always about Power and Control

Listening to clients can force a counselor to reconsider his or her assumptions about things. In the early years of my practice, I earnestly subscribed to the Duluth model (or, to be fair, to the Duluth model as it had been explained to me in partner abuse seminars). The Duluth model was the dominant treatment model of the time. Many still regard it as the treatment model of choice for partner violence. Over time, I began to question two of my widely held assumptions. I assumed that men hit women; the converse – the notion that women hit men–was so rare as to be unimportant in the overall scheme of things. If women did hit men, I believed, it was probably in self-defense.

Secondly, I assumed that partner abuse was all about power and control; men engaged in partner abuse in order to maintain control over women and maintain their status in a patriarchal society. Listening to men and women describe their abusive incidents, however, eventually led me to question both assumptions.

I say "eventually" because the shift in my thinking took time. In some cases, the Duluth assumptions were correct; men were clearly the abusers, and they clearly abused to maintain control over the women in their lives. For example, in reply to the question, "Why did you slap your girlfriend," one client replied, "Because she didn't do what I told her to do!" The "power and control" model easily accounted for his abusive conduct toward his girlfriend. Many times, however, the model accounted for only a portion of the problem. Joe was a good example.

Man Assaults His Spouse at LAX

Joe entered counseling expressing deep remorse and guilt for his abusive conduct toward his wife. He presented as jovial, eager to please, and somewhat self-depreciating. He characterized his seventeen-year relationship with his wife as one in which he was constantly striving to "keep her happy." Joe's wife was often verbally abusive to him. Although she was much smaller than Joe was, she frequently embarrassed him and humiliated him in front of others. She had slapped him from time to time, although her physical aggression was less frequent.

Joe did not retaliate for the abuse, either verbally or physically, for seventeen years. Indeed, he never even stood up for himself. When asked about his submissive behavior, Joe talked about his physical appearance; he was extremely overweight. Joe explained, "I was afraid to say anything back to her because I was afraid she would leave me. I'd be alone. No one else would want to be with a guy who looks the way I do. I'm just lucky that anyone wants to be with me."

One day, Joe and his wife were retrieving their luggage in an airport after a long and tiring flight. It was a hot summer day, and Joe sweated heavily as he struggled with all of their bags. His wife was angry about something, and she was giving Joe an earful as he struggled along. Joe kept silent. "Then something happened that's never happened before," said Joe. "My wife said, 'I'm going to the car and leave you here, and you can find your own way home!'". Suddenly, Joe just did not care anymore. He dropped the bags with a "plop" and punched her in the face, knocking her to the floor. "There was a policeman standing right there watching me," said Joe. "I saw him, but I didn't even care." (The officer who witnessed the assault produced a nightstick and, needless to say, Joe soon cared a lot.)

In counseling, Joe described sincere feelings of shock and remorse for his behavior that day. "Teach me everything you can, Doc," pleaded Joe. "I NEVER want to do anything like that again!" Power and control issues played a role in Joe's incident, but it would be overly simplistic to ascribe the incident to control issues alone. Joe's lack of assertiveness, self-devaluation, and insecurity played a large role. Passivity in the face of his wife's abusive behavior may have encouraged more of the same. Effective problem-solving skills were lacking. Most striking of all is the shift between long periods of passivity and brief but violent episodes of aggression.

Joe is not the victim in this case. Nothing justifies or excuses his abusive and violent conduct; Joe has to assume full responsibility for his behavior if he is to make progress. However, I do want to stress the variety of issues - *in addition to power and control* - which counselors often need to address over the course of treatment for partner abuse.

Woman Stabs Husband at Dinner

Counselors also need to be open to the possibility that women get violent too, and for the same reasons that men do. Think of partner abuse as a human problem, rather than a gender-specific one. The following vignette describes Maria, an immigrant from an Asian country. Her issues are similar to those of Joe.

Maria came to America to marry. Her marriage, arranged by her family, was to a man many years older than she was. By Maria's report, it was never a loving relationship. Her husband never hit or physically abused Maria, yet he frequently insulted and verbally humiliated her, both publicly and privately. Although she was unhappy with the marriage, she believed that she had no alternative to making the best of it. Given her cultural and religious values, she believed that divorce was unacceptable. Like Joe, Maria passively submitted to her spouse's verbal assaults.

As Maria cooked dinner one evening, her husband sat at the kitchen table. He began to harangue her, his words growing more cutting as he talked. Maria was doing some cutting of her own. She was chopping carrots, listening to him drone on and on. For the first time in her marriage, Maria crossed the "I don't care" line. She turned, flung the kitchen knife at her husband, and then stared in disbelief when it struck solidly in his abdomen – a professional knife-thrower could not have done better. He slumped to the floor, the kitchen knife protruding from his stomach and his blood soaking the floor. The husband survived; he filed for divorce while Maria served time in jail.

The relevant treatment issues in Maria's case closely mirror those of Joe. Her lack of assertiveness, her passivity in the face of overt verbal hostility from her partner, and the absence of effective problem-solving are most striking. Again, as in Joe's case, one finds the shift from long periods of passivity to a brief, violent episode of aggression. An imbalance of power in the relationship is also apparent, but it is one of several relevant treatment issues.

The Loss of an Ear

Janet was a strong and athletically-built woman. As a client, she presented with a different set of issues. Janet's childhood and adolescence were characterized by violent acting out. Physically aggressive to her peers, she often initiated physical fights. Due to the frequency and severe nature of her assaults on others, she spent time in juvenile hall as an adolescent, and served time in jail on numerous occasions as a young adult. During one jail term, she said that she had "found Jesus." She saw the light, she told those around her, and intended to start a new life, a Christian one, upon her release.

True to her word, Janet attended church regularly after her release. In time, she met a fine Christian boy and they soon became a couple. Janet's new life was very satisfying to her; things were going splendidly. She read the Bible with her new boyfriend, attended church regularly, and kept the terms of her probation. In time, however, the rose on her new relationship faded; she started to argue, and then to verbally quarrel with her boyfriend. It is unlikely that the young boyfriend had ever met anyone quite like Janet in his circle of friends at church, and he could not have known how ill-advised it was to fight with her.

One day, a verbal quarrel led to a push. The boyfriend pushed Janet back. Janet pushed harder. The boyfriend intended to push Janet again, but as he came near, Janet placed him in a headlock. They flailed around the living room, the boyfriend trying to break free and Janet tightening her grip. The harder the boyfriend struggled, the angrier (and less Christian) Janet felt. Then she saw his ear. She bit it.

Several months after the incident, and after serving another jail term, Janet described what happened next. "Dr. Adams," she said, "it was awful! I could feel my teeth go right through his ear, and then the ear came off in my mouth! I spit it out. Blood was everywhere. The worst part is, the doctors couldn't sew his ear back on. We never even found his ear. While I was trying to stop the bleeding and I was calling 911 . . . well . . . the dog ate it."

What are the salient treatment issues in Janet's case? The presence of a conduct disorder comes to mind, and ruling out the possibility of a personality disorder seems warranted. Janet is also distinguished from most of my clients in that her aggressive and violent conduct is generalized, rather than specific to the domestic relationship. Once again, power and control issues are one of many deserving of consideration in a treatment plan. Issues the dog may have are beyond the scope of this book.

A Domestic Violence Homicide

One might easily assume that all treatment models for partner abuse would give the detection and treatment of pre-existing psychiatric disorders a high priority. Unfortunately, it is my experience that this is not always the case. Some treatment models may over-emphasize the issue of "inequality" and "power" in relationships; as important as those issues are, they fail to address relevant psychiatric issues to the detriment of clients and victims alike. Put another way, some treatment models may follow a "social" model (re-socialization) in cases that call for a "bio-psycho-social" model. Do not make this mistake. Concurrent therapeutic and medical intervention for pre-existing disorders is an essential component of partner abuse counseling for many clients.

Mike, an early client of mine, provides an excellent illustration of the importance of multiple intervention strategies in cases of partner abuse. Mike made good progress in his early stages of counseling. I met his wife and children when they picked him up after his sessions, and his wife made a point of telling me how happy she was with the changes she saw in Mike. Mike was proud of his progress, and optimistic that he had put his abusive behavior behind him. Unfortunately, everything changed several months into his counseling.

Mike's demeanor grew sullen, and he became increasingly irritable and uncooperative. He was easily agitated, argumentative, restless, and pessimistic. Nothing pleased him. His dark transformation was so sudden and pronounced, so unlike the Mike I had come to know, that I pulled him aside after a counseling group.

When questioned, Mike eventually disclosed that he was under a doctor's care for a psychiatric disorder, and that he had stopped taking his medication. For reasons of his own, Mike failed to disclose this information during his intake. We addressed the issue of medical non-compliance, and the problem seemed to be resolved. Mike soon returned to his familiar ways. He was cooperative, productive in his sessions, and he made strong progress in his counseling program. By all accounts, Mike made excellent progress in partner abuse counseling; he had been an exemplary client.

I lost touch with Mike after he completed his partner abuse counseling. More than a year later, someone laid a newspaper clipping on my desk. It was about Mike. Mike had a verbal confrontation with his wife, the article said. According to the neighbors, she demanded that Mike leave the house. The evidence indicated that Mike started to pack his clothes, but for some reason he stopped. Instead of leaving, he retrieved a gun and shot his wife. He then turned the gun on his children. None of them survived. Mike then took his own life. The article reported that Mike's neighbors knew that he was off his medication again; they could tell that by the way he was acting.

In presenting these vignettes, it is not the intent to belittle treatment models for partner abuse centered upon establishing equality between genders and addressing men's power and control issues. In California, where I practice, many counselors in the field adhere to these models with an almost militant zeal. Sometimes power and control issues are extremely important. In many cases, however, power and control issues are not the only, or even the most salient, factors in partner violence. Some of my colleagues may brand me a heretic, but I am going to say it: it is not *always* about power and control.

A Review of Treatment Concepts

Let's take a moment to review the treatment approach discussed so far.

- Begin treatment with a thorough assessment. Objective measures such as the Conflict Tactics Scale greatly enhance subjective responses to questions such as, "Have you ever abused your spouse?" Give high priority to victim safety in the treatment plan.

- Identify stopping abusive behavior as the initial goal of counseling. Stopping verbally and physically abusive behavior is the primary treatment goal. Do not be side-tracked by other relatively unimportant points of disagreement between the partners. Specific points of disagreement between the partners cannot be resolved safely until problem-solving can take place in an abuse-free environment. Stop the yelling and hitting before moving on to other problems.

- Clients must assume full responsibility for their abusive behavior; allow no blaming, minimizing, or denying. When it occurs – and it often will – confront it. The counselor must keep the therapeutic spotlight on the abusive behavior. Practically, this requires keeping the spotlight on the abuser. Confront attempts to shift the spotlight away from the abuser and on to his or her partner. Depending upon the client, the strength of the therapeutic relationship, and the style of the counselor, confrontation may be direct or gentle. In all cases, counselors must be at ease with confrontation when clients attempt to avoid responsibility for their choices through blame, minimization, or denial.

- Give clear behavioral directives early in the counseling process. Clients rarely show much insight into their abusive behavior. The Box model organizes directives into a coherent model that provides structure for the client during interpersonal conflict. Directives should include self-monitoring when tension escalates (e.g., look for warning signs), and extrication from adverse stimuli when warning signs are seen (e.g., take a time-out). Time-out reduces the external stimuli, making it easier for clients to apply cognitive tools to reduce tension (e.g., self-talk) and maintain a problem-solving orientation. Cognitive skills are easier to apply when stimuli are minimized. As clients develop proficiency in the use of cognitive tools, they begin to apply them within the Box and they report less need for the time-out procedure. With a reduction of "out of The Box" behavior (verbal and physical abuse), more counseling time is given to the further development of cognitive interventions such as avoiding the abusive set, the modulation of affect, and modifying core beliefs associated with abusive behavior.

In the early stages of counseling, the client's primary goal is to "stay in The Box," or avoid further episodes of abuse, by following the behavioral directives implicit in The Box model. Expect that new clients will express understanding of the model, but that their early efforts to stay in The Box will often fail. Failure is usually due to a lack of skill in attending to or applying the directives in the model. When clients report new incidents of abusive conduct, the counselor should evaluate with the client which of the directives in The Box were ignored, and reinforce their importance. Did you see your warning signs? Were you looking for them? Did you call a time-out when you saw your warning signs? What was the first thing you said or did that was "out of The Box?"

Confront any attempt to avoid responsibility for abusive behavior, but be supportive of the client's efforts to change. Most clients will have to go through many episodes of conflict before they develop proficiency in "running the play" as it is meant to be run.

Clients often find it helpful to evaluate their own proficiency. I sometimes compare The Box to a designed play in a football game. The game starts when clients are "knocked out" of the OK Zone by a relational problem. Did they run the play as designed in the team meeting (the counseling session)? Asking clients to rate their "level of play" as amateur (I totally forgot everything the coach told me), as semi-pro (I ran most of the play as designed, but I could have done better), or as pro (I followed all of the directives with excellent results) often elicits surprisingly frank self-evaluations. Encouraging clients to search for opportunities to practice the play in all areas of their lives, at work, in rush hour traffic, and whenever tension rises, often speeds their proficiency.

Within 8 to 12 weeks, most clients demonstrate their ability to stay in The Box during relational conflict. They can run the play consistently. They are able to avoid verbally or physically abusive behavior through self-monitoring, recognizing their warning signs, maintaining a problem-solving focus, and detaching themselves from the conflict in time to keep their tension level below the "I don't care" lines. The first goal – eliminating out of The Box behavior – has been achieved. Clients have established a safe and stable environment in which problem solving can take place. It is time to introduce new skills.

Bob Attains Pro Status

During the past week, I met with two clients, Bob and Mark. They told me about two recent incidents that illustrate the concepts above. Both Bob and Mark have an extensive history of partner abuse. Bob has applied the directives associated with staying in The Box consistently for several weeks. When problems arose with his ex-wife, Sally, Bob watched for his warning signs, stayed focused on the problem, and disengaged when he saw himself about to get out of The Box. His primary goal was staying in The Box, rather than resolving the point of disagreement. When tension flared during arguments about visitation on the telephone, for example, Bob said, "I have to go now, but I'll call you back in a few minutes."

He hung up, took a few minutes to think rationally and lower his tension level below the "I don't care what I say" line, reminded himself to attack the problem rather than Sally, and called her back with a calm demeanor. Rather than fight about the problem, they talked about it. Recently, Bob and Sally attended their son's soccer game. Sally approached Bob during the game about a problem. As the tension rose,

Sally said some hurtful things to Bob, but rather than retaliate, Bob simply said they would talk later and returned to his seat.

Last week, Bob received a surprising email from Sally. She told Bob about the remarkable changes she had seen in him. After her sharp words to Bob during the soccer game, for example, she returned to her own seat, thinking, "Oh, shit! I'm in for it now." She expected Bob to bully her in the parking lot after the game. She also expected Bob to call her several times on the phone to rant, call her "a fucking bitch," and threaten her. Sally knew that Bob well. Sally was surprised, to say the least, when Bob took his son by the hand after the game, said goodbye to Sally, and left without incident. In her email, Sally told Bob that she wished he had taken counseling during their marriage. If he had, she said, things might have turned out differently for them.

Bob achieved his initial counseling goal; he stays in The Box. He has attained "pro" status. Bob knew it, and those who know him best see it. Notice, however, that while Bob is able to stay in The Box, the problems, that is, the specific points of disagreement, are not being resolved. Bob is "staying in" The Box, but he is not yet able to "work through" The Box and return to the OK Zone. There is still a lot of work to do. However, Bob has demonstrated his ability to maintain a safe environment wherein specific problems can be resolved; in his tenth week of counseling, he has laid the foundation for the next stage of the treatment protocol.

Mark, the Semi-pro

Bob's pro status contrasts sharply with the semi-pro status of Mark, another client I met with this week. Mark and Betty are married and have one child, but their marriage is in jeopardy and there are many stressors in their relationship. This is the second marriage for both Mark and Betty. Betty is a licensed medical professional, but she lost her employment several years ago due to a substance abuse problem. She is currently unemployed. Betty has relapsed a number of times. Her most recent relapse involved stealing her son's medication for hyperactivity.

Mark has grown increasingly controlling toward Betty. He sometimes lectures her like a child, and he acknowledges past episodes of abusive behavior towards her. Their efforts to resolve their problems are wholly ineffective, and usually result in abusive words and behavior. Incidents involving mutual combat between Mark and Betty are increasingly frequent. Frustrated, irritable, and mildly depressed, Mark decided to seek counseling.

In his last session, Mark talked about an incident that occurred a few days before. As he was brushing his teeth, he noticed that Betty had put a new tube of toothpaste in the medicine cabinet. He was sure that

Betty threw away the old tube of toothpaste, which was still half full. Mark thought, "That's just like her. Throwing away a half-full tube of toothpaste is like throwing away two or three dollars. We've been over and over this!" A moment later, Mark was in the bedroom lecturing Betty about the cost of things. Betty lay down on the bed and tried her best to avoid a confrontation by ignoring Mark. "When you throw away a half-full tube . . .," Mark droned on as he walked around the bed. Betty continued to ignore Mark, which aggravated him. He wanted to say something to get a response, and he did. "If I was irresponsible like you," he said, "if I didn't have to do anything but lay around all day, if I didn't have work and pay for stuff, I'd just throw shit out, too!" That hit the mark. Betty jumped up, lashing out with cutting remarks of her own. Mark started to yell back, but he stopped. He caught his warning signs (finally) and disengaged to give himself time to calm down.

Mark is an amateur trying to reach the skill level of a semi-pro. In our session, Mark evaluated his own status as an "amateur." He acknowledged that he did not think of looking for his warning signs when he first felt the tension inside himself start to rise. Further, he did not notice his warning signs until he was well out of The Box (attacking Betty rather than the problem). On a positive note, Mark checked himself before the incident escalated further, something that he certainly would not have done a few weeks earlier. Mark's story is characteristic of the learning curve reported by most clients. He will probably have many such experiences before he attains Bob's level of proficiency at following the directives in The Box, but I am confident that he will get there, as so many have before him.

OK, I'm staying In "The Box" – Now What?

Mark's story also illustrates how seemingly trivial problems quickly escalate when clients lack adequate problem-solving skills. In my experience, most abusive clients are in dire need of such skills. As clients such as Bob enter the second stage of counseling, they have minimized or eliminated verbal abuse, and physical abuse is typically absent. The affective tension and conflict between spouses over specific problems, however, remains high. Although clients now stay in The Box, their problem-solving efforts often have mixed results. The focus changes from "staying in" The Box to "working through" The Box (problem-solve and return to the OK Zone). The treatment plan focuses on developing greater non-abusive problem-solving skills to address specific points of disagreement. By working through The Box, rather than just staying in The Box, clients reduce partner conflict and lower the average tension level between the partners. As illustrated in The Box model above, returning to the OK Zone requires sound non-violent problem solving strategies.

Problem Solving

Clients must assume full responsibility for stopping their verbally or physically abusive behavior. Once they demonstrate the ability to stay in The Box, more attention can be given to resolving specific problems, or points of disagreement, between the spouses. Non-violent problem-solving strategies are established. The process usually begins by helping the client understand that partners who respect each other, who cooperate and work together as allies, can solve almost any problem. However, blaming, controlling, and hurtful behaviors cause fights, build walls between partners, and make it almost impossible to resolve problems. The client must learn how to create an environment in his/her relationship that is conducive to problem solving rather than fighting. Clients learn to eliminate behaviors that blame, control, or hurt their partners, and they learn to monitor their success by watching their partners' reactions to their words. Clients also learn to ask their partners to tell them whenever their words or actions are blaming, controlling, or hurtful.

The pages that follow will provide you with the concepts and skills our clients use to solve problems successfully and return to the OK Zone. One of the cornerstones of *The Choices Program* is helping clients become skilled problem-solvers. To understand why problem-solving skills are so important in this treatment plan, let us review some of the concepts of The Box model. The model suggests that life is good for our clients until a problem comes up—a point of disagreement that shakes our clients and their partners out of the safety and comfort of the OK Zone. Problems give rise to tension in the form of annoyance, resentment, anger, jealousy, or similar feelings. Tension grows and lingers until our clients and their partners solve the problem. Solve the problem successfully, and they return to the OK Zone. Fail to solve the problem and it can become an emotionally charged hot topic. The tension will intensify and threaten to push our clients out of The Box.

Some people are natural problem solvers. Unfortunately, abusive clients are not found among these people. Natural problem solvers resolve their relationship problems quickly and with minimal tension; abusive clients find resolving problems with their partners a daunting task. They usually end up outside The Box – verbally or physically abusing their partners – when a problem comes up, regardless of how minor the problem may be (remember Mark and his toothpaste issues). With practice, abusive clients can become intelligent and proficient problem-solvers who spend more time in the comfort of the OK Zone, reduce the average tension level in the relationship, and above all, stay in The Box.

Why Problem-Solving Fails

In the early stages of our program, we noted the difficulty that abusive clients had with solving relatively minor problems within The Box model. We made considerable efforts to interview clients about their problem-solving experiences in the hopes of understanding why their problem-solving endeavors so frequently failed. In the process, the themes of blame, hurt, and control consistently emerged. In response, the following strategies were developed.

Blaming, bossy and hurtful statements are the most common hazards that abusive clients blunder into when addressing specific problems with their partners. They block communication and they build walls between partners, making it impossible for them to solve their problems. They also increase the likelihood of verbal abuse and physical violence because they escalate anger, frustration, and defensiveness between the client and his or her partner.

Even worse, they have the power to turn spouses who should be allies against the problem into adversaries. The thing to remember about blaming, bossy and hurtful statements is this: if clients use them, they are sure to get into a fight. Blaming, bossy and hurtful statements almost always trigger fights. Whenever a client reports having a fight with his partner, the chances are high that the partner perceived our client as one or more of the following – blaming, bossy, or hurtful. These behaviors block problem-solving and cause fights. Blaming, bossy, and hurtful statements build walls between clients and their partners and keep them from solving their problems.

Blaming

It is easy to solve problems when clients and their partners work together as a team. When they cooperate and work together as allies, they can solve almost any problem. Blaming, however, destroys the feeling that they are working as the same team against the problem. When clients blame their partners for a problem, they become adversaries. It becomes the client against the partner, rather than the client and the partner against the problem. When the partner feels attacked and defensive, problem-solving comes to a standstill. Any feeling of cooperation and teamwork that once existed is lost. That is why our clients learn to avoid blaming their spouses for a problem, even when they think he or she is clearly at fault. Whether their partners are truly to blame for a problem or not, the results are always the same - defensiveness and fighting about whom is to blame.

Before our clients say anything to their spouses about a problem, they first stop and ask themselves, "Do I want to make my partner angry and defensive, or do I want my partner to help me solve this problem?"

It is always easier to blame someone for a problem than to solve it, but problems are not solved by pointing fingers and affixing blame. When a client blames his/her spouse for a problem, he is asking the wrong question: "Whose fault is it that we have this problem?" Better to ask, "What is the problem that needs to be solved?" and, "How can we work together to solve this problem?" Good problem-solvers do not waste time trying to fix blame. Like a dog chasing its tail, clients and their partners often argue endlessly about where blame lies. Even if they do finally agree about who caused the problem, the problem will still be there, unsolved and building tension.

Clients must learn that it is better to focus their efforts on how the two of them can work together to solve the problem, rather than on who should be blamed for it. When they skip the "Blame Game," they will have fewer arguments (and fights) and solve problems more easily. In the problem solving steps that come later, the question of blame never comes up. Teach clients that they do not have to assign blame in order to solve a problem. In fact, problem-solving is easier when the issue of blame never arises. The goal is not to fix blame. Rather, the goal is to solve problems and get back to the OK Zone.

To avoid the Blame Game, clients have to stay out of the "You Mode." You know what I mean by the You Mode. Clients are in the You Mode when they point their index finger at their spouses and shout, "YOU, YOU, YOU, YOU!" The You Mode guarantees an angry and defensive reaction from the spouse, and it is a great way to turn a caring partner into an angry adversary. It is also a terrible way to problem-solve.

Bossy

No one likes bossy and controlling people. Equality and mutual respect are imperative in an abuse-free relationship. There are no bosses in egalitarian relationships, and for good reason. Bossy people cultivate adversaries, not teammates. Good problem-solvers know better than to come across to their partners as bossy. When a client comes across to his spouse as controlling, he or she will resist what our client has to say, even if the solutions offered make sense. When a partner constantly rejects our client's solutions to problems, she or he may be rejecting the attempts at control rather than the solutions themselves. That is why clients should never try to force a solution on their partners, no matter how good they believe their solutions are.

To improve their problem-solving skills, clients must learn to approach their partners as equals and seek solutions through communication, negotiation, and compromise. They must learn that it is always more important to stay on the same team by showing mutual respect than to solve a particular point of disagreement. Allies eventually solve their problems peacefully, adversaries fight about them. Allies learn not to turn a partner into an adversary by being bossy.

To demonstrate what happens when one person tries to control another, just grab your client by the wrist. Slowly pull on his or her wrist and watch the reaction. Your client will pull away from you. No one likes being pushed or pulled, even when he or she is being pushed or pulled in the right direction. An attempt to control another person almost always gets a rebellious reaction. It is in our nature to resist bossy people. This is not the dynamic that clients want to create when problem-solving. Rather, they need to develop a spirit of cooperation and teamwork with their partners. For many abusive clients, this comes as a profound insight.

About Power and Control

Power and control issues are so prevalent among this population of clients that it is worth taking a close look at them. Power in relationships refers to the ability to get one's way and make all the important decisions. In some relationships, partners divide power equally. When it comes to decisions about things like where to live, access to money, time spent with friends, or the division of household chores, both partners contribute to the decision-making process. Both partners have the right to express their thoughts and feelings openly and without intimidation. They solve problems as equals through communication, negotiation, compromise, and mutual respect for each other's opinions.

Partners that share power in their relationships do not try to control their one another. They do not bully or force their partners to do something against their will. They understand that attempting to get control or power over their partners turns them into adversaries. In an atmosphere of anger, resentment, and intimidation, partners never really resolve their problems, and they never get back to the OK Zone. Couples that value equality in their relationships know that in forcing solutions upon one another, partners will not resolve their differences, however "right" the solutions seem to be.

Tom and Chris

Unfortunately, not all relationships are founded upon mutual respect and an equitable distribution of power. One person sometimes convinces his or herself that he/she is the boss of the spouse, the king of the castle, the lord of the house, or whatever. These people do not share power; they covet it. Whenever one person has more power than one's partner, there is the potential to abuse that power.

Tom, a client of mine, was such a man. He reveled in power. Like a king in his realm, Tom brandished total control over his partner,

Chris. She and the children lived in abject fear of Tom, because he was capable of terrible acts of abuse when he did not get his way. In order to maintain power over Chris, he socially isolated her. He objected to her leaving the house without him. He even enraged himself whenever he checked the telephone bill (he did this every month) and saw that Chris had talked to her mother (long distance) or friends (trouble-makers) on the telephone. One by one, family and friends drifted away from Chris until she was socially isolated.

Chris was a free citizen in this country; she did not surrender any of her rights when she married Tom. Unfortunately, he did not see it that way. Tom refused to let Chris work, and she had to ask Tom for money to buy groceries. After going to the store, Chris gave Tom the receipt and the change, which Tom pocketed. Of course, Tom made sure that Chris' name was not on the family checks, credit cards, or bank accounts. Tom often accused Chris of cheating, and used that as an excuse to beat her, although he acknowledged later that he knew that he was the only one who cheated in the marriage. Chris eventually got away from Tom. She left, barefoot and without a cent, with the kids in tow. She ran all the way to the women's shelter when she left, because she was sure he would kill her if he found her leaving.

I wish that I could say the story ended happily, but that was not the case. After giving lip service to counseling for a time, he stopped attending. Counseling threatened his control over Chris, who eventually returned to Tom. He promised her that things would be different, and she told me that she believed him. In the end, I lost contact with them. While not all clients are as controlling as Tom, I present their story here to illustrate how controlling some clients can be, and how resistant they can be to surrendering control.

While either gender can engage in controlling behavior, some argue that men have a cultural predisposition to seeing themselves as boss. After all, men have historically held most of the power in relationships. Men have traditionally held a privileged position in which they were the "head of the household," and the home was their "castle." Women traditionally yielded to the husband's decisions on matters of importance, as though his needs, wants, and opinions were more important than hers were.

In the eyes of many male clients, that is as things should be. After all, they reason, men are the traditional "breadwinners" for the family. Shouldn't the fact that his partner depends upon him for her financial well-being earn him some extra privileges around the home? Doesn't he "pay to have the say?" Hasn't he earned the right to have the final word about important family matters? The proper answer is no, he has not. Power in an adult relationship should not be based upon who earns a larger paycheck. How many men would be willing to assume a traditionally "female role" the moment she earns a larger income? Not many. I've known more than a few clients who lost their jobs and were forced to depend upon their spouses' income. To a man, each complained – loudly – that the spouse was abusing her new financial power to control and manipulate him. They did not like it a bit. I do not think women care for it either.

Other men have argued that they should be the head of the household (have their way all the time), arguing that that is the way things have always been. I point out that there are many traditions in our society, but not all of them were good. Slavery was a "tradition" in this country, but today no reasonable person looks at slavery with anything but regret and outrage. The old ways were not necessarily better ways. Just because something was a tradition doesn't mean that it was the right way, or the best way, only that it used to be that way. Be prepared to address these issues with your clients; they will come up often over the course of counseling.

When it comes to power and control issues, remind clients of this: even if they succeed in forcing their partners to do something against their will, the partner will resent them for it. No one likes to be bullied.

The three stories that follow illustrate this point. While the stories do not involve physical violence, they are presented as examples of how problems can be handled when partners see each other as equals, and neither partner tries to force his or her will on the other.

Samantha and Laura

Samantha and Laura had been together for years, but they were on the verge of breaking up when I met them for couple's counseling. The problem was that Laura had a friend whom Samantha disliked intensely. Samantha firmly believed that Laura's friend was a bad influence on Laura. When Laura visited her friend she usually drank a lot, and Laura would come home late at night and intoxicated. Every time this happened, Samantha and Laura got into a verbal fight. Samantha blamed Laura's friend for their problems. It seemed like the friend deliberately tried to cause problems between Samantha and Laura. For example, Laura always promised Samantha that she would be home by midnight. Once Laura's friend learned of the promise, she would try to make Laura late, knowing that it would provoke an argument between the couple.

Samantha tried everything she could think of to get Laura to stop seeing her friend. She reasoned, shouted, pleaded, and finally threatened to break up. Nevertheless, Laura was determined to keep seeing her friend. Laura admitted that her friend was a bad influence, but she wouldn't let Samantha say with whom she could and couldn't go out. Unable to resolve the issue, Samantha and Laura seriously considered ending their relationship.

Through counseling, Samantha learned to stop pushing Laura on the issue and she stopped trying to control Laura. She told Laura, "It hurts me that you want continue to go out with your friend. I think she likes to cause problems between us. When you go out with her, I feel like you're choosing her over our relationship. But I'm not going to ask you to stop seeing your friend. You have the right to see anyone you want. I don't like her, but you have the right to decide whether to continue your friendship with her. I just wanted you to know how I feel."

After Samantha told Laura that she would respect her decision about her friend, the power struggle stopped. Laura no longer felt controlled, and both were free to focus on the things that they valued in their own relationship. About two weeks later, Laura surprised us all by announcing that she had stopped seeing her friend because she was a negative influence on her. Samantha was as surprised as anyone.

Gamblin' Joe

Joe loved to gamble. In fact, Joe gambled on anything and everything, no matter what the odds. The problem was, Joe was the worst gambler ever, and he was always broke. Though he was penniless, Joe fell in love a beautiful young woman named Naomi and asked her to marry him. Naomi loved Joe as much as he loved her, but being a sensible woman, she was worried about his gambling. Joe promised to stop gambling once they were married, and after that, Naomi agreed to marry him. I met Joe some thirty years later, and he told me the following story.

"I broke my promise twice in all the years we've been married. The first time, I lost most of my money, but Naomi didn't say a word about it. A few months later, I got the urge again. This time, I drove to Las Vegas after work without even telling Naomi. I gambled all night until I lost every dollar of my paycheck. There was nothing to do after that but go home and face Naomi.

When I got home the next morning, I expected the worst. I'd broken my promise, stayed out all night, and lost my whole paycheck. I walked in the house expecting her to be mad. Who wouldn't be, after what I did? But she just smiled at me and said, 'You must be hungry, sit down and I'll fix you some breakfast.' I couldn't believe it! I sat at the kitchen table while she made bacon and eggs, coffee – the biggest breakfast ever. She didn't say one word about me being gone all night, the money, or anything. I sure didn't bring it up. After all these years, she's still never said a word about it."

Joe smiled as he thought back over the years and said, "I've never gambled since."

The Lonely Sailor

In his book, *Thunder Below*, Admiral Eugene Fluckey tells a story about his life as a young naval officer in Panama during World War II. One of his duties in 1942 was to censor the mail of sailors stationed at the Coco Solo Submarine base. This was a dull and time-consuming job, but one day an interesting letter caught his eye. A sailor wrote to his wife that he had not left the base on liberty since the war began. He was so desperate for a woman that he could not trust himself to be faithful off the base. Abstinence, he wrote, was driving him crazy. He just had to have a woman, but he would never do such a terrible thing without her permission. Would she think it over and give him her answer – *quickly*?

Two weeks later, her answer arrived. In her letter, she told her husband that she loved him, and the letter had brought tears to her eyes. She wished they could be together, but she never wanted him to change. She gave him permission to have another woman, with the provision that he did not fall in love with the woman, did not bring home something that he did not go away with – or pay too much for it. The sailor, noted the admiral, never left the base.

In telling the stories of Samantha, Joe, and the lonely sailor I am *NOT* suggesting that anyone should become passive in their relationships. To the contrary, both partners must be free to state how they feel, and free to bring up problems. *NOR* am I condoning alcohol abuse, reckless gambling, or infidelity. There are some behaviors that no partner should be expected to tolerate in a relationship. I AM suggesting that pushing one's will on his or her partner blocks problem solving, while accepting your partner as an equal – as a person whom you have no right to control – makes problem-solving easier. Controlling behavior builds a wall between partners that keeps them from resolving problems and prevents them from getting back to the OK Zone, as illustrated below.

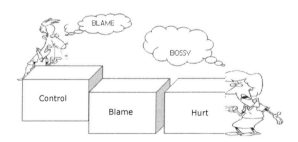

Hurt

Hurtful comments are things said to hurt, insult, or humiliate a partner. They have no place in problem-solving, and they should have no place in our clients' relationships. When clients say hurtful things, anger spirals upward, battle lines are drawn, and the fight is on. Teaching clients to avoid hurtful statements – even in retaliation for something said to them – is an important component in problem-solving. Our clients cannot be part of the solution when they contribute to the problem. Whenever clients find themselves looking for a fight and feel that they just cannot help making irresponsible and hurtful comments, they should take a time-out and pull themselves together. Until their attitude improves, no one will want to talk to them anyway. To summarize, work with clients to help them:

- Choose not to blame, even when your partner is blameworthy.
- Choose not to control, even when you are sure what your partner should do.
- Choose not to hurt, even when your partner hurts you.

Teach Clients to Watch Their Partners' Reactions

Sometimes clients come across to their partners as blaming, controlling, or hurtful when they are not trying to be. More often, they are not aware of how blaming, controlling, or hurtful their words really are. The best way for clients to screen for their own blaming, bossy, or hurtful behavior is to watch their partners' reactions to what they say. If their partners respond to their words with anger, defensiveness, or rebellious resistance, they are probably coming across as blaming, controlling, or hurting, and they need to change their approach.

If your clients are to become good problem-solvers, it is important to communicate that it does not matter whether they INTEND to blame, boss, or hurt their spouse. The reactions they get from their partners are the same, whether they intend to come across that way or not – problem-solving ends and the fight is on. Anytime our clients find themselves in a fight, the odds are good that their partners PERCEIVE them as blaming, bossy, or hurtful. The table that follows is a rough guide that my clients use when they are talking to their partners about a problem. It tells them whether they are blaming, controlling, or hurting by watching their partners' reactions to their comments.

When I:	My Partner Will Feel:	And React To Me By:
Blame	Defensive	Blaming me back
Control	Rebellious	Criticize my solutions
Hurt	Angry	Hurting back

The hard part is getting abusive clients to understand that the decision not to blame, control, or verbally hurt a partner has nothing to do with who is right and who is wrong. Avoiding these behaviors is simply good strategy. Effective problem-solvers choose not to engage in blaming, controlling, or hurting behavior because it is harmful to their relationships and blocks problem-solving efforts.

Encourage Clients to Become Leaders

I often tell my clients, male and female alike, that I expect them to become leaders in their home. "If you and your partner constantly fight about problems rather than solving them," I say, "someone needs to start showing some leadership. That might as well be you." I am VERY CLEAR, however, to explicitly explain what I mean by "leadership." Leadership does not mean telling a partner what to do or trying to be the boss in the home. Leadership means leading by example. It means putting the welfare of the relationship first. Leadership means showing respect to your partner, handling your anger responsibly, and showing a willingness to make meaningful changes in your own behavior to make your relationship better. It means handling problems skillfully and above all, staying in The Box.

Responding to Partners Who Blame, Hurt, and Control

Clients often ask, "What do I do when my partner blames, bosses, or hurts me? What do I do then? Do I just sit there and take it?" "When that happens," I say, "your first impulse will be to blame back, rebel, or hurt back. Don't do it. Think of times such as these as opportunities to make the relationship better, to lead by your example. Every time your partner attempts to blame, control, or hurt you, you have a chance to lead your relationship in a better direction by putting your ego aside and responding in a positive and constructive way. You need to be a leader and not a follower."

Clients must learn that they do not control what their partners say or do, but they always choose their responses. Teach them to choose not to retaliate by blaming back, rebelling, or hurting back. These reactions only escalate anger; they intensify the argument and make problem-solving impossible. Clients cannot get ahead when they are trying to get even. Moreover, the blame, control, and hurt in their relationships will not stop as long as they willingly participate in it. To solve problems, clients must see their partners as allies rather than adversaries. One can be willing to tell the partner how he/she feels if he or she is mistreating, but avoid participating in the destructive behavior.

"Change has to start somewhere," I tell them. "Rather than showing your willingness to fight, demonstrate your willingness to accept responsibility for your behavior and to cooperate in finding solutions to your problems." My clients use the concepts below as a basic guide when they feel blamed, bossed around, or attacked by their partners.

- *When I feel blamed: "I'll listen without getting defensive. I'll keep an open mind and accept responsibility for my role in the problem. I'll say how I feel, but I won't play the Blame Game. I'll let my partner know that I'm willing to make reasonable changes in my behavior to help solve the problem."*

- *When I feel controlled: "I won't be controlled, but I won't get rebellious either. I'm an equal partner in the relationship. I'll say how I feel about bossy behavior, but I'll also try to understand my partner's concerns and seek solutions through negotiation and compromise."*

- *When I feel hurt: "I won't return abuse with more abuse. The hurting has to stop somewhere. This is a time to show leadership by my example. I'll tell my partner that I won't be verbally abused. I'll try to get us re-focused on the problem, and let my partner know that I'm willing to listen, but we need to respect each other to solve the problem."*

The first step in effective problem-solving is to create an environment in your relationship that is conducive to solving problems. Learning to discuss problems without blame, control, or hurtful behavior, (and learning to respond appropriately to a partner's blame, control, and hurt) is a big step in the right direction. As long as these behaviors persist in our clients' relationships, they have an environment that is more conducive to fighting than problem-solving.

The concepts presented here, and the homework assignment that follows, help clients create an atmosphere in which problem-solving comes naturally. Getting back to the OK Zone becomes easier once clients learn to avoid the barriers to problem-solving that blame, bossy, and hurtful behaviors produce.

A Useful Homework Assignment

Years ago, before these concepts were organized into a treatment plan, my clients and I spent a lot of time trying to understand why their problem-solving efforts sometimes failed. As time passed, we recognized that the failures were nearly always associated with blaming, controlling, or hurtful things our clients said to their partners. Whenever this occurred, a fight ensued and one or both partners got out of The Box. About this time one brave soul in the group, whom we shall call Bill, offered to conduct an experiment. "When I go home tonight," he said, "I'll ask my wife if I ever come across as controlling and see what she says." The group thought that was a good idea, and Bill offered to tell us how the experiment went the following week.

When the group met the following week, we were curious about Bill's experiment. How did it go? "Well," said Bill, "the first thing I can tell you guys is this: if you don't want to know the answer, DON'T ASK!" Bill went on. When he asked his wife if he was controlling, she rolled her eyes and exclaimed, "All the time! You're ALWAYS trying to tell me what to do!" Bill was surprised, to say the least. "No I don't!" he said defensively. "Oh, yes you do," his wife countered, "and I hate it."

As the week went on, Bill and his wife talked a lot about his controlling behavior, and how it made her feel. To his credit, he eventually accepted her criticism. "She was right," he told us in the group. "I've been pretty bossy to her all these years, and I didn't even realize it. No wonder we fight so much."

We asked him how he was going to stop his controlling behavior, since much of the time he did not even seem to know that he was doing it. "I'll do two things," Bill promised. "First, when we start to get mad and fight, I'll ask myself if I'm trying to solve a problem by telling her what to do. If I am being bossy, I will apologize and start over. I also asked her to tell me whenever she felt like I was being bossy to her. That way, I'll see my controlling behavior even quicker and I can stop it before we get into a fight."

As the weeks came and went, we often asked Bill how his "experiment" was going. "Great!" he would say. "We're actually talking about our problems instead of fighting all the time. I can't believe the difference!" Bill got such good results with his experiment that it became an important part of our counseling program.

Step One: Ask clients to take the first step towards removing blame, control, and hurt from their relationships by removing them from their own behavior. Change has to start somewhere; it might as well start with them. To begin the change, they will ask their partners each of the three questions below:

1. *Do you feel like I try to boss you around and tell you what to do?*
2. *Do you feel like I blame you for our problems?*
3. *Do you feel like I say things just to hurt you?*

The client should listen carefully to the partner's answers and write them down. Even better, clients can ask their partners to write their answers on a sheet of paper. Advise clients to be prepared for criticism and to avoid getting angry and defensive, which defeats the purpose of the exercise. "Show your partner that you can be trusted," I say, "even when you do not like what you hear. Just listen."

Step Two: If their partners answer "yes" to any of the questions above, have clients follow Bill's example and ask their partners the question: "I want to change, and I can use your help. The next time you feel like I'm being bossy (or blaming or hurtful), will you tell me?"

Step Three: Have your clients record incidents in which their partners tell them that they are coming across as blaming, controlling, or hurtful when they discuss a problem. A format like the one below to record these interactions is helpful. If a few days go by without anything to record, clients should remind their partners that their feedback would help them make important changes. Repeat the invitation. Partners should be encouraged to let our clients know whenever they feel like they are being blaming, bossy, or hurtful toward them.

Homework Exercise

Recording Blaming, Controlling,
And Hurtful Statements

Have the courage (and the humility) to create the proper environment for problem-solving. When your partner tells you that you are controlling, blaming, or hurtful, set your pride and your ego aside for the good of your relationship. Stop, apologize, and start over. Do not get defensive.

Thank your partner for helping you make meaningful changes in your life. You will find that you are starting to solve your problems rather than fight about them.

1. My partner said I was coming across as: (Circle one)

      Blaming   Controlling   Hurtful

2. Record your response to your partner's feedback to you. What did you say to your partner after he or she told you that you were acting in a blaming, controlling, or hurtful manner?

3. How did the situation turn out? Were you able to resume problem-solving and return to the OK Zone? Be specific.

Six Steps in Problem Solving

When clients adhere to The Box model, they apply the concept that non-abusive problem-solving is the only way to remove tension between themselves and their partners. Problem-solving skills assume much importance in maintaining an abuse-free relationship. By applying effective and appropriate problem-solving strategies, they stay in The Box during times of conflict. The following six-step problem-solving strategy is used in our program, and it is recommended as a starting point for most abusive clients.

By ridding themselves of blame, control, and hurtful statements, clients break down the walls between themselves and their partners, and create an environment in which problem solving can be successful. Clients then learn a step-by step procedure that will guide them through the problem-solving process and back to the OK Zone of The Box.

In introducing these problem-solving steps, it helps to review some of the basic concepts of The Box model for your clients. The model suggests that conflict usually follows a predictable cycle. At first, everything is OK between clients and their partners. That is, there are no major problems or stressors, and both partners are generally satisfied with the way things are going. Tension grows between the couple when a problem surfaces.

If the couple is unable to reach an agreement about how to resolve the problem, tension mounts and an argument occurs. Among this population, arguments escalate until one or both partners get out of The Box, and enter the domains of verbal abuse and partner violence. Effective problem-solving eliminates the tension, which is an important step toward maintaining an abuse-free relationship.

With practice, clients in my program have been able to effectively apply the following six-step method for solving many relational problems. At first, the steps feel unnatural to them, but that is only because the steps are new. The steps feel more natural as they get accustomed to them. The important thing is that these steps get clients back to the OK Zone. As with any of the other skills discussed in this book, however, they take time and practice to master. When you introduce clients to the steps in this problem-solving procedure, have them keep the following points in mind:

- Some problems do not lend themselves to quick resolution. Some problems are challenging and complex, and the best you can do is own up to the fact that you do not know the answer to a problem, but that you will keep working on it. Do not get frustrated if you cannot solve a tough problem the instant that it comes up.

- Sometimes there is no perfect answer. People sometimes feel that a problem has not really been solved until a solution has been found that has no down side, and that makes both partners ecstatic. With some problems, the best solution comes down to a choice between the lesser of two evils. You and your partner may have to go along with a solution that you are not completely comfortable with because it is the best solution you can come up with at the time. At times like these, you have to be content in knowing that you are doing the best you can with a difficult problem.

- Stay on the same team! It is generally more important for you and your partner to stay on the same team than to resolve a point of disagreement. Do not create a bigger problem by blaming your partner, saying hurtful things, or trying to push your partner into doing something that he or she does not want to do. These tactics sever the lines of communication at the very time you need them most. Remember, problem-solving requires teamwork. It should be you and your partner against the problem. If it starts to become you against your partner, stop and do whatever it takes to get back on the same team before you go any further.

- Stay focused on the problem. Do not ask the question, "Who is to blame for the problem?" That question is divisive and leads to defensiveness. The important questions to ask are: (1) "What is the real problem?" and (2) "How can we work together to solve it?"

- Pick the right place and time for problem solving. Pick a time and place when you can both give the problem the best that you have to offer. Bringing up a problem the minute your partner returns from a long day at work, or during his or her favorite television show, is not a good idea. You may have to schedule a time to talk, so that neither of you is distracted. Saying, "I need to talk with you about something that is bothering me. How about talking about it after supper?" is better than demanding immediate attention. Do not expect your partner to drop everything and give you her full attention the moment that you bring up a problem. Likewise, if she brings up a problem at a time that is bad for you, propose a better time: "I want to talk about this when I can give you my full attention. I will be free in an hour. Will that time work for you?"

Introduce the Six Steps

I tell my clients that the problem-solving area in The Box is exactly six steps wide. Take those six steps, and they will re-enter the OK Zone; the tension behind that specific problem will go away. However, "mine fields" surround each of the six steps. "Mine fields?" they ask, "What the hell do you mean, 'mine fields?'"

"Well," I say, "the problem-solving area of The Box is littered with hidden mines that can derail the whole problem solving effort if you step on one. You have to know where the mines are to avoid them. Relax. I'll tell you where the mines are located each step along the way. Before talking about those explosive mines, take a look at the six problem-solving steps you will have to take every time a problem knocks you and your partner out of the OK Zone."

The Six Problem-Solving Steps:

1. Identify the real problem.
2. Tell your partner how you view the problem.
3. Understand your partner's point of view.
4. Work together as a team to create as many solutions as possible.
5. Mutually pick a combination of solutions to try for a week.
6. Evaluate your progress one week later.

Step One: Identify the Real Problem

Clients often acknowledge that they had a fight with their partners, but the next day, they could not remember what the fight was about. Alternatively, clients felt that the problems that they wanted to talk about were different from the issues that their partners saw as important. In instances such as these, the chances are good that the client poorly defined the problem to begin with. Before bringing up a problem, clients should be sure that they understand what the real problem is. The client has to know what the real problem is before he or she can work with the partner to solve it. They should take time to think about what is really bugging them (or bugging their partners), and try to be clear in their own minds what the problem is before they start fixing things. Like a carpenter, they need to know what they want to build before they pick up their tools and start hammering away.

 CAUTION: MINEFIELD #1

The task of identifying the right problem brings clients to the first "mine field" in the problem solving area. When clients identify the problem incorrectly, problem-solving often ends before it gets started.

Even worse, couples find themselves fighting the same battle repeatedly, never finding a solution. That is what happened to Joe and his partner, Carla. They repeatedly stepped on this mine, which caused frequent fights and deep-seated resentment between them.

Joe liked to go out with his friends for a few drinks from time to time. He did not do this often – he met his friends at a club once a month or so – and he always let Carla know about his plans ahead of time. One day, Joe told his counseling group, "I don't get it. Carla and I have been fighting all weekend. It's the same old problem. Every time I go out with the guys she gives me hell, and I'm sick of it!"

We asked Joe to tell us more. "Well," he said, "I hardly ever go out with the guys, but every time I do Carla gets mad. She says I always go out with the guys, but I never take her anywhere. She knows that's not true! I always come home right after work, and we do stuff together almost every weekend. Just last week, we went to Las Vegas. We've been fighting all weekend about whether I spend enough time with her. I've even asked her to go with me when I see the guys, but she won't go. We go through this every time I go out with my friends."

After all the arguments and fights about whether Joe spent enough time with Carla, they never addressed the real problem.

Can you guess what the real problem was? The real problem became clear later, and it had nothing to do with the amount of time that Joe and Carla spent together. The real problem had to do with Carla's insecurity about what took place on Joe's nights out. It turns out that Danny, one of Joe's friends, was a real womanizer. Carla knew it. Hell, everybody knew it. Danny chased women in the singles' clubs, and Carla knew that Joe would be with Danny when he went out with the boys. The thought of Joe being part of that scene made Carla angry and insecure. Once the real problem came out, Joe and Carla were able to talk about it openly and find a solution by following the rest of the problem-solving steps. Joe still spends time with his friends, but he participates in activities that are more sensitive to his girlfriend's concerns. More importantly, the fighting has stopped.

Sometimes, what our clients and their partners argue about is not the real problem. Clients must understand the real problem before they try to solve it. Uncovering the real problem may take some digging, but once it is identified, a workable solution can usually be found.

Step Two: Tell Your Partner How You See the Problem

After clients identify the problem, they bring it to their partners' attention. This sounds easy, but this is the step where problem-solving often goes wrong. Clients do not want to make a partner defensive – they are not looking for a fight. They must present the problem in a way that promotes cooperation and a feeling that the client and his or her partner are working together against the problem. Clients must remember that the partner is not the problem, and that the partner is a most important ally in resolving the problem. "Attack the problem," I advise my clients, "not your partner."

 CAUTION: MINEFIELD #2

The most common mistake new clients make is asking a partner the wrong question. They ask, "Who's to blame for this problem?" rather than "How can we work together to solve this problem?" Nothing derails problem-solving quicker than bringing up an issue in an accusing and blaming manner. That approach puts clients and their partners on opposite sides of the fence; they become adversaries rather than allies, and that is not a smart thing to do if they really want to solve problems.

Partners can argue for years without agreeing about who is to blame for a problem. Like a dog chasing its tail, that argument just goes on forever. It is a wiser strategy to avoid the whole question of blame. It is important to stress that it is not necessary to assign blame for a problem to solve it. For many abusive clients, this concept comes as a revelation. In our problem-solving steps, the question of blame never comes up. To avoid stepping on the "blame mine," I have my clients avoid using words that convey blame, such as "YOU" and "YOUR" when telling their partners how they see the problem. They try to restrict themselves to words like "WE" and "OUR" because they are inclusive and foster a feeling of teamwork. This is harder to do than it sounds.

Here is an example. Dan, a newer client, received a bill from the bank for a bounced check that his girlfriend Kelly had written. This is how he brought up the problem: "YOU have a problem. YOU bounced another check! I don't understand how YOU can be so irresponsible. Do YOU have any idea how much YOU are costing us? What are YOU going to do about it?" He acknowledged that his attempt to resolve the problem ended in disaster. Kelly became defensive and angry. "There would be money in the account if YOU didn't spend it all on that damn car of yours!" shouted Kelly. The fight was on, and so ended any real chance to solve the problem.

Dan's group members helped him rehearse a different approach to the same problem. To a group member playing Kelly, Dan said, "*WE* have a problem. *WE* don't have enough money in *OUR* account to cover all the checks *WE* write. *WE* are getting bounced check charges, and it's costing *US* money. Let's think about what *WE* can do to keep this from happening again."

We asked Dan which problem-solving approach he thought would work best, and which approach was more likely to keep them on the same team and maintain a spirit of cooperation. Further, which

99

approach is likely to generate defensiveness and lead to a fight about whose fault it is? The group reminded Dan that the words used to bring up a problem matter. Stay focused on the problem, rather than who is to blame.

Assigning blame is provocative. Moreover, blame is irrelevant once clients become skillful problem-solvers. Clients also learn to stay in control of their voices – never shout or yell, swear, threaten, or verbally assail a partner. Body language is also important. When it comes to non-abusive problem-solving, how clients say something is just as important as what they say. The key to avoiding the "mine fields" in the second problem-solving step is to avoid blaming. When clients report that they are fighting about their problems rather than solving them, blame is often the "mine" that has been derailing them.

Step Three: Demonstrate Understanding of Your Partner's Opinion

In step three, clients ask their partners how they see the problem. The client's goal is to demonstrate understanding of the partner's opinion. The goal is not to reach agreement or to make the partner see things differently. Clients often report that it is helpful to reflect their partners' opinions back until they demonstrate to their partners that they understand them.

Once again, the client's goal is to be able to see the problem through the eyes of the partner. It is often helpful to rehearse using language such as, "Let me be sure I understand you. The way you see it is ___, right?" Clients keep reflecting with their partners until they get it right. It is important to understand the partner exactly. The better that partners understand each other, the easier it will be to find a solution that both find acceptable, and the more effective the problem-solving will be.

Clients usually feel better about this step when I explain that the goal is to show understanding, and that demonstrating understanding of their partners' opinions does not mean that they must agree with their partners. It only shows that they understand and respect their opinions. Feeling understood usually reduces anger and defensiveness. Again, the better that partners understand each other's concerns, the better they will be able to find workable solutions to their problems.

 CAUTION: MINEFIELD 3

Derailment of the problem-solving process during step three usually happens when one partner invites the other to give an opinion, and then tells him or her how stupid and misguided the opinion is. A "who's right" argument follows, which escalates into a fight. A "who's right" argument is one in which each partner tries to win and make the spouse say, "You're right and I'm wrong." I have known "who's right" arguments between family members that have gone on for years without resolution. When this occurs, the real problem is forgotten and unsolved.

Step Four: Create As Many Solutions as Possible

Clients work with their partners to make a list of as many possible solutions to the problem as they can. This is a time to be playful and creative. Neither partner should be afraid to include solutions that seem impossible or unworkable; solutions are not evaluated as "good" or "bad" at this point. Have clients write down all of the ideas, no matter how unlikely the ideas seem at first. Make sure that both partners contribute to the list of possible solutions.

 CAUTION: MINEFIELD 4

When the problem-solving process gets derailed in step four, it is usually because one partner insists upon evaluating the other partner's solutions as silly or unworkable, or because one partner tries to control what gets on the list. When that happens, the other partner does not feel like an equal partner. He or she feels frustrated, causing the problem-solving process to break down. Every suggestion should make it onto the list, and each partner should get an equal opportunity to contribute. If clients do not like their partners' suggestions, advise them to keep their opinions to themselves.

Step Five: Mutually Pick Some Solutions

After clients and their partners develop a list of possible solutions, they work together to pick a solution, or a combination of several solutions, that they both agree to try. Key words to remember here are communication, negotiation, and compromise. Fairness and evenhandedness gets the job done, but trying to bully a partner into accepting unwanted solutions derails the process. Forcing a solution on a partner will not work. The solutions chosen must be mutual. Clients keep working with their partners until they come up with a set of solutions with which they can both live. Partners should write the solutions down, so they have a record of what they have agreed to do.

 CAUTION: MINEFIELD 5

Controlling behavior comes into play here. If clients attempt to dominate this step, if they refuse to negotiate and compromise, they will step on a major "mine." Suppose the illustration below represents a couple's list of possible solutions to a financial setback:

1. *Make a budget*
2. *Ask for more hours at work*
3. *Have a yard sale*
4. *Get a second job*
5. *Go out to eat less*
6. *Cut back on expenses*

7. Sell stuff online   8. Win the lotto

Maybe our client starts by suggesting solutions 3, 7, and 6. His partner does not like solution 7 at all, and thinks solution 1 is better. Our client does not like solution 1 at all, but he is willing to compromise – he will accept solution 1 if his partner will try solution 7 for a week. His partner says, "No way, but how about solution 4 instead?" Solution 4 was not the first choice for either of them, but it is something they are both willing to try. In the end, our client and his partner agree on solutions 3, 8, and 4. You get the idea; negotiation and compromise win the day when it comes to non-abusive problem-solving.

Step Six: Evaluate Your Progress

This is perhaps the most important step in the whole process. Partners take time to sit down and evaluate how successful (or unsatisfactory) their solutions are. Sometimes their solutions will need adjustment and further experimentation before they develop the best solution. Problem-solving is really a series of experiments. Clients keep experimenting with solutions until the problem is resolved.

 CAUTION: MINEFIELD 6

When partners do not evaluate their progress, they tend to slip back into old behaviors and the problem returns. This can be a frustrating experience for both partners. Clients should always set a time to review their progress with their partners, and to make any needed adjustments to the problem-solving plan.

When Problem Solving Succeeds

When clients and their partners successfully work through a problem, they know they were successful because they "feel" it. The tension between them disappears, and they feel closer to each other than before the problem came up. They have entered the OK Zone of The Box. The tension caused by the problem ceases to exist; it is not there anymore, and the relationship feels healthier and stronger.

Letters that Supplement Problem-Solving

When a couple is unable to resolve problems to its satisfaction, the tension intensifies. The tension can grow so strong that partners stop talking altogether. Letters that openly communicate feelings other than anger can open the door to communication, making problem-solving possible. The letter-writing strategy below opens the lines of communication with a partner by revealing the client's feelings about anger, sadness, fear, regret, understanding, and love.

The skills and concepts in the preceding pages usually make a significant difference in the way clients handle problems in their relationships. At least, that is what usually happens if our client and his or her partner are still talking to each other. But what can be done when there is so much anger and animosity between them that communication has broken down? How can they work on their problems when they are hardly speaking to each other? In cases such as these, the letter-writing strategy that follows often gets clients and their partners talking again. Letter-writing exercises do not solve their problems, but they do open the door to communication, and that makes problem solving possible.

Many clients have never written a letter before, and they need a lot of help in this regard. They have found it helpful to use a structured letter to say what is on their minds in a constructive way. These letters follow a template that we have developed in our counseling groups. It allows clients to work on their letters at their own pace. The great thing about letters is that clients can think about what they want to say before they say it. Words can be selected carefully and thoughtfully, the letter set aside for a time, and read again later to make sure it is just right before giving it to a partner. What really makes this letter work, however, is that it says the things that need to be said, but rarely are.

How the Letters Work

Couples who are unable to resolve their problems experience an increase in tension between them as time goes by. Feelings of affection that they had for each other when the relationship was new become buried beneath a mantle of hostile feelings like anger, resentment, hurt, and frustration. Abusive behavior becomes more frequent. Tension can grow so strong that talking only makes matters worse. Everything said seems to be misinterpreted; every attempt to bring up a problem triggers a defensive response; the fighting grows more and more hurtful. Finally, the partners stop talking altogether.

When couples experience chronic conflict, they express anger clearly and loudly, but gentler feelings such as affection go unexpressed. In this environment of open hostility, neither partner trusts the other well enough to reveal feelings that could be seen as weakness and make him or her vulnerable to attack. Affection is hidden, if it is still experienced at all, and neither partner trusts the other. Neither wants to be the first to open up, or to reveal him or herself in a way that they could be taken advantage of, or hurt. An oppressive and unforgiving silence permeates the home.

If a client's relationship has devolved into one like I describe above, the partner already sees him or her as abusive, uncaring, unwilling to listen, and unable to deal with problems in a mature way. That has to change. If clients and their partners are to start talking again (and they must talk to resolve their problems – there is no other way), they have to start giving voice to feelings other than anger. Venting anger during conflict comes easy, but the open hostility has transformed them into adversaries. It is time to end the war.

The letter in this chapter has helped many clients break the silence and start talking to their partners again. Through the letter, clients reveal feelings other than anger – feelings like sadness, regret, and appreciation. Many times, clients are unaware that they have such feelings. Expressing them to their partners helps break through icebound communication by creating a new atmosphere – one of warmth, openness, and trust.

Six Key Feelings

The six key feelings that clients express in the letter are anger, sadness, fear, regret, understanding, and love. Each of the six feelings in the letter has three sentences attached to it. Clients complete each sentence by "filling in the blank." The author John Gray suggested a similar letter in his popular book, *Men Are from Mars, Women Are from Venus*.

The letter touches on six feelings: Anger, Sadness, Fear, Regret, Understanding, and Love. The actual sentences that clients complete are shown below. I have included letters written by people in my counseling groups to help you understand how the letters are written. The letters vary in quality. Some of them were very good, and they got great results. Some of the letters are average, and one of them is…well…terrible! I have included the good, the bad, and the ugly to read so that you can tell the difference between a well-written letter and one that is poorly written. It is important to know the difference. A poorly written letter can make things worse rather than better. The format of the letter is shown below.

ANGER
I'm angry that . . .
I get mad when . . .
I feel frustrated . . .

SADNESS
I'm sad that . . .
It hurts me when . . .
I'm disappointed that . . .

FEAR
I'm afraid that . . .
I'm worried that . . .
I don't want . . .

REGRET
I'm ashamed . . .
I was definitely wrong . . .
I apologize . . .

UNDERSTANDING
I understand . . .
I see your point about . . .
I know you feel . . .

LOVE
I love . . .
I appreciate . . .
I thank you for . . .

Bob's Letter

Bob, a client of mine, wrote the following letter to his girlfriend, Alison. The letter surprised Alison, and the exercise had its intended effect of bringing them closer together. It opened doors, and they talked constructively about their problems for the first time. The letter had a positive effect because this was the first time that Bob really took responsibility for his abuse and openly expressed remorse to Alison for his behavior. Bob still had a lot of work to do to make meaningful changes in his life, and he still had to prove that his words were sincere and not just a ploy to keep Alison from leaving. Words are cheap.

Nevertheless, his letter got things moving in the right direction; it was a place for Bob and Alison to start. It was important that he acknowledged the pain that his abuse caused Alison.

Dear Alison,

I'm angry that . . . I put my hands on you and called you out of name.

I get mad when . . . I think about what I did to you.

I feel frustrated . . . that I caused you to fear me and not trust me.

I'm sad that . . . instead of me talking to you I chose to hit you.

It hurts me when . . . I look in your face and see the pain I caused.

I'm disappointed that . . . I put my hands on you.

I'm afraid that . . . one day I will lose you.

I'm worried that . . . you think I'm going to hit you again.

I don't want . . . to lose my family.

I'm ashamed . . . that I hit you.

I was definitely wrong . . . for ever putting my hands on you.

I apologize . . . for all the wrong I caused.

I understand . . . why you don't trust me.

I see your point about . . . my big mouth and your fear.

I know you feel . . . hurt and betrayed.

I love . . . you and the kids.

I appreciate . . . the way you hang in there and have hope.

I thank you for . . . all that you ever did and never walked out on me.

Bob openly acknowledged the hurt that he caused Alison. He admitted the shame he felt when, in his words, "I look in your face and see the pain I caused." He also acknowledged that he had "hurt and betrayed" Alison, and that he was ashamed of himself for hitting her. Good. Bob should have said these things long ago, and they are things that Alison needs to hear.

Also, notice that Bob tells Alison that he loves her, and that his greatest fear is that "I will lose you." This emotional honesty and opening up to Alison was new ground for Bob. As you will see, the fear of losing one's partner is a common theme in these letters. Some people react to that fear by becoming even more abusive and controlling, hoping to make their partner too afraid of them to leave. With counseling, other clients realize that their abusive behavior is pushing their partners away, and that realization motivates them to stop the abuse.

Remember, it is not the purpose of the letters to resolve significant problems in the relationship. The purpose is to open lines of communication so that clients and their partners can address the problems constructively – by talking again. In addition, this exercise is appropriate for clients who, at a minimum, have shown sincere motivation to stop their abusive behavior, and who have demonstrated

106

their ability to stay in The Box. It is not a tool for abusive clients to keep their victims emotionally tied to them by false hope and empty promises to change.

Donald's Letter

Donald had just started counseling when he wrote this letter to his wife, Emily. They continued to see each other every week, although they were legally separated. Donald and Emily still seemed to care for each other, but they continued to have verbal sparring matches and reported a high level of anger and conflict in the relationship. Here is Donald's first draft of his letter to Emily.

Dear Emily,

I'm angry that . . . we argue every other week.

I get mad when . . . you leave there are rude messages on my answering machine.

I feel frustrated . . . because we are not on the same page.

I'm sad that . . . our marriage hasn't worked out like it should.

It hurts me when . . . we go days without seeing or talking to each other.

I'm disappointed that . . . I haven't been more responsible towards my family.

I'm afraid that . . . if I get close to you I will get hurt.

I'm worried that . . . we might not stay together forever.

I don't want . . . us not to be together.

I'm ashamed . . . that I have pushed you and verbally abused you.

I was definitely wrong . . . for all the times I didn't tell you I loved you.

I apologize . . . for not being more supportive.

I understand . . . your frustration and feelings of resentment.

I see your point about . . . how spending more time together will bring us together.

I know you feel . . . a little scared, nervous, and unsure.

I love . . . that you have stood by me through thick and thin.

I appreciate . . . you and how you have raised my kids.

I thank you for . . . not jumping ship when the going has gotten tough.

As Donald read his letter to his group, he became deeply emotional. After he wrote the letter, he said he went to Emily and asked her, "Why are you still with me after all the things I've done?" Emily replied, "Because I love you." Emily's response deeply affected Donald, and he was ashamed of himself. It had been a long time since either had said the words "I love you." He told her that he was determined to change himself. Emily deserved better, and he knew it. Once again, they were a long way from solving major problems in the relationship, but they had created an environment in which change was possible.

Notice that Donald crossed out the words *you leave* in the second sentence of his letter. Although he was relatively new to our counseling group, he was applying what he had learned so far by staying out of the "You Mode." He also opened up to Emily in ways that were new to him. For example, he told her about the ambivalence and fear he felt about being so close to her. He acknowledged that it hurt him to "go days without seeing or talking" to her, but that he was also afraid that "if I get close to you I will get hurt." This was an important insight for both of them, and it helped explain the mixed messages that Emily often got from Donald, such as all the times when Donald "didn't tell you I loved you."

Donald also expressed his shame about his abusive behavior toward Emily, and the commonly expressed fear that she might leave him. Donald's letter was not perfect. His expression of gratitude towards Emily for "how you have raised MY kids" (instead of OUR kids) smacks of male privilege, an issue that had to be addressed in counseling. Nevertheless, Bob did a good job in his first letter-writing exercise. He discovered a lot about himself, and he revealed it openly to Emily. With communication established, problem-solving could begin.

Jose's Letter

Jose wrote the following letter to his girlfriend Veronica. He did not follow the suggested format for the letter, and he did not address all of the feelings that are important to address. Jose liked to go his own way. I have included his letter here so you can compare it to the previous letters.

Dear Veronica,

I'm angry that I have put ourselves in such an awful position and the abuse I've caused you. I'm hurt that I have lost the trust you once had in me. I'm sad we don't make love the way we used to. I'm afraid the happiness we once shared got lost and I'm going to work very hard to get it back and more. I'm happy you are here more than anything else. I appreciate all your patience and understanding, your kindness and most of all your love. I love you so very much, the last thing I want to do is lose you. We will overcome these obstacles and have a happy home once again.

Jose reported to the group that he left the letter out for Veronica to find and read. He said that Veronica cried when she read it. Then she came to his room, kissed him, gave him a hug, and they made love. Jose was all smiles, and he thought it was a great homework exercise.

"Wow, Dr. Adams," he said, "these letters work great!" I told Jose that while I was happy he got laid, that was not the purpose of the letter.

Jose should have put more effort into his letter. Notice that clients sometimes use tools such as these for purposes other than those for which they are intended. On the positive side, Jose did acknowledge that his actions had cost him Veronica's trust and their happiness, and that he was committed to working hard to get it back. Considerable minimizing is evident, however, especially when contrasted with the preceding letters. While Veronica seems to have appreciated the letter, it concerned me that Jose was not very specific about how he planned to change himself to make their "happy home," nor was he specific about his past abusive behaviors. Maybe I am a pessimist, but I suspect that Jose had other motives for writing the letter.

Peter's Letter

When Pete read his letter, the more experienced men in his counseling group confronted him strongly. See if you can identify their concerns about his letter as you read it.

Dear Sandra,
I'm angry that . . . my girlfriend and I argue about everything.
I get mad when . . . my girlfriend calls me names.
I feel frustrated . . . when she don't stop when I ask.
I'm sad that . . . we get into it so much.
It hurts me when . . . she doesn't like to talk.
I'm disappointed that . . . when I get upset.
I'm afraid that . . . if this keeps on we will break up.
I'm worried that . . . my son will suffer the most.
I don't want . . . visitation of my son only on court ordered days.
I'm ashamed . . . for going to court.
I was definitely wrong . . .
I apologize . . . for the name-calling.
I understand . . . your feelings.
I see your point about . . . arguing.
I know you feel . . . bad.
I love . . . you.
I appreciate . . . you being such a good mother.
I thank you for . . . understanding.

I hope you were able to identify some of the problems in Peter's letter. My first impression was that Peter put as little effort and thought into the letter as possible. "I know you feel bad . . . I'm disappointed when I get upset . . . I understand your feelings." Sentences like these lack substance. They indicate that Peter has little motivation to establish communication or work through problems with his girlfriend. That may be for the best. Partner abuse counseling is not marriage counseling, and partners should never be encouraged to stay in an abusive relationship. On the other hand, this is the attitude that many clients bring to their initial counseling sessions. Bob, whose letter was discussed earlier, had an attitude similar to that of Peter when he started his counseling.

My second impression was that Peter blamed his partner for their problems. Peter's letter is full of information about the things he resents about his girlfriend, but he does not have much to say about his own history of abuse towards her (yes, there was an extensive history of abuse). For example, he did not bother to respond to the sentence that begins, "I was definitely wrong..." In another sentence, Peter apologizes for some name-calling, but does not mention his physical abuse. The only thing he is ashamed of is going to court for his acts of partner abuse. This is an example of the type of letter that can do more harm than good. The worst example, however, is yet to come.

Martin's Letter

Martin is an angry man. In his letter to his wife, he is too angry to communicate without trying to hurt and abuse. Martin is not ready to solve problems or look at his own behavior objectively. Indeed, he used his letter as an excuse to vent his hostility and heap more destruction on an already battered relationship. It speaks for itself.

Dear Donna,
I'm angry that . . . you lied.
I get mad when . . . you quit your jobs.
I feel frustrated . . . when you lay around all day.
I'm sad that . . . you took my daughter away from me.
It hurts me when . . . you lie.
I'm disappointed that . . . that you lied.
I'm afraid that . . . our relationship is doomed.
I'm worried that . . . you will never understand.
I don't want . . . you to be my wife anymore.
I'm ashamed . . . that I had to go to jail.
I was definitely wrong . . . to marry you in the first place.
I apologize . . . for nothing.
I understand . . . that I can't change you.
I see your point about . . . getting a divorce.

110

I know you feel . . . bitter.
I love . . . someone else.
I appreciate . . . our separation.
I thank you for . . . our beautiful daughter.

Martin's letter was included an example of what clients should not to do in a letter. Martin's letter is an example of the behaviors that clients should avoid: blame, avoidance of responsibility, the YOU mode, deliberately and recklessly saying things to hurt, and so on. Thankfully, Martin's spouse never read the letter.

Letters such as this last one underscore the importance of reviewing exercises before clients present them to their spouses. Martin's letter also speaks to the importance of setting proper priorities in partner abuse counseling. Help the client develop the skills and concepts he or she needs to stay in The Box before addressing specific problems in the relationship.

After clients finish their letters, have them read them over once or twice. Have them consider how their words would sound to their partners, and ask themselves if they are being fair to him or her. Try to avoid the YOU mode, and follow all of the guidelines for problem-solving covered in the previous pages. While it is appropriate for clients to express their anger, they need to remember that the purpose of the letter is to say how they feel in a way that increases communication. Never use it as an excuse to punish a partner.

Clients sometimes invite their partners to write their own letters. If so, talk to the client about how to respond to a letter from the partner. Communication is not easy, and it always involves some risks. It is often hard to express anger or other negative feelings without hurting, and it is equally hard to remain respectful when your feelings have been hurt. Nevertheless, a successful relationship requires that clients learn to do both of these things reasonably well – not necessarily perfectly, but reasonably well. A partner must be able to listen to one another's feelings in a respectful way, and express feelings of his or her own with respect and sensitivity.

It is helpful to develop the right perspective about the anger and hurt that our clients' partners may express in letters. When a partner expresses anger, criticism, or hurt, the client often reacts as though the partner has said such things as:

- *"I don't love you."*
- *"I don't respect you."*
- *"I'm going to leave you."*
- *"You aren't good enough."*

- *"I'm better than you."*
- *"I'm your boss."*

Most often, none of these things were said. Defensiveness and hurt often grow out of the erroneous meanings that a client gives to the partner's expressions of anger or criticism. Anger is not a declaration of war, and criticism is just a request that some changes be made. Most often, no one was really wronged; the partner simply told him how she felt. To the contrary, there is much that is good about a partner's willingness to trust you with his or her feelings. Opening up and being honest probably was not easy for a partner, especially an abused partner. It took trust, courage, and caring about the welfare of the relationship. Clients need to remember that the partner is taking a risk by opening up to them, just as they are taking a risk by inviting him or her do so.

Encourage clients to respond to a partner's letter in a respectful manner, and never punish a partner for expressing feelings they do not like. If they cannot say anything positive at the moment, say, "Thanks for writing this letter. Give me some time to think over what you told me, and then we'll talk about it some more." If the client gets defensive and angry, the partner will have a hard time trusting them enough to open up in the future.

When clients write letters to their partners, remind them that they can express anger with consideration and respect, as in the first examples, or in manner that is hurtful, demeaning, and mean-spirited, as in the last example. Clients can be truthful without insensitivity, and open without malice. Be mindful that the goal of the letter is to open communication and bring clients and their partners closer together.

Create a Big Picture

Keeping a "Big Picture" in mind can make a big difference in the way clients choose to behave during times of conflict. A Big Picture allows them to see past day-to-day problems and focus on long-term relationship goals. The pages that follow present a strategy to help clients develop and maintain their own Big Picture. When problems come up and tension starts to build, clients stop to think about their Big Picture. They also bring the Big Picture to mind during self-talk and in time-out periods to put things into perspective. For example, the client remembers to whom they are talking, how important that person is to them, and what they want their relationship to become as the years go by. With a Big Picture in mind, they are more likely to act in a way that is consistent with it.

It is surprising, I tell my clients, that so many people lack the basic rudiments of a Big Picture for their relationships. Having no Big Picture, they get caught up in daily quarrels and act towards their partners as if tomorrow didn't matter. Unable to "see the forest for the trees," they say and do things that no relationship can long withstand. Common sense tells most of us that we cannot engage in verbally and physically abusive behavior that is certain to destroy our relationships. We know that we cannot swear at our partners, call them demeaning names, physically attack them, and expect that they will continue to love, trust, and respect us. Yet many people who are reasonable and responsible in other areas of their lives do just that. In giving vent to destructive and hostile anger over some perceived slight, they assault their partners with words and behaviors that are sure to antagonize and hurt. In time, feelings of resentment, bitterness, and disappointment replace feelings of affection, tenderness, and hope that were once a source of happiness and optimism for the future.

The daily news talks about war, crime, violence, and brutality in the world. However, not all warfare is waged between nations. Too often, the home is a battlefield in which family members wage vicious verbal and physical combat that erodes love and inflicts lasting emotional scars. Brutality and violence occur not only on dark streets at the hands of strangers, but also in our own homes at the hands of family members.

Although people are often aware of what they're doing, they persist – sometimes as a matter of stubborn pride, sometimes because they smugly believe that they're "right" and their partners are "wrong" – until there is no hope at all that the relationship can be saved. All the while, they soothe their guilty consciences by telling themselves that it

113

was all their partners' faults, that they "pushed my buttons," and that there was nothing else that they could have done. The result is one of the greatest sicknesses in the world today: the feeling of being unwanted and unloved.

Why do perfectly reasonable adults do and say things that they know will hurt their partners and destroy their relationships? Part of the answer, I tell my clients, may be that people lose sight of the Big Picture. The Big Picture means seeing past day-to-day squabbles and problems; problems are an inevitable part of two people trying to adjust to each other's differences. The Big Picture means knowing why you got into a relationship with your partner in the first place. It means keeping sight of how you want your relationship to grow, and what you want it to become as the months and years go by. It means letting the power of love replace the love of power.

Many clients have told me that the process of developing a Big Picture for themselves was among the most powerful components of their counseling program. As they thought about why they are in their relationships, what they want it to grow into, and how they see themselves and their relationships twenty years from now, their lives and relations with the people in it assumed new meaning. Talking about the Big Picture requires talking a lot about family and love, although some clients are uncomfortable talking about such things. To introduce the concept, I like to define what "home" means to my clients, and begin by giving clients my own Big Picture. I tell them what my family means to me:

> To me, forming a family means doing something great and noble. My family is where "I love you" is expressed sincerely and often. It is the only place on earth where I can know that the most powerful force in the universe is not hate, greed, or some other vice, but love. It's where I experience love as a verb. It's where I learn that it is not how much I give that is important, but how much love I put into the giving.

> In my family, I find support and relief from the pressures and problems of life, and gain courage from the knowledge that at home there are people who will always be there for me, and upon whom I can always rely. Family is where I experience what it means to be a husband and father. My family is the greatest source of happiness that is within my power to reach. While the work that I do brings me happiness for a time, my family will be a source of joy for my entire life. It is the most important work I'll ever do.

> Through my shared experiences with my family, I will build a storehouse of contentment and glad memories upon which to draw. Long after I leave this earth, I will leave something of

myself behind – something good that just may, if I set a good example and do my best as a husband and a father, continue to have a positive effect on the lives of my children, and of their children after them.

These are more than just words. It is my Big Picture. This is what I want my relationships to grow into as the years go by. Being far from perfect, I sometimes forget my Big Picture, and when I do, I act foolishly. Sometimes I do and say things that I regret. But I keep coming back to this Big Picture of mine, and I try to keep it in mind when I feel angry or frustrated about something. I stop and remind myself that these people I am speaking to are my wife and children, and I remind myself what they mean to me. I remind myself that my relationship with these people, my connection to the people I love, is all that really matters to me in this world. Then I try to act accordingly.

While I do not dwell on it, I know that one day I will inevitably leave this world. When that day comes, I want my wife and children to know beyond doubt that they were loved deeply and profoundly. I regret that I fail at this far too often, but I am trying to improve, and am trying to keep my Big Picture in mind every day.

Many others have written in a similar fashion. One such man was Sullivan Ballou, who served as a Major in the 2nd Rhode Island Volunteers during the American Civil War. An ardent patriot, Major Ballou believed deeply in the cause for which he was fighting, but he was not a fool; anyone could see that many men from both sides would die on this battlefield. Preparations had been underway for some time, and by July of 1861, over 60,000 Union and Confederate soldiers gathered along the banks of Bull Run for the imminent battle. Nearly 5,000 men were about to lose their lives.

One week before the battle started, Major Ballou's mind was on his two children, Willie and Edgar, and on his wife, Sarah. As sometimes happens on the eve of battle, he had a premonition that he would not survive. There were things he wanted to tell Sarah, things he wanted her to know before he died. On July 14th, in the calm of a summer night, the Major opened his heart to her in a letter. Excerpts from his letter follow.

July 14th, 1861
Camp Clark

My very dear Sarah,

The indications are very strong that we shall move in a few days – perhaps tomorrow. Least I should not be able to write you again, I feel impelled to write a few lines that may fall under your eye when I shall be no more.

Our movement may be one of a few days' duration and full of pleasure – and it may be one of severe conflict and death to me. If it is necessary that I should fall on the battlefield for my country, I am ready. I have no misgivings about, or lack of confidence in, the cause in which I am engaged, and my courage does not halt or falter. I know how strongly American Civilization now leans upon the triumph of the Government, and how great a debt we owe to those who went before us through the blood and suffering of the Revolution. And I am willing – perfectly willing – to lay down all my joys in this life, to help maintain this government, and to pay that debt.

I cannot describe to you my feelings on this calm summer night, when two thousand men are sleeping around me, many of them enjoying the last, perhaps, before that of death – and I, suspicious that Death is creeping behind me with his fatal dart, am communing with God, my country, and thee.

Sarah, my love for you is deathless, it seems to bind me to you with mighty cables that nothing but Omnipotence could break; and yet my love of Country comes over me like a strong wind and bears me irresistibly on with all these chains to the battlefield.

The memory of the blissful moments I have spent with you come creeping over me, and I feel most gratified to God and to you that I have enjoyed them so long. And hard it is for me to give them up and burn to ashes the hopes of future years, when God willing, we might still have lived and loved together, and seen our sons grow up to honorable manhood around us. I have, I know, but few and small claims upon Divine Providence, but something whispers to me – perhaps it is the wafted prayer of my little Edgar – that I shall return to my loved ones unharmed. If I do not, my dear Sarah, never forget how much I love you, and when my last breath escapes me on the battlefield, it will whisper your name.

Forgive me my many faults, and the many pains I have caused you. How thoughtless and foolish I have oftentimes been! How gladly would I wash out with my tears every little spot upon your happiness, and struggle with all the misfortune of this world, to shield you and my children from harm, but I cannot. I must watch you from the spirit land and hover near you, while you buffet the storms with your precious little freight, and wait with sad patience till we meet to part no more.

But, Oh Sarah! If the dead can come back to this earth and flit unseen around those they loved, I shall always be near you; in the garish day and in the darkest night, amidst your happiest scenes and gloomiest hours, always, always; and if there be a soft breeze upon your cheek, it shall be my breath; or the cool air fans your throbbing temple, it shall be my spirit passing by.

Sarah, do not mourn me dead. Think I am gone and wait for thee, for we shall meet again.

Major Ballou died at Bull Run one week later. Major Ballou, like many soldiers moving toward the field of battle, had the Big Picture when he wrote this letter to Sarah. People in life and death situations often do. Unfortunately, it seems clear to him that there were times when he lost sight of the Big Picture. The lines, *"Forgive me my faults and the many pains I have caused you. How thoughtless and foolish I have oftentimes been!"* suggest that there were times when he forgot how important she was to him. It often works that way. Too often, we do not appreciate what we have until it is gone. It is not until we have lost the people we love that we realize how much they mean to us. The realization comes in divorce court, in a child custody hearing, or with the death of a loved one. The Big Picture comes, but it is too late to do anything about it.

Regret is a terrible thing, regret about things we should have said but did not say; regret about wounds we wish we could undo but cannot. As the Major wrote to Sarah, "How gladly would I wash out with my tears every little spot upon your happiness . . . But I cannot." How much better life would be if we always kept the Big Picture! Losing sight of it always leads to regrets. Arturo, a client of mine, had such regrets. Like Major Ballou, Arturo was a good man, but he sometimes lost sight of the Big Picture.

Arturo and the Towels

Arturo loved his daughter Julia, and she loved her father. Julia was soon to be married to a fine young man of whom her father approved. One day, Arturo came home and found that his daughter and several of her friends had left their towels by the pool. Arturo was annoyed that they had not put the towels away, and he snapped at Julia. Jabbing his finger in her face he shouted, "If you can't get your friends to clean the place up, then you do it!" It was not so much his words as the harsh tone in his voice, with her wedding only days away, that hurt Julia. She did not say anything, but excused herself and went to her room. A while later, Arturo's wife told him that Julia was in her room crying. Arturo's only response was a shrug of his shoulders.

When Arturo told me this story, I asked him why he had not gone to Julia to talk with her. "I never apologize!" Arturo said. "That's one thing I never do!" Knowing that he adored Julia, I asked him to consider the Big Picture. "Is this the last memory you want Julia to have as your daughter in your home?" "What do you mean?" Arturo asked. I reminded him that his and Julia's lives were about to change forever. In a few days, she would be married, with a husband and a home of her own. Did he really want to end this phase of their lives with such an ugly memory? "Were the beach towels," I asked, "worth even one of your daughter's tears?"

"Try to see the Big Picture, Arturo," I said. "Remember who Julia is and what she means to you. When you react to small problems with an aggressive attitude, you give her the impression that the towels are more important to you than her feelings. Julia is about to take a big step in her life. In her few remaining days with her father, she needs to feel your love, support, and encouragement. She needs to know that she can turn to you for advice and relief from the problems and pressures that she will have to face over the years to come. This is a time to let her know that you will always be there for her, and that she can confide in you without fear. Isn't that part of your Big Picture, Arturo?"

Arturo regretted having lost sight of the Big Picture. Beneath his gruff exterior, he cherished Julia, and he set about the job of putting things right between them. This is a relatively minor incident when compared to the other stories in this book, but it illustrates the hurt that we inflict upon the people we love when we lose sight of the Big Picture. On the other hand, keeping the Big Picture in mind when we are angry can make a big difference in the way we choose to behave.

The Client and His Cat

I once had a client who lived alone; he had done a good job of driving most of the people who cared about him out of his life. He took his counseling to heart, however, and bought a kitten so he would have someone with whom he could practice the skills that he was learning. The cat had a habit of jumping up on a chair and pawing at him every morning when he left for work. One day, the cat scratched him badly enough to draw blood. He told us that his first reaction was to hit the cat, but he stopped himself and thought, "I'd rather have the cat try to stop me from leaving each day than to have it run from me when I come home." That is using the Big Picture. By keeping sight of the Big Picture of our relationships (even with our pets), we avoid behaviors that damage them and cause regrets later on.

The Big Picture is an important part of self-talk and time-out exercises. When a problem comes up and tension starts to build, clients should stop to think about their Big Picture until the problem is resolved. They should also bring the Big Picture to mind during a time-out period to help them put things into perspective. Again, consider to whom they are talking, how important they are, and what they want their relationship to become as the years go by. With the Big Picture in mind, they are more likely to act in a way that is consistent with it.

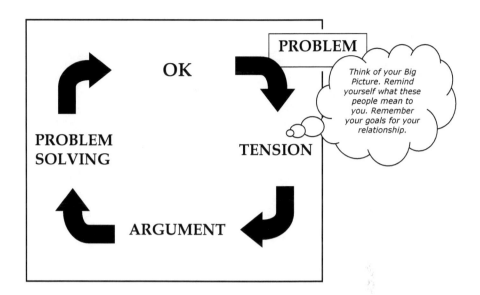

OK

PROBLEM

Think of your Big Picture. Remind yourself what these people mean to you. Remember your goals for your relationship.

PROBLEM SOLVING

TENSION

ARGUMENT

Emotional Numbness

Why do so many of relationships fail to become what they could and should become? Why do so many people lack a clear Big Picture? One reason is that many people are taught from childhood how to be tough and strong, but not how to give and receive love. Uncomfortable with strong emotions (except anger), they tune out their emotions because the softer feelings of love and affection make them feel weak and vulnerable. In fact, the mere mention of the word "emotions" can send many clients running for cover. Not only are many uncomfortable with their own feelings, but they are also uncomfortable with strong expressions of love from their partners or their children. They stumble over the words "I love you," and avoid real intimacy in their relationships. As one client said, "I'd never hug my son! I might shake his hand, but I'd never hug him!" His son was about eight years old.

Typically, these people do not see their "emotional numbness" or emotional inhibition as a problem. Rather, they see their partners as the problem; he or she is "too emotional." They believe that everything would be fine if their partners would stop trying to get them to talk about their feelings so much. Their inability to feel and talk about any emotion but anger isolates them and takes the warmth and closeness out of their relationships; they disconnect from others and from themselves. If you never tell and show people that you love them, how are they to know? Our partners and children need to hear the words. I am not saying that we need to wear our feelings on our sleeves and cry at every movie (many clients are relieved to hear me say this). I am saying that we should be at least as comfortable in expressing love as we are in expressing anger. The words "I love you" need to be a substantial part of our Big Picture.

Destructive Anger

Another cause of failed relationships is destructive anger. "Anger doesn't solve anything," it has been said, "but it can destroy everything." Freely venting anger without regard for the hurt it inflicts upon your partner, or the harm it does to your relationship, is childish and irresponsible. The things we say when we are angry matter, and they can't be taken back once they are said. Vicious verbal attacks scar a partner and injure a relationship deeply, possibly beyond repair.

What do we say to clients about relationships that are already crippled by the things that they have said or done? The Big Picture may help. More to the point, clients need to remember the words of Karl Menninger who wrote, *"Love cures people – both the ones who give it and the ones who receive it."* If you want to turn your relationship around, I tell them, you have to see the Big Picture. A large part of the Big Picture is to start to give and receive love. In your words and behavior toward your partner, act as though you were as deeply in love as you wish you could be, and keep at it. Do not expect to undo all the hurts overnight, but persist in loving your partner in your words and actions.

In time, unless too much damage has already been inflicted, you will see a change in your relationships. The important thing is to begin to really give and receive love, and to keep your eyes on the Big Picture. The choice is up to you. You have the power to make your relationships a heaven or a hell. For the most part, our relationships are what we made them. They are as poor or as great as our own Big Picture.

Encourage clients to take their time and put some thought into writing their own Big Picture. Why are they in the relationships they have chosen? How do they want their relationships with their partners to grow over the years to come? What do they want their relationships to be like? How will they treat each other during times of problems and conflict? How do they want their relationships with their children to develop over the years? What do they want their children to learn from the way their parents treat each other? If they are not in a relationship currently, describe the kind of relationship they hope to have one day.

Advise them to avoid the temptation to talk about how big their house will be, or about the expensive car they will drive one day. The Big Picture is not about material things, but about the quality of their relationships. It is also helpful to have clients describe several specific behaviors that they can start doing today to make their Big Picture a reality.

Social Influences and Violence

As clients reflect about their Big Picture, it is a good time to ask male clients to think about their basic beliefs about manhood and aggression. In their adolescent years, most males ask themselves whether they are tough enough. As adults, we need to ask a different question – whether tough is enough. To be successful in adult relationships, many of us need to redefine what it means to be a strong man. At some point in the counseling process, most men will have to examine their core beliefs about what it means to be tough and strong, and develop a more mature understanding of what it means to be a strong adult.

Why are people so violent? Watch the local news, see a movie at the theater, or pick up a local newspaper and you will see how pervasive violence is in our society. Most violent crime, I am told, is committed by men against other men. However, much of the violence in our society is of the domestic variety, between partners in their own homes. To get a picture of the extent of the problem, consider the number of domestic violence cases filed in the city of Long Beach, California (the city in which I practice) in 1994. During that year alone, there were 4,030 partner abuse cases filed in Long Beach Superior Court. The sheer number of cases shows the extent of the problem of violence in many American homes.

Two nationwide studies of American families (*Straus & Gelles, Physical Violence in American Families: Risk Factors and Adaptations to Violence in 8,145 Families, 1990, 2nd printing 1999*) indicated that 8,700,000 couples experience at least one incident of domestic violence per year, and that's probably an underestimate of the actual number.

A large portion of the violence was relatively minor in nature (not likely to cause severe injuries that require medical attention). However, 3,400,000 of those couples experienced the more severe levels of violence (kicking, punching, choking, hitting with an object, etc.) that *are* likely to require medical attention. One-third of the couples studied had experienced at least one incident of domestic violence during the course of their marriage. Two-thirds of the couples reported that they had never experienced an incident of domestic violence. The same survey found that about 1,500,000 children per year are severely assaulted (kicked, punched, beaten up, burned) in their homes.

To their surprise, the authors also found that the violence was not confined to male on female violence. Women in the study were full and equal partners in the violence. By their own report, the men and women who participated in the 1985 survey (84% of those contacted agreed to participate) revealed the following rates of violence in their relationships:

1985 Survey Results (Straus & Gelles, 1990) Violence Rates Between Partners	
Any violence by the husband	11.6%
Any violence by the wife	12.4%
Severe levels of violence by the husband	3.4%
Severe levels of violence by the wife	4.8%

As can be seen in the table, women in the studies reported that they carried out domestic assaults at about the same rate as men did. (About 30% of the people referred to my program by the court for partner abuse counseling are women.) In an effort to find out how many of the women were acting in self-defense from assaults initiated by men, Straus (1980) found that among couples reporting one or more domestic violence incidents, about half of them reported mutual violence (they were hitting each other). In a quarter of the cases, only the man had committed violent acts, and in a quarter of the cases, only the woman had committed violent acts. In cases where the violence was mutual, women were the first to hit about half the time, and men were the first to hit about half the time.

While the incident rates reported above continue to be controversial, similar rates have been found in more than two dozen studies of domestic violence (for example, O'Leary, Malone, & Tyree, 1994). In their book, *Domestic Violence: The Criminal Justice Response (Third Edition, 2003)*, Eve and Carl Buzawa reviewed the partner abuse research in depth and concluded, *"The preceding recent studies collectively suggest that female-on-male violence is a widely underreported phenomenon. (The research] also simply does not fit into the image that many authors, activists, and politicians have of a crime that is almost exclusively within the province of men" (p.22).*

Male clients should not take this information as justification for their acts of violence towards their female partners. No act of partner abuse is justifiable, not a single one. In addition, there are important differences between men's violence and women's violence. As Eve and Carl Buzawa also acknowledge, *"the impact [of violence] in the form of actual injuries and death is demonstrably less [with female violence] than [with male violence]" (p.22).*

In other words, male-on-female violence is much more likely to result in severe injury or death. Men inflict far more severe injuries on women. When a partner is seriously injured in a domestic assault, the vast majority of the time the victim is a woman. Women, for example, are far more likely to receive emergency room attention due to domestic violence, and women are far more likely to be murdered by male partners in domestic violence situations. In 1994, according to the California Department of Justice, 78% of the people killed by their partners or ex-partners in California were women.

Another difference is that male violence is much more likely than female violence to induce fear in the victim. With fear comes the potential to use violence or the threat of violence to intimidate and control the partner. Studies of couples who report mutual violence in the relationship (both the husband and the wife have been violent towards each other) show that, for the most part, only the wives are fearful during arguments (Jacobson, et al., 1994). While there are exceptions, it is generally true that only male violence induces fear in the partner. Female violence generally produces anger in their male partner.

On the other hand, female clients should not minimize the abusive nature of their own violence. You do not have to severely injure or kill your partner to abuse him. The point I want to make is this: partner violence, at least in my clinical experience, is not a gender issue. Nor is it a straight, gay, or lesbian issue. It is a human issue. All partner violence, regardless of the gender of the person doing the hitting, and regardless of the gender of the person hit, is abusive, destructive, and in most instances, a criminal act.

Social Pressure

To return to the original question, why are people so violent? To understand violence we must understand how we are socialized. From a very young age, boys, and an increasing number of girls, come to believe that certain characteristics are strong and admirable, while other characteristics are weak and contemptible. Ask clients, especially your male clients, to remember what it was like to be a 13- or 14-year-old adolescent. How did they want to be seen by their peers? What kind of characteristics did they think were strong? What characteristics did they think were weak and unmanly? I have conducted this exercise with groups of men for many years. They consistently give the following answers:

As an adolescent, I wanted to be seen as:

Strong
Tough
Confident
Unafraid
Experienced, Street smart
Don't take any bull from others

Don't show feelings (except anger)
Sexually experienced

I did <u>not</u> want to be seen as:

Weak
Easily pushed around
Unsure of myself
Frightened
Naïve and gullible
Cowardly
Emotional
Sexually inexperienced

If you take the characteristics that clients thought were strong and put them in a box, you have an adolescent's idea of what it means to be strong and manly. One could call this box "The Adolescent Idea of a Real Man." Many young women also come to see this image as one of a "Strong Woman."

The Adolescent Idea of a Real Man

A real man is . . .

Strong
Tough
Confident
Unafraid
Experienced
Street smart
One who does not take any bull from others
One who does not show feelings (except anger)
Sexually experienced

As adolescents, we sought after the characteristics we associated with being a "REAL MAN." We saw examples of "real men" in movies, sports, among our peers, and frequently in our homes. The social rewards for being a "real man" seemed obvious. We saw our favorite film and sports heroes get the respect of others, win beautiful women, and make lots of money by being tough. In the movies and on the field, we saw them solve their problems with aggression. They never cried, they were never afraid, and they never let themselves be pushed around by others, no matter what the odds. We did not realize it at the time, but our adolescent ideas of a real man were based on two lies:

Lie Number One: A real man can solve his problems with violence. In fact, the stronger, tougher, and more violent you are the better you will be at solving your problems.

Lie Number Two: A real man doesn't have to pay negative consequences for his violence.

If you want to see examples of these two lies in action, just go see the latest action movie at your local theater. The action hero on the screen will be tough and strong, live totally inside the Adolescent Box, and solve all his (or her) problems by shooting someone, bashing them around, or blowing something up. The hero will not get in serious trouble for this violent behavior – no jail, probation, destroyed lives and relationships, or mandated court counseling – and our hero will never die.

The most significant training, however, comes from teenage peers. We train each other to be tough and strong, and to live according to adolescent ideals of manhood. While the rewards for being strong and tough seem wonderful, punishment from our peers for weak or unmanly behavior is swift and terrible (Weak behavior is any behavior other than that in the Adolescent Box.). Adolescents put tremendous pressure on themselves and on each other to act tough and strong, like a "real man." Those who dare to act in ways regarded as weak, or effeminate, are subject to vicious ridicule by their peers, such as the name-calling below.

Names we call each other when we get outside the Adolescent Box:

wimp	mama's boy	queer
punk	pansy	pussy-whipped
sissy	pussy	bitch
fag	cry-baby	girl

These names have a common theme. They all question our manliness. They accuse us of "acting like a girl" rather than a "real man." These names apply social pressure to get us to act tough and strong, to stay inside the Adolescent Box, and be a "real man." The name-calling, ridicule, and rejection last until we begin to live up to the adolescent ideal of what a "real man" should be. (In ridiculing others in this way, boys also try to ease their own insecurities about being tough enough.)

When directed at us, this type of ridicule from peers hurts deeply; fear of such ridicule and the need to avoid it motivates us to appear tough and strong to our peers, no matter how we really feel. When we feel hurt, sad, afraid, or unsure about ourselves, we cover it up and hide it from others, for fear of inviting further ridicule and rejection.

I suggest to my clients that we were all subjected to this socializing by our peers. To illustrate the near universal nature of the training, I ask clients in the group to raise their hands if, as an adolescent, they ever . . .

- *Exercised or worked out to get stronger.*
- *Took turns trading punches on the arm with another guy. (Or played any other game where the goal is to get the other guy to show fear or hurt while hiding your own.)*
- *Did something they did not really want to do because a peer "dared them" to do it.*
- *Covered up feelings of fear, sadness, or insecurity because they did not know how their peers would react to them.*
- *Did something they did not really want to do in order to appear tough or brave to others.*
- *Were told, "Big boys don't cry."*
- *Were called any of the names listed above.*
- *Got into an avoidable fight because they were afraid their peers would think they were afraid if you did not fight.*
- *Refrained from showing affection to another peer because you were afraid he might take it the wrong way.*
- *Pretended that they had more sexual experience than they really did.*

I also give a short quiz to see how well they learned their lessons from adolescence about being a "real man." What is a "real man" supposed to do, I ask, if . . .

On the way home from school someone gets in your face, pushes you, and calls you names. You should:

    a. Ask him to stop annoying you.
    b. Ask a teacher for help.
    c. Tell him how his behavior makes you feel.
    d. Punch him in the face.

You really hurt yourself sliding into home plate during a high school baseball game. You should:

    a. Cry.
    b. Tell the coach you quit.
    c. Show no outward signs of pain and try to "walk it off."
    d. Ask someone to go get your mom.

Clients always know the "correct" answers. They were trained well. As an adolescent, I ask, what kind of reaction would you have received from your peers if you took any course but the "approved" one? Can you see how thoroughly you were trained to act like a "real man"?

As a man, you were trained to prove your toughness by following the manly rules of adolescence, some of which are shown below:

- *Show no feelings except strong, manly ones, such as anger and sexual prowess.*
- *Especially, don't show it when you are feeling hurt. (People will know you care and use it against you.)*
- *Never cry. (People will think you are not strong, and your partner might not respect you.)*
- *Never show affection for other men, even those you love. (They will think you aren't tough and strong.)*
- *Avoid talking about personal problems with other guys or turning to them for emotional support. (You might seem wimpy and not in control.)*
- *Take no crap off anybody. (Everyone will try to push you around.)*

By living scrupulously by these adolescent rules of conduct, I say, you may have minimized ridicule and rejection from your peers during your adolescent years. The problem is that when you entered the world of adults, you found that these rules no longer worked. Rather than helping, you avoid problems. In actuality, these rules from your adolescence caused bigger problems, some of which are shown below:

- *Because men are accustomed to hiding most of our feelings, our partners think we are uncaring and distant. They think we don't love them.*
- *We try to handle problems by getting angry and being tough, but this only makes the problems between you and your partner worse.*
- *Because we are used to avoiding personal problems, our partner is frustrated in her attempts to discuss problems with us. No one told us how to "open up" and talk problems through.*
- *We don't show feelings of hurt until we explode like a volcano.*
- *We are more comfortable with sex than with intimacy.*
- *Because we have learned to get aggressive when pressured, we resort to abusive violence when we feel threatened by our partners' angry words or behavior. Sometimes we even get arrested for our abusive aggression against our partners. We are surprised when we get arrested, because we were only behaving like we learned to behave as adolescents – like "real men."*

Real Men and Their Children

One of the saddest and most destructive aspects of adolescent thinking about manhood is the effect it has on the relationship between a father and his children. Too often, fathers think that children (especially sons) need "toughening up." In reality, what they need most from us is understanding, love, compassion, respect, and patience. They need to know that we understand what they are going through, and that we are proud of them. They need to know that manhood means being strong at times, but it also means being gentle, kind, and loving. They need to learn by our example to control their anger and solve problems non-violently. Far too often, what children receive instead are harsh words and physical ill-treatment.

Many fathers feel uncomfortable demonstrating affection, even to their own sons. They think that showing affection is a woman's job; and that a father's job is to make them "tough." If they show affection to their sons, it might make them "soft." Through this attitude, we reaffirm the myths of adolescence to our children, and they perpetuate the cycle with their own children.

The Adolescent Man Falls Short

We learned as young men to adopt an adolescent idea of what it means to be a "real man." Given the pressure from our peers and others, we were afraid to act any other way. The problem is that the adolescent man is woefully unprepared to handle the complex problems and issues that adults must face in their relationships. How do we get these bills paid? I don't know if my partner loves me anymore. I'm afraid my daughter's using drugs. My son's failing school. Is my wife having an affair? My boss doesn't like me. My doctor told me I may have a serious illness. Why is my daughter afraid of me? Adult problems require adult skills to handle them. If all we have in our toolbox to deal with problems is being tough, strong, aggressive, and showing no feelings but anger, we are going to fail.

As adolescents, we often asked ourselves, "Am I tough enough?" As adults, we have to ask ourselves, "Is tough enough? The answer is no, tough is not enough. Being tough is not enough to be successful in adult relationships. Success in the adult world requires a set of skills that were not in the Adolescent Box. What are the skills needed? Many of these skills are taught in this counseling program, such as staying in The Box and non-violent problem-solving, but there are others as well. Ask them to answer this single question: When I was an adolescent, what did I need more of from my father? If your clients are like mine, they will give answers similar to those below.

What I needed more of from my father
<u>*as I was growing up:*</u>

Time
Love
Support
Understanding
Advice
To know he was proud of me
Listen to me
Talk to me about stuff I was going through
Do things with me
Patience

To succeed in the adult world, our clients (and the rest of us as well) needed to cultivate these attributes. They are the things our partner and our children need from us to make our relationships work. I do not want to imply that many of the characteristics in the Adolescent Box are of no value. There is nothing wrong with being tough sometimes. When we are parenting a gaggle of teenagers, we may need to be tough in setting limits and rules of conduct. There is nothing wrong with being physically strong, and how could children's burn clinics operate if the people who work there could not "turn off" their emotions at times? Certainly, there is nothing wrong with being a good sexual partner. These attributes can help make relationships successful.

However, *being tough is not enough*. Being tough is not enough to successfully solve the complex problems that adults often face. I'm afraid I am going to get laid off; I think my son is using drugs; I don't have money for the rent; I'm not sure my wife loves me anymore. If, when faced with difficult problems, our only strategy is to be tough, show no emotion but anger, and take no crap off anyone, we are in trouble. We need additional strengths. We need patience, the ability to listen and to show understanding, the ability to give support and receive it from others, and the willingness to show feelings other than anger. These characteristics, in addition to being tough, provide the flexibility and range of skills that strong adults need.

In many ways, I advise clients, partner abuse counseling is about growing up. It is about learning skills and tools that we were not taught as adolescent boys. It is about learning to be more than tough and strong. It is about leaning to be an adult.

Breaking Free

If partner violence in the home is to stop, and if relationships are to be successful, clients must break free from adolescent thinking. I also suggest that we have not been talking about "manliness" at all; we have been talking about becoming a mature adult, and the concepts apply equally to women as to men.

Core beliefs about being strong and manly must change. Mature, adult thinking and behavior must replace adolescent thinking and behavior. Adult beliefs about strength and manliness need to be restructured to include the following principles:

- *A strong person does not have to hide feelings from his or her partner. A strong adult has the courage to share anger, as well as a wide array of feelings, with his or her partner appropriately and honestly, including feelings such as love, hurt, and insecurity.*

- *A strong person never resorts to violence to resolve problems with his or her partner. A true adult understands the negative effects of abuse, and knows that verbal and physical aggression only make matters worse. Personal dignity and self-control are more valued than getting control over one's partner.*

- *A strong adult is willing to talk about problems with his or her partner, and does not avoid them. Wise strategies for solving problems are used, such as communication, negotiation, and compromise, rather than intimidation and bullying.*

- *Adults do not blame their partners for their own mistakes. A strong adult accepts full responsibility for handling anger inappropriately, and for stopping his or her own abusive behavior.*

- *A strong adult can tolerate the anxiety that comes from trusting and opening up to his or her partner, so that they can be truly intimate.*

- *A mature adult has the courage and self-confidence to turn to other men for support, both to give and to receive it. He sets precedent, rather than follows suit. In other words, a mature adult is not overly concerned or intimidated by the perception of others, and is not afraid to engage in behaviors that less mature people perceive as signs of weakness.*

- *A strong adult shows affection for his or her children without fear of making them "soft." A mature adult teaches his or her children through example – by his or her behavior in relationships – that real strength includes things like kindness, patience, understanding, and love. A mature and strong adult never abuses others.*

Personality Differences

It is helpful for a client to understand how his or her personality differs from the partner's personality, and how the differences can affect their relationship. When our client's personality differs sharply from his or her partner's personality, the differences can contribute to discord in our relationship. Marital discord is correlated with domestic violence – couples with more marital conflict have more incidents of domestic violence. If the strategy for dealing with differences includes a willingness to engage in controlling and abusive behaviors, the relationship can become volatile. It is in our client's interest to understand how personality differences are affecting the relationship, and to have an effective strategy to address them.

To introduce this concept it is helpful to describe the course of a typical relationship from the beginning of the relationship to the end of the honeymoon period, usually 6 -18 months later, as in the following excerpts from *The Choices Program: How To Stop Hurting the People Who Love You*.

When relationships are new, it's natural to feel overly optimistic about the future. Infatuated with our partner, we feel the wonderful emotional high that comes from romantic love. We think about our lover constantly, and even brief separations are difficult to bear. We call from work to leave intimate love messages, we buy small gifts as tokens of love, and we demonstrate affection in infinite ways. Attentive to their every mood, we use pet names such as "darling," "my love," "honey," and "sweetheart." It is the nature of infatuation that we focus on the qualities in our new partner that are attractive, and ignore or minimize the less attractive traits. (We can always change those little annoying habits of theirs later, right?) No, we can't change our partner, and the belief that we *can* marks the beginning of the end for the honeymoon period.

As time goes by, each partner is faced with a disconcerting and indisputable fact: *my partner is different from me!* My partner is too emotional, or doesn't show enough feeling. My partner spends too much time socializing, or never wants to go out. My partner always wants to try new things, or never wants to do anything new and different. My partner forgets to pay the bills, or has to plan everything. My partner is grumpy and rude to people, or is too nice and always gets taken advantage of by others. My partner wants different things, likes different things, has different opinions, and acts in ways that annoy me. *Why can't my partner just be more like me?*

The discovery that you and your partner are different is inevitable because you're both individuals with your own personalities. There are *always* differences between people. People differ in personal habits, ideas about the way money should be spent, their choice of friends, beliefs about the way chores should be distributed, and even expectations about the way a husband or wife should act. The specific differences vary from couple to couple, but because no two people are ever exactly alike, differences are always there. Even if you leave your partner (which many people do when the honeymoon ends) and find a new partner, you will discover a new set of differences between you and your new partner. The problems may be different, but there will still be problems. *Having to cope with individual differences is the price you pay for being in a meaningful relationship.*

The success of your relationship does not depend on whether you have differences. Every relationship has them. *The success or failure of your relationship depends upon how you and your partner handle your differences.* If differences are handled wisely, the feeling of affection will grow. You will experience a renewed confidence in the strength of the relationship, and lay the foundation for real love to flourish. But if differences are handled unwisely, by trying to change each other, anger and resentment will flourish instead of love.

When differences are encountered, people often expect their partner to change in order to make them happy and resent their partner if they don't change. If our clients desire abuse-free relationships, they need a more effective strategy for dealing with the differences between them. A fundamental part of this strategy should be *acceptance* and *encouragement*.

Acceptance

Introduce the concept that acceptance of differences is a more effective strategy than demanding change through coercion and intimidation of the partner.

If you choose to live with someone, the sooner you can learn to accept each other the better. Unfortunately, as soon a couple gets together they usually set about trying to change their "perfect" partner into something else. He should be more this way; she should be less that way. I'm not suggesting that you accept behaviors like infidelity, substance abuse, or domestic violence – there are some things that no partner should tolerate. But I am saying that you should accept your partner as a separate individual. You need to accept that you are different in some ways, and stop trying to change or control each other.

When you accept your partner as he or she is, you send a powerful message: *"You are O.K. as you are. You don't have to change. I accept you as you are. You don't have to meet my standards or be just like me for me to love you."*

Acceptance is an important and powerful message for partners to send to each other. It helps couples feel intimate. Feeling free to be themselves, without fear or coercion, they're able to open their innermost thoughts and feelings to each other. You demonstrate acceptance of your partner when you do the following things:

- *Choose not to point out your partner's faults.*
- *Focus on your partner's strengths.*
- *Choose not to criticize when your partner makes a mistake. Instead, offer your support and understanding.*
- *Show faith in your partner's decisions.*
- *Give your partner positive messages every day.*
- *Avoid telling your partner how he or she should or must do things.*
- *Listen to your partner's thoughts and feelings respectfully, even if you disagree.*
- *Don't blame your partner for your unhappiness.*
- *Don't demand that your partner think and feel the same way you do.*
- *Be emotionally available to your partner.*
- *Be willing to say "I'm sorry" when appropriate.*
- *Control your anger and accept responsibility for past abusive behaviors.*
- *Learn to enjoy the ways that your partner is different from you.*

Group members often ask what to do about a partner who consistently does something that irritates or annoys them. Often, the partners have had repeated arguments about some issue, but the annoying behavior continues. First, realize that *you don't have to have everything your way in order to have a happy and satisfying relationship.* Whenever two people choose to live together, there will always be differences that annoy and irritate. You won't always want the same thing or see things the same way. It would be foolish to expect it to be otherwise.

Understand that there are also things that *you* do that irritate and annoy your partner. You each must learn to accept each other's annoying behaviors in order to share your lives. Don't allow yourself to turn a minor annoyance into a major problem. Sometimes people get so focused on a relatively minor annoyance that they forget what attracted them to their partner in the first place. Ask yourself: "Do the good things about this relationship outweigh the bad?" If so, you may have to learn to accept some of your partner's annoying habits, just as your partner may have to accept yours.

It is also important to be able to tell the difference between a real problem and an annoyance. Too often, partners treat small irritations or annoyances as serious problems. They *"awfulize."* Annoyances are just a part of life, and should be accepted as such. Don't demand perfection from your partner, don't let small annoyances rob you of the good things about relationship, and don't sweat the small stuff. Endless bickering about the small stuff drains the joy from your relationship.

Personality Traits

Help clients develop realistic expectations about trying to change their partners. Help them understand that personality traits are stable characteristics that tend to endure throughout a lifetime.

Here's another reason why you should learn to accept your partner as he or she is: *your partner isn't going to change much, whatever you do.* So what does this have to do with acceptance? Just this: with all the complaining, cajoling, and criticism in the world, your partner isn't going to change much – and neither are you. That's because personality traits, the enduring characteristics that define our personalities and make us the person we are, are very stable. For the majority of people, their basic personality traits don't change much over their entire lifetime.

This does *not* mean that couples shouldn't try to work through their differences and resolve their problems. Relationships are more satisfying if both partners allow themselves to be influenced by each other. People can and do make meaningful changes in their behavior. But the changes that can and will take place are usually constrained, or limited, by each person's basic personality.

134

For example, it's unreasonable to expect John, a life-long introvert, to become the unfailing "life of the party," no matter how much Jill, a life-long extrovert, wants him to. He may work to become a bit more outgoing, but it's unlikely that he'll change to the extent that a real party animal might like. Also, if Jill is a dedicated hedonist (she cares mostly about the pleasure and fun she can have today), she's never going to turn into as conscientious a person as her CPA husband John, no matter how much they fight about it. Jill will never care as much as John whether the bills are paid on time, and all his lecturing about credit ratings won't change that. If they're wise, partners can find ways to compromise on some issues. But many couples launch headlong into vicious fights without any regard or appreciation for the fundamental differences in their personalities.

Five-Factor Model

The Five Factor Model (**FFM**), is a widely researched model of human personality based on common language that describes personality characteristics (good-hearted, rude, open-minded, outgoing, etc.) The model theorizes that society has developed words to describe the personality characteristics that are important to us. These descriptors are statistically grouped together using a statistical procedure called factor analysis. The five main factors consistently emerge: neuroticism, extraversion, openness to experience, conscientiousness, and agreeableness.

The Five-Factor Model presents an easily understood way to teach clients about personality traits, and to illustrate how personality differences can lead to conflict within relationships. The following excerpts from *The Choices Program: How to Stop Hurting the People Who Love You* illustrate how these concepts can be taught to clients.

To illustrate my point, let me tell you more about personality, and how personality differences can be a source of unceasing conflict in relationships. One prominent theory of personality is called the Five-Factor model. The five-factor model identifies, as you can guess, five major parts to every personality: *Neuroticism, Extraversion, Openness, Agreeableness, and Conscientiousness*. Every person in the world, including me, your neighbor, and you and your partner, can be measured on each of these five dimensions of personality.

Here's a general idea of what the scales mean. A score of 1 is on the low side, 5 is on the high side, and a score of 3 would be somewhere between the two extremes. Keep in mind that there are no "good" or "bad" scores. One score isn't better than any other. Some personalities are just a better fit to than others to certain situations.

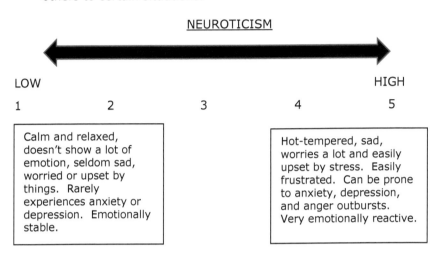

NEUROTICISM

LOW ← → HIGH

1   2   3   4   5

Calm and relaxed, doesn't show a lot of emotion, seldom sad, worried or upset by things. Rarely experiences anxiety or depression. Emotionally stable.

Hot-tempered, sad, worries a lot and easily upset by stress. Easily frustrated. Can be prone to anxiety, depression, and anger outbursts. Very emotionally reactive.

Where would you rate yourself on the "Neuroticism" scale? Are you low, high, or somewhere in the middle? Where would you rate your partner? Can you imagine how differences between partners on this personality trait can lead to conflict? Suppose that John is low on the scale, and Jill is on the high side. John may be baffled why Jill is so emotionally reactive, and Jill may see John as emotionally detached and unavailable.

John says, "why do you have to get so emotional all the time? Can't we just once have a calm conversation?" Jill responds, "How can you just sit there show no feeling? If you loved me you would show me your feelings." Mary, a patient of mine, was very high on this scale. She often criticized her husband, who was on the low end of the scale, for rarely showing strong emotion. One night at a restaurant, the waiter was very slow to take their order. Mary was boiling mad, but her husband seemed not the least upset. Her only explanation was that he must be stuffing his anger. "Why," Mary asked him, "do I always have to experience your anger for you? It's not fair!" It never occurred to her that his personality is such that he just does not experience strong anger as frequently as she does.

Personality differences can be easily misinterpreted, and that can lead to a lot of conflict unless they understand that, in some ways, they are fundamentally different. If they're wise, John will see that Jill brings a lot of emotion and color to his life that he might otherwise miss, and Jill will understand that John can be a calming influence that adds stability to her life. In truth, that's probably what attracted them to each other in the first place. *The choice is this: accept your differences and appreciate the positive contribution that the differences bring to each of your lives, or reject each other's differences as bad and engage in endless, futile attempts to make your partner be more like you.*

The next scale is Extraversion. It describes how important socializing is to people. If you are high on the scale, you enjoy being with others a lot. If low on the scale, you prefer more solitary activities.

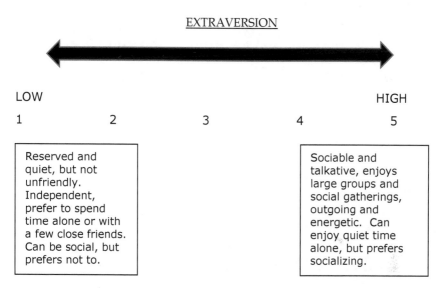

EXTRAVERSION

LOW   HIGH

1   2   3   4   5

| Reserved and quiet, but not unfriendly. Independent, prefer to spend time alone or with a few close friends. Can be social, but prefers not to. | Sociable and talkative, enjoys large groups and social gatherings, outgoing and energetic. Can enjoy quiet time alone, but prefers socializing. |

Rate yourself and your partner on the Extraversion Scale. What type of conflict could personality differences on this scale lead to? John, who is low on the scale, has his heart set on spending their vacation in their cabin on a lake. Jill, who is high on the scale, craves the nightlife and action of Las Vegas. John says Jill never wants to stay home and needs to settle down. "Can't we ever have a quiet night at home?" Jill complains that John is a couch potato and that never wants to go out anymore. If they're wise, they will learn to accept their differences, find ways to compromise, and have the best of both worlds.

The next scale is Openness to Experience, which I've described below:

OPENNESS TO EXPERIENCE

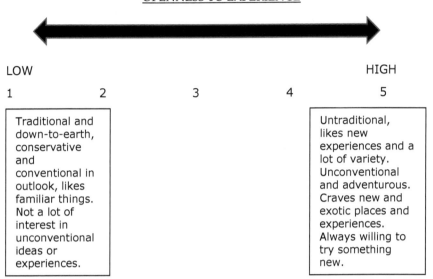

LOW   HIGH

1   2   3   4   5

Traditional and
down-to-earth,
conservative
and
conventional in
outlook, likes
familiar things.
Not a lot of
interest in
unconventional
ideas or
experiences.

Untraditional,
likes new
experiences and a
lot of variety.
Unconventional
and adventurous.
Craves new and
exotic places and
experiences.
Always willing to
try something
new.

The next scale is Agreeableness. People high on this scale want very much to be liked. They are uncomfortable with direct expressions of anger. Those who are low on the scale generally don't trust or like others, express their anger easily, and can be rude to others.

AGREEABLENESS

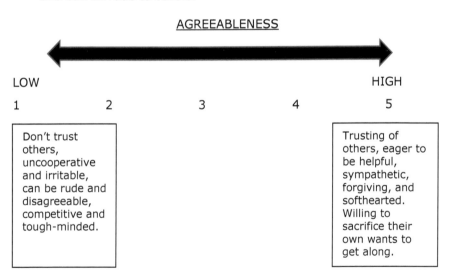

LOW   HIGH

1   2   3   4   5

Don't trust
others,
uncooperative
and irritable,
can be rude and
disagreeable,
competitive and
tough-minded.

Trusting of
others, eager to
be helpful,
sympathetic,
forgiving, and
softhearted.
Willing to
sacrifice their
own wants to
get along.

138

You may think that it's better to be high than low on this scale, but that's not necessarily the case. I'd want a lawyer who is defending me in court to be on the lower side of this scale. On the other hand, I'd like my children's kindergarten teacher to be high on the scale. The best personality type depends on the situation you're in. Some situations are a good fit for your personality, and some are not. A person who is very low on the Extraversion scale would be miserable as the Activity Director on a cruise ship. A person who is very high on this scale would probably be unhappy as a Forrest Ranger in an isolated part of the country.

Differences between partners on the Agreeable scale can lead to conflict if they're unable to understand and accept each other, and find some way to be influenced by each other. For example, John is low in Agreeableness and Jill is on the high side. John accuses Jill of spoiling the kids and thinks she's foolish to spend so much time and money on charities. He thinks people walk all over her and take advantage of her kindness. Jill accuses John of being too gruff with their children and rude to others. She thinks John is uncaring about the plight of less fortunate people, and cares more about money than people. In reality, sometimes John is too hard, sometimes Jill is too soft. If they could be more accepting of each other, respect each other's point of view, and find ways to be influenced by each other, both would be better off. Where do you and your partner fall on the Agreeableness scale?

The last scale is Conscientiousness. People high on the scale are very conscientious. They are organized, pay their bills on time and arrive early for their appointments. They schedule their day and have long-term career goals. Disorganization is stressful for them. People low on the scale are hedonistic and pleasure-seeking. They like to live moment to moment, and rarely stress out. Being organized, staying on top of things at work, and meeting deadlines are not very important to them.

CONSCIENTIOUSNESS

← ────────────────────────────────── →

LOW   HIGH

1   2   3   4   5

Lives for the moment, careless about deadlines and appointments, unmotivated, pleasure seeking, lacks clear goals or direction in life. Likes to have fun.	Well organized and disciplined, always make appointments and pays bills on time, very reliable and well organized, neat and goal oriented.

Rachel and Joe were instantly attracted to each other. Rachel was on her way to a business meeting when she saw Joe sitting on his surfboard, soaking up the sun and laughing with his friends. She wished she had more time for fun. Joe noticed Rachel too. He thought she was sexy, and her new Mercedes was cool. They got together. Joe moved in, and at first it was fun for both of them. But now they fight a lot. Rachel expects Joe to "grow up" and get a serious job. Joe complains that Rachel worries too much and tries to "plan their whole lives." He thinks she just needs to "chill" and have some fun. Rachel calls Joe a lazy beach bum. Joe calls Rachel a control freak. They both need to stop trying to change each other.

Joe is never going to be as conscientious as Rachel, no matter how hard she pushes him. He's never going to become a CEO for a top corporation; he's probably not even going to become a great surfer. But he does bring a lot of fun and spontaneity to Rachel's life. Rachel is never going to be as "laid back" as Joe wants her to be. But with Rachel's conscientious ways she provides greater stability to Joe's life - great "digs," the bills get paid, and things get done. If Rachel and Joe are going to be happy together, they'll want to understand and accept each other, be willing to make some compromises, and appreciate the unique qualities they each bring to the lives of the other.

By including this chapter in the book, I hope to help you understand that a lot of the conflict in relationships is unnecessary and futile. Much of the fighting that goes on has its source in basic personality differences – differences that just aren't going away. Why not learn to accept your differences and stop trying to change each other? If you're going to stay together, you'll need to appreciate that your unique personalities can actually enhance your lives. The aim is not to change each other, but to accept each other and to look for ways to make each other happier by finding ways to compromise.

Challenge Beliefs about Fear and Respect

In addition to challenging beliefs about strength, aggression, and manliness, it is also important to address the belief held by many abusive clients that they are both feared and respected. The section that follows provides strategies that introduce the concept that leaders win the love and respect of others, while tyrants are feared but not respected. Clients learn that leaders and tyrants use very different behaviors in their relationships. Leaders use tools like patience, understanding, and self-sacrifice, while tyrants use tools like intimidation and violence.

Clients are encouraged to choose respect rather than fear by using leadership skills during times of conflict, applying tools that foster love and respect, and avoiding tools of the tyrant that create an environment of fear.

Clients often find it helpful to discuss the concepts of respect and fear and of leaders and tyrants, to clarify these concepts, and to make a conscious choice about the sort of people they want to be in the future. These issues fit nicely into the treatment plan when addressing concepts such as the Big Picture, strength, and manhood. I begin by asking clients whether they would rather be respected or feared. Do they want to be a leader or a tyrant? Do their partners and children respect or fear them? Do they see themselves as a trusted leader in the relationship, or as a despotic tyrant? Are they neither a leader nor a tyrant, or do they think of themselves as a little of both, depending on their mood on a given day?

How do the partners and children of our clients behave when our clients get angry? Do they get anxious and shy away? Are they afraid? One client, discussed earlier in this book, wrote, "I physically and emotionally damaged my wife and caused my children inestimable pain and distress. I have seen fear in their eyes as they recognized my rage. I have noticed their avoidance of me at times and their timid demeanor with me." To his credit, he was ashamed of the fear he had caused in his family, and he made meaningful changes.

I ask clients whether they see the same fear in the eyes of their families when they recognize the clients' rage. If so, I tell them, they need to listen carefully to the concepts that follow. Significant changes are in order.

The first thing to know about respect and fear is that respect and fear never occur at the same time. No person is simultaneously feared and respected. Although people may say, "I want to be feared and respected," it is not possible. A feared person is not respected; respect goes to different kinds of people, people who do different sorts of things. In the same way, a respected person is not feared. Respect is the exact opposite of fear. If clients want respect, they must treat people in ways that engender respect – if they want to be feared, they must behave in ways that engender fear. They can have either fear or respect, but not both.

When I teach this concept, it often provokes an argument from at least one or two of the men or women in the group. From a young age, some people believe that fear and respect go hand in hand like burgers and fries. They do not. The following exercise is used to illustrate how different fear and respect are.

First, ask clients to think of the person they feared most in their life. Have them take their time. The person feared may be someone currently in their lives, or it may be a person from their childhood: a bully in the neighborhood, an abusive stepparent, or some tormentor from their teenage years. The important thing is to think of a person whom they really feared. (Understand that I'm not talking about the kind of fear engendered by a strict parent who would spank them if they cut school or stole candy. I'm talking about genuine fear. Clients who were exposed to a truly abusive parent or stepparent know the kind of fear I'm talking about.)

After clients have a person in mind, ask them to make a list of the characteristics of the feared person. What was the person like? They will come up with a list that looks like this:

The Feared Person

Got violent and abusive when they were angry
Was angry most of the time
Took advantage of people smaller and weaker than themselves
Was unpredictable, especially when using drugs or drinking
Couldn't be trusted
Had no respect for the rights of others
Liked to boss people around and order them about
Only cared about themselves
Had no self-control
Was feared and hated by almost everyone

Next, ask clients to think of the person whom they most respect in their lives. Out of all the people they have known, whom do they respect the most? Have them make a list of the characteristics of the respected person. The list will look something like this:

The Respected Person

Respected me

Took time to listen to me

Had good moral character, he or she usually did the right thing

Cared about me as a person

Respected the rights of other people

Was willing to sacrifice for the good of others

Had wisdom and knew right from wrong

Could be trusted, and I could depend on them

Had self-control, even when angry or disciplining me

Tyrant or Leader?

Now compare the two lists to illustrate the difference between the feared person and the respected person. As you compare the two lists, clients can see that they describe two different people. Not only are the feared and respected people different, they are the exact opposites of each other. The feared person, I say, is a tyrant.

You can tell tyrants by the tools they use to get what they want: fear, intimidation, and violence. The tyrant gets what he or she wants by bullying others, but they are fooling themselves if they think they can act this way and also be loved or respected. Tyrants believe that fear, intimidation, and violence are the best ways to control others and get what they want out of life. If they persist in acting this way, they eventually find themselves alone, despised even by their own family, and very frequently incarcerated.

A respected person is the opposite of a tyrant. They are leaders. The people who know them do not fear them. They are not avoided, and people don't have a timid demeanor around them. In fact, people like to be around people they respect, and look forward to their coming home because they make their families feel safe and secure. They have no desire to engender fear or to intimidate others, and they are loved and respected. You can tell a leader by the tools they use: respect for others and self-control, they are trustworthy and self-sacrificing. They are true leaders in their homes.

Fear and intimidation are the tools of a tyrant; mutual respect and trust are the tools of a leader. I tell my clients that whenever your partner does what you say out of fear of you, rather than from his or her own free choice, you have become a tyrant rather than a leader. Act like a tyrant and you will be a tyrant, a person feared but not respected. Respect goes to different kinds of people who do different sorts of things. In the same way, act like a leader and you will be a leader, a person respected but not feared. Respect is the exact opposite of fear. If you want respect, you must treat people in ways that engender respect – if you want to be feared, behave in ways that engender fear. You can have either fear or respect, but not both.

Frequently, clients will say, "Sometimes I act like a leader, and sometimes I get mad and act the way you say a tyrant acts. Doesn't that mean I can be feared and respected at the same time?" No, I tell them, it does not. As I have said, fear and respect are polar opposites. You cannot have both. It works this way: to the extent that you act like a tyrant, you will be feared. To the extent that you start acting like a leader, people will stop fearing you and slowly start respecting you. The diagram below illustrates the concept.

FEAR   RESPECT

Act Like a Tyrant:
Use abuse, intimidation, and violence. Disrespect others, bully and force people to do what you want, ignore the concepts and skills learned in counseling.

Act Like a Leader:
Show respect and kindness to others, show self-control when you are angry, put the welfare of the family first. Use the skills and concepts learned in counseling.

To the extent that clients act like tyrants, people's feelings toward them will move toward the FEAR end of the spectrum. To the extent that they act like leaders, their feelings will move toward RESPECT.

What It Means To Be a Leader

There is nothing wrong with clients wanting to be a leader in their homes. In fact, I encourage them to become leaders. If clients have a history of getting out of The Box, if there is abuse, or if the verbal or physical hostility is evident, the relationship is crying out for someone to start to show some leadership. That person might as well be the client. Before clients take on the mantle of leadership, however, reiterate what leadership means, and what is required of a leader. Being a leader does not mean being the boss!

A leader and a boss are NOT the same thing. Being a leader does not mean controlling a partner. Being a leader does not mean getting power and control over others. Being a leader does not mean that clients get their way or tell their partners what to do.

Being a leader means leading by example. It means mastering skills and concepts learned in counseling and applying them in their lives. It means making meaningful and lasting changes in their own behavior first, and then inviting others to follow their positive examples. It means respecting one's partner at all times, staying in The Box from now on, and abandoning efforts to control or manipulate others. If that is what clients want (and they should want it), then they are on their way to becoming inspiring leaders. In time, they may become loved and respected, rather than feared and rejected.

I encourage clients to add the following concept of leadership to their Big Picture: *"I want to become the best leader I can be for my family, to be a real leader. I know I have to give up any ideas about controlling others. I have to accept my partner as an equal in every way, and the only influence I will have will be through communication, persuasion, negotiation, compromise, and the example I set through my own choices."*

Address Male Privilege Issues

It is wise to address leadership issues in conjunction with "male privilege" issues. Male privilege is the belief that any man has the right to be "the boss" in any relationship with a woman. It is the belief that men should have special privileges, power and control over women, and that what a man wants, thinks, and feels is somehow more important than what a woman wants, thinks, and feels. This attitude can be expressed in countless ways in a relationship, some subtle and others not so subtle. Below are some examples of male privilege. If clients agree with any of them, the counselor has some male privilege issues to address.

People who believe in male privilege:

• *Believe that it is a man's right to be the boss of the house.*

- *Believe that it is worse for a woman to have an affair than it is for a man.*
- *Believe that a woman should ask the man's "permission" before she gets a job.*
- *Believe that it is the man's right to make the major decisions for the family.*
- *Believe that disagreeable chores like changing diapers, doing the laundry, and washing dishes are "women's work."*
- *Believe that the man has the right to demand sex from his female partner whenever he wants it.*
- *Believe that a man should have the last word.*
- *Believe that a woman's place is in the home.*
- *Believe that men are natural leaders, and women are natural followers.*
- *Believe that women are naturally inferior to men.*

Some men argue that they have special rights over women because men are supposed to be the "head of the family." They argue that because men pay the bills (a questionable belief), because men are the protectors of the home, because it has always been that way, and for a number of other reasons, men should have more power in a relationship than women have. They believe that they should be the "king of the castle," and that their female partners accept them as the boss of the home. They should always get their way, and they should have the final say about all the important decisions in the home simply because they are men. Such men may not feel guilty about violence toward their partners because they believe that when their partners challenge their authority as head of the home, it is their "privilege" to use violence to maintain their power and control. "I'm the boss," they say, "and if I have to get tough to control things, I will, and if I get tough it's her fault for not doing what I said in the first place."

There is no rational, moral, or legal reason why one partner should expect to have any special power or authority over another partner. When people strive to gain power and control over their partners they do harm to themselves, their partners, and their relationships. They harm themselves because they push others away through their attempts to dominate and control them. They waste time and energy trying to control others, rather than learning to gain control of their own lives and resolve problems. They harm their partners through endless power struggles and erosion of their self-esteem and self-confidence. They harm their relationships because their partners regard them with fear and resentment rather than love and respect.

Who should be the "head of the home?" In the sense that being the head of the home means that one partner dominates or holds power over the other partner, there should be no head of the home. Successful relationships do not have bosses; they have equal partners. The foundations of successful relationships are mutual respect, freedom of choice, and equality. Every adult has the right to live his or her life as he wishes. No partner surrenders that right when entering into a relationship with another adult. Neither partner has the right to force his or her will on the other. Once clients accept that reality – once an egalitarian relationship is established – the qualities of leadership in the home may start to emerge.

Leadership is a powerful concept for this population, and most clients respond in a positive manner. I emphasize, however, that leaders lead by changing themselves. Lead by example, by doing the things that need doing in your relationship. Stop trying to get your partner to change, focus on yourself, and start setting a positive example for others to follow. If your relationship needs more respect, start respecting more. If it needs more tolerance, start tolerating more. If it needs more communication, start communicating more. If it needs more love, start loving more. Leadership is like trying to move a string in a straight line – it must be pulled from the front, not pushed from the rear.

Change the House Rules

Every relationship has unspoken rules about the way anger is expressed. When relationships are new, there is an unspoken rule that says, "No hostility allowed." Over time, verbal and physical hostility may find their way into the relationship. Clients can change the unspoken "house rules" back to the original "no-hostility rule" if they learn the process by which rules in their relationship change, and apply their new skills to assertively remove hostility from their relationships.

Every relationship has rules about how to express anger. Generally, the rules are unspoken. That is, no one says, "This is how we will act when we get angry." Thought rules are unspoken, your clients and their partners understand the rules, and the rules determine how they express anger to each other. When relationships are new (in the honeymoon period), the rule is, "We can be angry with each other, but we cannot be hostile with each other." In most new relationships, hostility is prohibited.

It helps clients understand this concept if you define the difference between anger and hostility, as used here:

Anger: Anger is a feeling, not a behavior. It describes the way you feel, not the way you behave. For example, you can be angry about something but not let it show. You may simply "stuff" your anger.

Hostility: Hostility describes a certain way of acting. It describes what you say or do. Hostile behavior is openly aggressive, abusive, sarcastic, or antagonistic. Examples of hostile behavior are yelling, swearing, name calling, threats of violence, and violence itself. Everyone recognizes a hostile attitude when they see it.

The Honeymoon Period

In the beginning, I tell my clients, there is a honeymoon. When you first started to date your partner, how did you act when you were angry about something? Most likely, you were on your best behavior because you wanted to create a good impression. You were attracted to your partner, and because you wanted him or her to like you, you were on your best behavior. When you were angry about something, you probably just blew it off. If you are like most people, statements like, "That's OK, don't worry about it" were common. You instinctively knew that if you were openly hostile toward your partner on your first date, there would not be a second date. Let's face it, no one goes out for a movie, dinner, and a beating later.

This is the unspoken rule of all new relationships, I continue. How did you act the first time you met your boss? You were on your best behavior, right? All new relationships have a honeymoon period. How did you act the first time you met your neighbors or your in-laws? Same thing – if you want a relationship to continue past the first few meetings, you have to avoid a hostile attitude. The rule about anger during the honeymoon period is, "No hostility allowed."

Unfortunately, the rule forbidding hostility between clients and their partners did not last. They may even remember the first time they yelled at their partners, or their partners yelled at them. There was a first time. They may remember the first incident of swearing or name-calling. There was a first time for that, too. There was a first time they said something cruel or hurtful. They may not remember it, but there was a very first time. Those incidents changed the rules about the way anger was expressed in their relationships. Hostility was accepted, and a new rule emerged.

The First Rule Change

To change the rules in a relationship, the consent of both partners is usually required. It only takes one partner to suggest a rule change, but both partners must agree before the rule changes. Relationships start with the unspoken rule that no hostility is allowed, but at some point a new rule came into effect, "Verbal hostility is OK." Clients and their partners changed the no-hostility rule and allowed hostility to become a part of their relationships.

The change probably occurred in the following manner. A problem came up, and our clients and their partners started to argue about it. The tension caused by the problem grew to levels they had not reached before. As the tension grew higher and the argument more heated, either our clients or their partners crossed the "I don't care what I say line." One of them became verbally hostile; one of them started to yell, swear, insult, call names, or engaged in some other form of verbal hostility.

This first open expression of hostility was reckless and irresponsible. It did two things. First, it greatly escalated the anger between the two of them, making it harder to solve the problem. Second, it created a "pull" for the other partner to join in the hostilities. When someone yells at you, what do you want to do? If you are like most people, you want to yell back. This desire to participate in the hostility is "the pull." Verbal hostility is always hurtful, destructive, and selfish. When it comes to making permanent rule changes, it does not matter who offers the invitation first. As far the rule changes go, the important thing is whether the invitation is accepted. That is what seals the deal.

Accepting the Invitation

The first time one partner expresses verbal or physical hostility to another partner, he or she extends an invitation similar to the one below:

An Invitation to My Partner

Dear Partner of Mine,

This is a formal invitation to join me in changing the rules we live by. From now on, I'd like to adopt verbal hostility as a part of our relationship. If you care to join me in this rule change, please respond by:

1. Participating in the hostility with me, or
2. Passively accepting my hostility without objecting to it in a meaningful way.

Lots of love,

Me

Any incident of open verbal hostility is an invitation given to the other partner to change the rules about how couples treat one another when they get angry. Although abusive clients often assert that their partners "started it," it is not particularly important which partner starts the process. Suppose, for example, the client's partner really was the first to yell. Does that mean that the rule change was his or her fault? No, it does not. A rule change is not complete until the other partner accepts it by (1) giving in to "the pull" and participating in the hostility, or (2) passively accepting the other person's hostility without objecting to it in a meaningful way.

Either course of action is a way of saying, "I accept this rule change. From now on, hostility can be a part of our relationship." When clients chose to participate in the verbal hostility they are saying, through their behavior, "I'll show my partner that I can't be pushed around. I'll give back as good as I get. I'm OK with this change in our relationship. I'm willing to change the rules."

On the other hand, when clients passively accept the hostility without assertively objecting to it in a clear and decisive manner, they also communicate to their partners that they accept the rule change. Behaviorally, they communicate the idea, "Hostility is OK with me." By accepting the invitation by getting verbally hostile back or through passive acceptance, the process is complete. The unspoken no-hostility rule has changed. Hostility will now become an ever-present part of their lives, and their relationship is going to be very different from now on.

The first incident of verbal hostility unlocks a door that was closed during the honeymoon period. Once unlocked, it becomes easier to go through that door again. The next time the partners get angry with each other, the yelling comes a little quicker and grows a little louder. From now on the rule is, "When we are angry with each other, verbal hostility is expected." The hostilities increase in frequency and in severity as they grow to be comfortable with the hostility in their relationship. After a while, it seems normal. As the comfort level develops, so does the anger and frustration between them. On the other hand, expressions of love and affection come less frequently than before. The relationship is in trouble.

Before the rule change, the average tension level between them was low. There was a time when it took a lot to get them anywhere close to the "I don't care what I say line" and out of The Box. Allowing open hostility into their relationship changes that. With every new expression of hostility between them, the average tension level rises. Eventually, any small problem or minor increase in tension can push one partner or the other over the line.

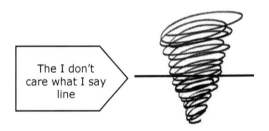

The I don't care what I say line

The Second Rule Change

Living with such a high level of tension is no fun for anyone. It is no fun for the partners, who find themselves in constant verbal combat. It is certainly no fun for the children, who have to endure the unrelenting tension in the home. They cannot escape it, and may try to cope by discharging their anger and anxiety with hostility of their own. Extended family and friends often see what is happening, but they are helpless to do anything about it. Meanwhile, with every new insult and shout, the comfort level with verbal hostility grows higher.

Problems are almost unsolvable in this environment. As you have read, partners solve problems by working together as a team. In

154

this atmosphere, unfortunately, teamwork is impossible. With all the yelling going on, the partners spend more time attacking each other than attacking the problems they face. Like ghosts that refuse to go away, old problems that were never solved continue to haunt them, and new problems give rise to even higher levels of hostility. The average tension level can even rise above the "I don't care what I say line." When that happens, every word between the partners carries animosity and anger.

Eventually, the second invitation is offered: "From now on, let's get verbally AND physically hostile with each other." This does not happen in every relationship where the door is opened to verbal abuse, but at least eight million couples a year take this next step.

An Invitation to My Partner

Dear Partner,

This is a formal invitation to join me in changing the rules we live by. From now on, I'd like to adopt verbal AND physical hostility as a part of our relationship. If you care to join me in this rule change, please respond by:

1. Participating in the physical hostility with me, or
2. Passively accepting my physical hostility without objecting to it in a meaningful way.

I hate you,

Me

The second rule change happens the same way as the first. The average tension level between the partners may already be well above the "I don't care what I say line" and dangerously close to the "I don't care what I do line," with one or both partners spending a lot of time outside of The Box. One day, there is an incident of open verbal hostility, but this time one partner escalates beyond verbal hostility to physical hostility. The first incident of physical hostility may be relatively minor (a punched wall, a thrown dish, a pushed partner), or it may come as a vicious physical assault like an exploding volcano. Either way, the invitation is made to change the house rules.

Any physical assault upon a partner is inexcusable and outrageous. But how does the partner respond to it? The invitation to change the rules again has been made, but will the victim of the assault accept the invitation? Remember, the rule change is not complete until the second partner accepts the invitation by (1) giving in to "the pull" and participating in the physical hostility, or (2) passively accepting the other partner's physical hostility.

Either course of action is a way of saying, "I accept this rule change. From now on, physical hostility will be a part of our relationship. I'm OK with this change in our relationship. I'm willing to change the rules. From now on, when we are angry with each other, physical hostility is OK." Once again, if partners participate in the violence or passively accept it without assertively objecting to it in a clear and decisive manner (calling the police, following the advice of a woman's shelter, separating, etc.), they show through their behavior that they accept the new rule change. By accepting the invitation, by getting physically hostile back or through passive acceptance, the process is complete. The unspoken no-violence rule has changed. Physical hostility will become a part of their lives. As with verbal abuse, the comfort level with physical hostility grows with each new incident. Once the door to physical hostility is unlocked, it becomes more frequent and more severe over time.

Once more, *participating* in verbal and physical hostility is not the only way that rules are changed. Rules also change if one partner is *passive* or *submissive* when the other partner is abusive. Moving from hostility to passivity is common among the clients that I work with, and it creates its own set of problems. When one partner abuses the other, and the abused partner passively accepts it, the rule change is complete. The abusive partner will usually continue to be abusive. This is seen in the "battered woman's syndrome," in which the battered woman continually forgives and submits to the abusive partner. If accepted passively, abuse often escalates in frequency and severity.

Assertive Behavior

To avoid hostile or aggressive behavior, clients must become well-versed in assertive behavior. I begin by making sure that clients understand the difference between hostile, passive, and assertive behaviors.

HOSTILE BEHAVIOR: I have rights but you do not, so it is OK for me to express my anger in an aggressive and hurtful way. I do not have to take responsibility for my behavior toward you, because you deserve it. I do not care if my behavior is harmful to you and to our relationship. I want the immediate gratification of going off on you.

PASSIVE BEHAVIOR: You have rights but I do not, so it is OK for you to express your anger in an aggressive and hostile way. You do not have to take responsibility for your words and behavior towards me because I deserve it. You do not have to worry if your behavior is harmful to me and to our relationship. You can go ahead and get immediate gratification by going off. I will hold on to my own anger and find a way to stuff it. I will say nothing about the verbal abuse directed at me; I will just keep silent and apologize even when I have done nothing wrong. I will agree with my partner when I really disagree.

ASSERTIVE BEHAVIOR: We both have rights. I can express my anger to you, but I will do it in a way that is respectful and non-abusive. I take responsibility for my words and behavior towards you, and I expect you to do the same. Neither of us will abuse. We must both take responsibility for the way we express ourselves, and do so in a way that does not harm our relationship. I will put the long-term good of our relationship over the immediate gratification of expressing my anger inappropriately. I will tell you when I do not appreciate the way you are talking to me. I will remind you that yelling and insulting each other will not help. I do not talk that way to you, and I want the same consideration. I am willing to listen to you and work with you on our problems, but I am not going to be yelled at. Let's both calm down and see what solutions we can come up with.

Turning Back the Clock

The goal of counseling is to remove verbal and physical hostility from your clients' relationships. The skills and concepts presented in this course help them change the rules once again – to return to the time when they expressed anger without hostility. To be successful, they must make a personal commitment to avoid hostile speech and behavior in the future, and remind themselves continually that the hostility in their relationships will not stop as long as they are willing participants in it. Making a serious commitment to remove hostility from their behavior is always the first step.

Because hostility has been a part of their relationships for so long, it is going to take some time to remove it. Meaningful change does not happen overnight. Removing hostility from their own behavior will not immediately heal the wounds they have inflicted on their partners. Some clients find that they stop their hostile behavior, but their partners do not. It is important to prepare once-abusive clients for situations in which their partners abuse them. Suppose a problem comes up, and the partner starts to yell and insult the client. What should clients do? The first thing they will feel is that familiar "pull" to yell or hit back. They must not give in to it.

Clients cannot always choose the situations in which they find themselves, and they certainly do not control the way their partners behave. They do choose, however, how they respond to their partners. If they choose to respond with hostile or passive behavior to a partner's hostility, their attempt to change the rules will fail. Clients should behave assertively when confronted with hostility from a partner. For example, they need to respectfully but assertively address the issue of the yelling by telling their partners how it makes them feel, how they are trying to change their own behavior, and why it's important that the yelling stops. Now is the time to apply everything they have learned so far about staying in The Box: warning signs, self-talk, problem solving, time-out, keeping the Big Picture, all of the homework assignments they have done; every concept in this program has prepared them for this.

Clients must apply what they have learned, and lead by example. Use self-talk and stay focused on the problem. Do whatever they have to do to keep themselves from responding in a hostile or a passive manner.

When clients handle conflict respectfully, assertively, and without hostility, it creates a different kind of pull on their partners. If they apply their skills and abide by the "No Hostility" rule, it creates a pull on their partners to stop the yelling and join them in stopping the hostilities. That is how they turn back the clock. Change will not happen overnight. Meaningful change takes determination and work; it does not come easy. They will have to resist "the pull" to become hostile repeatedly. However, every time they successfully resist the pull, they come closer to changing the rules and removing hostility from their relationships for good.

Children and Family Violence

A staff member of a women's shelter related the following incident to me. The shelter admitted a mother and her three young children into the shelter after enduring years of horrific abuse at the hands of her alcoholic husband. Temporarily safe from their brutal father, the children talked about their experiences at home. "What was it like at home?" asked the shelter worker. "My daddy would come home drunk at night," replied one of the children. "He would make us go to bed and turn out the lights. Then he would beat up mommy. We were afraid to get out of bed, but we could hear him hitting her. We could hear mommy crying." The shelter worker asked, "Wasn't it awful laying there in the dark listening to your mommy being hurt?" "No," the child answered. "The worse part was when he stopped. Then it was quiet, and we didn't know what happened to mommy."

Of all the different groups in our society, children are the most vulnerable to abuse and exploitation. Children do not choose their parents. Dependent upon the adults around them, they have no control over the way their parents act. The adults in their lives have the power to make their world warm and safe – or brutal and frightening. Whether parents make their children's world a heaven or a hell, children must live in it. They cannot leave when things go wrong at home.

For many children, things at home are terribly wrong. Child abuse, in its various forms, is a horrifying reality for far too many children. One estimate (Carlson, 1984) is that over three million children witness acts of domestic violence in their home every year. Straus and Gelles (1990) estimate that at least one-third of American children have witnessed violence between their parents. Straus (1990) reported that of the 46 million American children who were living with both parents in 1975, approximately 1.7 million were subjected to "very severe violence" at the hands of their parents.

Although clients may assert that they hit their spouses, not their children, they need to understand that they cannot abuse their partners without hurting their children. Here is a brief review of research on the subject.

- In a 1983 study, sixty-five percent of the children who attempted to kill themselves had witnessed violence in their own homes (Kosky, 1983).

- A study of violent teenage boys found that exposure to family violence was associated with a positive feeling about using violence to solve their problems (Spaccerelli, Coatworth, & Bowden, 1995).

- Compared to other women, Kalmuss (1984) found that battered women were six times more likely to have been subjected to physical violence when they were children.

- Women who were abused by their husbands were found to be twice as likely to abuse their children, as compared to women who were not abused. The more violent a husband is to his wife, the more violent the wife is to her children. Women who are battered may commit the highest rates of child abuse (Straus & Gelles, 1990).

- The same study found that seventy-six percent of children who were repeatedly abused by their parents repeatedly and severely assaulted their brothers or sisters. The more violent parents were to their children, the more violent children were to their own siblings (Straus & Gelles, 1990).

- Sons who witnessed battering between parents were found to be ten times as likely to abuse their own partners. This does not mean that every child who witnesses abuse between his or her parents will eventually abuse his or her own partner. Many people who abuse come from non-violent homes, and some children from violent homes do not abuse. However, witnessing abuse as a child does seem to increase the risk of becoming an abusive partner (Straus, Gelles, & Steinmetz, 1980).

As you might expect, exposure of a child to family violence is associated with a number of significant childhood problems, including antisocial behavior, depression, anxiety, and school problems (Adamson & Thompson, 1998). It seems that parents who abuse each other also abuse their children, even if the children are not the ones hit. That is why many perceive children as the "hidden victims" of the violence between their parents.

Physical Abuse of Children

In a national survey of violence in American families, 90% of the parents of three-year-olds, and 34% of the parents of 15- to17-year olds, reported that they had hit their child one or more times during the year (Straus & Gelles, 1990). In most of these instances, the violence was relatively minor. However, the survey also found that at least 1.5 million children per year are subjected to severe physical abuse (such as punching, kicking, and burning) at the hands of their parents. Among this unfortunate group of children, infants were physically assaulted an average of 19 times a year, three-year-olds were assaulted an average of 32 times a year, and 17-year-olds, an average of about six times a year.

Keep in mind that these are the rates of violence towards children in a national study of American homes. The problem of child abuse appears to be much more severe in homes where the mother is battered by the husband. In one study of the children of battered women, 90% of the children had also suffered physical abuse (Giles-Sims, 1985).

Parents who hit their children are probably teaching them that violence is an acceptable way of handling family problems. In the Straus (1990) survey, for example, teenagers were found to hit their parents about as often as the parents hit each other. Research also indicates that parents who engage in abusive violence toward their children or their spouses had themselves received more physical punishment as a child (Straus & Gelles, 1990). It is also the opinion of many that while most physical punishment does not turn into physical abuse, most physical abuse begins as ordinary punishment (Kadushin & Martin, 1981).

Spanking is also a model for the child's own acts of violence. As the saying goes, violence begets more violence. When spanked, a child can easily develop core beliefs that it is OK to control and coerce another person through physical violence, and that when you are angry, it's alright to express the anger by hitting the person you're mad at. The studies above suggest that the more violence children experience in their homes, the more favorably inclined they are towards violence against other children, and even toward their own parents. An article in *Newsday* (August 15, 1978) reported that one in five parents suffered objects being thrown at them, pushing, shoving, and furious verbal abuse at the hands of their own children. It is likely, observed *Newsday*, that this abuse was learned "at the knee of the parent."

I am sure that I am not alone in my belief that physical punishment is not the most effective way to teach a child to behave. To be effective, I teach my clients, discipline must educate a child. Punishment alone is not education. Punishment usually does not elicit true remorse for misbehavior, nor does it foster true sorrow for the harm that a child's misbehavior may have caused others. Rather, physical punishment fills a child with fear, anger, and defiance, and while violence may make a child fear his or her parents, it does not effectively teach a child to respect them. More importantly, it does not teach a child how to behave more responsibly in the future. Having children take a time-out, withdrawal of privileges, rewarding positive choices, and taking time to communicate and teach are more effective methods of discipline than corporal punishment alone.

Abusive clients must not mistake hitting or spanking for discipline. Hitting and spanking are forms of punishment, and punishment alone is woefully inadequate in raising a child. Parenting takes more than punishment. Discipline and setting limits are important, but effective discipline involves finding a way to communicate values and ethics to the child. When parents are not present to watch over them, it is the values and ethics that parents have taught their children that guide them in making the right choices and doing the right thing. On the other hand, if parents rely on spanking to get their children to behave, children may do the right thing when they are watching; they want to avoid punishment. However, when parents are not present and the children are not afraid of being caught, the fear of punishment loses its influence, and children may not make the right choice.

I remember one study of moral development in children that compared delinquents in juvenile hall with schoolchildren of the same age from the same neighborhood. Both groups of children were asked questions like, "Why shouldn't a person steal?" The schoolchildren provided answers like, "Because it is wrong to take something you haven't earned. No one will trust you if you steal. It hurts when people steal something from you." The delinquents, on the other hand, provided answers such as "Because you might get caught, and you might end up in jail." Do you see the difference in their answers? The schoolchildren had internalized important values and social ethics, while the delinquents had not.

When the two groups were compared further, it was found that the delinquents had been subjected to far more physical punishment by their parents than the school children had. The lesson is this: spanking alone does not teach children how to live their lives responsibly, and it may make the situation worse. When children misbehave, they need more than punishment. They need to learn from their parents:

- What he or she did that was wrong.
- Why that behavior was wrong.
- The natural consequences of wrongful behavior.
- How misbehavior makes others feel.
- Better choices that the child can make in the future.
- Non-violent ways to handle problems with which they are faced.

It is important to counsel clients that slapping and hitting cannot teach children the things they need to learn, no matter how often or how hard they are hit. Some parents hit their children so often that the children eventually lose all fear of parental punishment.

Effective parents take time to teach their children right from wrong. When the subject arises in counseling, I advise clients that good parents control their own anger, and use their heads rather than hands to solve discipline problems. They remember that children have legal and moral rights of their own, and that they have no right to injure or inflict unjustifiable suffering upon a child in the guise of "discipline."

Clients need to understand that verbal abuse, psychological abuse, and neglect are also ways in which parents can inflict mental pain and suffering on their children. Verbal abuse, as I am sure you know, is the use of words to deliberately inflict fear, embarrass, degrade, humiliate, or otherwise inflict emotional pain on a child. Some examples of verbal abuse are:

- You're so stupid! You're disgusting! You make me sick!
- One of these days, you're going to wake up and I'll be gone.
- I could get married again if it weren't for you.
- You're the reason your father and I got divorced. He couldn't put up with you.
- I wish you had never been born.

Psychological abuse and neglect refers to non-violent actions intended to cause fear, inflict emotional pain, or cause a child humiliation. Here are some examples:

- Locking a child in a dark closet or room.
- Withholding reasonable access to clothing (forcing them to go naked), food (starving them until they are below their natural body weight), or denying children other essentials of living.
- Embarrassing or humiliating a child in public or in front of their peers.
- Forcing a child to witness violence to another member of the family.
- Refusing to speak to a young child for long periods of time.
- Inflicting pain and suffering on a child's pet, or destroying a child's favorite toy.

It is important that clients understand the extent of the pain and suffering that their abusive words and actions cause, and that no child, no matter what he or she has done, ever "deserves" such abuse. Verbal abuse, psychological abuse, and neglect are always destructive. If repeated over a period of years, it can result in life-long problems from which the child may never recover.

There is an old saying that goes, "Sticks and stones may break my bones, but words will never hurt me." This is most definitely not true. Take time to teach clients that verbal abuse is destructive, and it has long-lasting negative effects on children. In terms of the emotional pain caused, it can be just as traumatizing as "broken bones."

When a Child Witnesses Violence

Research on children who see domestic violence in the home consistently shows that these children experience significant emotional trauma (e.g., Jaffe et al., 1989). Children who must live in a home where one or both parents suffer abuse at the hands of the other parent are denied the security and nurturing that they deserve. They live in an environment of fear, anger, resentment, shame, and guilt. Speaking of the consequences of spouse abuse on the children in the home, psychologist Lenore Walker wrote:

Children who live in a battering relationship experience the most insidious form of child abuse. Whether or not either parent physically abuses them is less important than the psychological scars they bear from watching their fathers beat their mothers. (From *Battered Women*, 46, 1979)

Children who witness abuse between parents often experience short-term and long-term developmental problems that are similar to those of children who are themselves the target of abuse. Chief Justice Margaret Workman of the West Virginia Supreme Court, writing about the effect of family violence on children, wrote:

Partner abuse has a tremendous impact on children. Children learn several lessons in witnessing the abuse of one of the parents. First, they learn that such behavior appears to be approved by their most important role models and that the violence toward a loved one is acceptable. Children also fail to grasp the full range of negative consequences for the violent behavior and observe, instead, the short-term reinforcements, namely compliance by the victim. Thus, they learn the use of coercive power and violence as a way to influence loved ones without being exposed to other more constructive alternatives. In addition to the effect of the destructive modeling, children who grow up in violent homes experience damaging psychological effects. (What Therapists See That Judges May Miss, 11-12, Spring, 1988).

When addressing these issues, I ask clients to write a letter that starts with the words, "The Promises I Make to My Children." Clients are encouraged to write down the promises that they are willing to make to their children as a parent. If they do not have children of their own, they write down the promises that they are willing to make to their future children. They are encouraged to avoid talking about material things, and to write about the kind of parental relationship and home environment they promise to provide. Ideally, clients will put some thought into their promises.

These promises are not like New Year's resolutions that people make and then forget the next day. I advise clients to write down only things to which they are willing to make a real commitment. When they finish, clients put the letter somewhere handy, so they can bring out the letter and read the promises they have made when tensions in the home are running high. Clients also ask themselves whether they have kept their promises during the past week. If so, they congratulate themselves. If not, they resolve to do better during the week to come.

To help them get started, I list some of the things that I believe all children have a right to expect from their parents, such as:

- A home free of violence, neglect, sexual, psychological, and physical abuse
- A loving and supportive relationship with both of their parents
- A home where they feel safe and protected, and where their parents show consideration for each other and treat each other with respect
- To be corrected and disciplined as appropriate, but in a manner that respects them as a people in their own right
- Parents who provide for their basic emotional, educational, and material needs
- To be taught the difference between "right" and "wrong" through their parents' words and example.

The letter can have a powerful effect upon clients. I have included parts of the letters written by two prior clients, Laura and Steven, below.

Laura's Letter to her son, Danny

Dear Danny:

Hey baby its mommy. I want to start this letter by telling you that I'm sorry for putting you through the pain that you're going through. I know that I've made a lot of mistakes in my life and because of them you are suffering. I'm sorry that you would see your daddy and I fight, you should have never seen those things.

I want to make things better. That's why I'm taking these classes, so I can learn to be a better mommy. When I'm done I know that you're going to be coming home, and when you do no matter who I'm being with I promise that you won't see mommy getting hit or me hitting someone else. I promise that when I get frustrated I won't take it out on you. I'll take time for myself until I cool down. I know you love me. I'm learning a lot, and now I understand why you would start crying and screaming when you would hear me yelling. I know that I've made a lot of bad choices, but I'm going make things better and we're going to be happy again.

Love,

Mommy

Steven's Letter to his Children David and Christina

Dear David and Christina,

I want to start by telling you that I'm the happiest father in the world. You guys make me very proud to be your father. I know that you are very young, and this is only the beginning of the long road ahead of us, but the day you guys were born I knew in my mind and my heart that I would do whatever it took to be with you forever. I want to be able to show you by example that no matter what the situation may be, I will always be there when you need me. I want you to be able to trust and respect me, the way I will show trust and respect for you. I will treat you as fair as I would want to be treated, with the love and respect that you deserve.

Through our years I will maintain a relationship in which you will never feel a doubt about my commitment to you. I think the most important thing growing up is feeling love and respect from your parents. If I am able to make this happen I feel our relationship will be everything I wanted from the start. We would be able to talk about anything with the confidence of knowing it will be treated with honor and respect, not ridicule. We have a long road ahead and I know it is my responsibility to keep us in the right direction, and that is my promise to you. Well, here we go on our way. I love you guys very much.

Love,

Your father xxoo

To my knowledge, both Laura and Steven have kept their promises. Before moving on to another subject, I wish to emphasize to the reader the opportunity that these issues offer as a motivation for abusive clients. Meaningful change is a long and arduous process. Applying the skills and concepts necessary to stop abuse and stay in The Box requires constant vigilance and effort, especially in the earlier stages of counseling.

Some of my clients simply lacked the motivation needed to apply themselves. They no longer cared about their relationships with their partners. Nor did they care about the potential consequences of abuse, such as going to jail or losing their jobs. They did, however, care about their children. In their love for their children, they found the will and the motivation they needed to learn, accept responsibility for their behavior, and to change.

David, a prior client, comes to mind. After talking about the issues above, he started to make meaningful progress in his counseling. When I asked him about the obvious change in his attitude, he told me that he had gone home after this "lesson" and put a picture of his son on a mirror. He looked at the picture a lot. "When I look at his picture," David said, "I think about him and about this class, and then I want to stay in The Box."

Alcohol, Drugs and Violence

Alcohol and drug abuse are often associated with higher rates of partner abuse. Although there are inconsistencies in the literature, there is a significant body of research suggesting that the greater the drug or alcohol problem, the greater the risk of a domestic violence incident. As clients may reduce the risk of future incidents of partner abuse by seeking help for a drug or alcohol problem, they should understand the relationship between substance abuse and partner violence. Counselors should encourage them to evaluate the role of drugs and alcohol in their lives and seek appropriate help if needed. Francisco, a former client, had an experience that illustrated the importance of this issue:

It was one week before his daughter's birthday party, and Francisco was worried. "My wife wants a big party at the park, and so do I," he told the men in his group. "We rented one of those inflatable things the kids like to jump in, and there will be clowns, and a barbecue, and the whole family's invited." When Francisco said "the whole family," he meant everyone even remotely related to his daughter, grandparents, aunts and uncles, nieces and nephews, second and third cousins, everyone on the block where they lived – and their children and friends of their children. Francisco liked to do things in a big way. One person said the birthday party sounded like fun, and asked Francisco why he was so worried. "Well," Francisco said, "my wife invited her two cousins to the party, and there's always been bad blood between us. They're trouble-makers. I just don't want any problems with them. I asked my wife not to invite them, but she did anyway."

Francisco took his counseling very seriously, and he had made strong progress during his six months in the group. We were not too worried about him. We thought he had the skill to stay in The Box and handle any problems that came up. The following week, however, Francisco was missing from the group. Three weeks passed before we saw him again.

When Francisco returned to the group, we asked him where he had been. "In jail," he told us. "Everything was fine at the party at first," he explained. "We started the party about ten in the morning, and everyone was just having fun. I didn't allow any drinking at the party, and my wife's cousins weren't causing any trouble. Everything was going so good that about five o'clock I gave in and let someone go on a beer run. By six o'clock, the police were there. A fight broke out and I was arrested along with her cousins. It was like I forgot everything I knew."

I do not think it was a coincidence that the fighting started after the drinking. According to Francisco, everything was peaceful for the first seven hours of the party, but one hour after the booze arrived things turned ugly. There was a lesson to learn from Francisco's experience. There is a long tradition of research linking alcohol and drug abuse to family violence. The National Violence Against Women Survey reported that binge drinkers (people who consume excessive amounts of alcohol when they drink, but don't drink on a daily basis) are three to five times more likely to assault their partners than those who don't drink (Tjaden & Thoennes, 1998, 2000).

A study in Memphis found that 92% of the victims of domestic violence said that the attacker used drugs or alcohol during the day of the assault, and that 67% of the aggressors had used a combination of cocaine and alcohol (Brookoff, 1997). A study of Indiana men arrested for domestic violence (Roberts, 1987) found that 60% of the men were under the influence of alcohol during the domestic violence incident for which they were arrested. Another study reported that 70% of the abusers studied were under the influence of drugs, alcohol, or both at the time of the attack (Roberts, 1988).

Yet another study reported that a Latina who was in a relationship with a binge drinker was ten times more likely to be assaulted than Latinas with partners who drank less (Kaufman, Kantor, & Straus, 1990). In a study of marital violence among military personnel (Pan, Neidig, & O'Leary, 1994), researchers interviewed 11,870 randomly selected men on 38 different Army bases. They found that 5.6% of the men had engaged in severe spouse abuse (choked, beat up, threatened with a gun, etc.) at least once during the past year. They also found that compared to non-violent men, the presence of an alcohol problem elevated the risk of severe partner violence by 128%. The existence of a drug problem increased the risk by 121%.

Other studies have found that more than half of prison inmates serving time for violent crimes were drinking or using drugs at the time of the offense, and that 40% of people who killed their partners were drinking at the time of the murder (Greenfeld, 1998; Willson, 20000). In a nationwide study of over 8,000 families (Straus & Gelles, 1990), researchers found a strong link between drinking and family violence. The greater the drinking problem was, the higher the rate of violence in the home. Among the men who abstained from alcohol, 6.8% had one or more violent acts against their spouse during the year of the study. In contrast, binge drinkers had a violence rate that was three times higher (19.2%).

Many researchers agree that there is a strong, if imperfect, correlation between drinking, drug use, and family violence – the greater the drug or alcohol problem, the greater the risk of violence. In an effort to reduce the risk of further acts of violence, it seems appropriate to

170

encourage abusive clients with a substance abuse problem to obtain alcohol or drug abuse counseling as a part of their treatment plan for partner abuse. By reducing the frequency and severity of the substance abuse, they are likely to reduce the risk of new episodes of violence. On the other hand, failing to maintain sobriety may increase the risk of new incidents of abuse.

Over the years, I have heard many of my clients tell stories like the one Francisco told at the beginning of this section. A man or woman will be making great progress in his or her counseling when, confident in their new skills and accomplishments, they get drunk or use drugs. Under the influence of drugs or alcohol, they seemed to forget everything they had learned in their sessions and abused again. In one intoxicated moment, they lose the trust that their partners and children have slowly gained in them – the trust that they had worked for months to regain by using their skills and staying in The Box.

Increased Risk

Advise clients that the following issues probably contribute to an increased risk of violence when they are under the influence:

Alcohol and drugs impair our judgment. Let's face it, when we are under the influence, we lose a whole bunch of IQ points (we all do) and it's easy to get stuck on "dumb." For clients who have already demonstrated a history of poor judgment via their violence towards family members, further impairment of judgment through alcohol or drug intoxication seems a risky thing to do. I remind clients that the more frequently they drink or use drugs, the more likely it is that they will be under the influence when a crisis arises between them and their spouses. If a conflict arises between them while they are under the influence, they could be in trouble. They will not have the ability to think as clearly as they normally do, or to apply their skills as well as they ordinarily can. Many people in our program have said that they would never have done the things they did if they had been sober at the time. Because they were under the influence, they just did not think or care about the consequences of their behavior. (They cared a lot when they sobered up, sometimes in jail, but they did not care when they were drunk or high.)

Like an athlete who shows up for the game drunk, they were not up to the challenge. That is how it is when clients use drugs or alcohol when there is a lot of conflict and hostility in their relationships. I remind clients that they never know when "the game" is going to start. There is always the chance that the day you decide to have a snoot full will be "game day."

To illustrate the point, let us use Larry and Bob as examples. Larry does not drink as often as Bob and he never uses drugs. Suppose

171

Larry has a few beers on Friday at a barbeque, but he does not drink the rest of the week. Also, suppose that we know for sure that a major conflict between Larry and his partner is going to come up sometime during the week. What are the odds that Larry will be under the influence when the conflict starts? The calendar below shows the days of the week. The "B" indicates Larry's "Beer" day.

Larry's Week:

Mon	TUE	WED	THUR	FRI	SAT	SUN
				B		

Larry is drinking one day out of seven, so the odds that he will be drinking when a conflict comes up are 1/7 = 0.14, or about 14%. There's a 14% chance that Larry will be under the influence when "the game" starts for him and his partner, and he'll be called on to use all his skills to stay in The Box. (Yes, I know this is an over-simplification, but stick with me while I make my point.)

Bob is a different type of man than Larry. In fact, some of the people who know him best will tell you that Bob is a drunk. During the week in question, Bob drinks six days of the week. Suppose that Bob is also going to have a major problem come up between him and his partner during the week. His week looks like the calendar below, and the "B's" stand for Bob's "beer" days.

Bob's Week:

Mon	TUE	WED	THUR	FRI	SAT	SUN
B		B	B	B	B	B

What are the odds that Bob will be intoxicated on the day that the conflict comes up? The answer is 6/7 = 0.86, or 86%. The odds are 86% that Bob will be under the influence on "game day." There is an 86% chance that Bob will be under the influence when he needs his skills the most. "Given what you have learned about the link between alcohol and violence," I ask, "who do you think is more likely to have another incident of partner abuse, Larry or Bob?" Their answer, of course, is Bob.

I used a sports analogy to make my point, but there is, of course, a big difference between our Bob and a professional athlete. If a baseball player shows up drunk to a game, his next appearance may be in the minor leagues. Partner abuse has more severe consequences. If Bob shows up drunk at his game and abuses his partner again, his next

172

appearance may be in criminal court, divorce court, the unemployment line, or in family court asking for supervised visitation with his children.

If Bob is wise he will put the beer (or dope) down and get in the best rehabilitation program he can find. His family will thank him for it, and it may greatly reduce the likelihood of another incident of violence.

There are other ways that substance abuse increases the risk of violence. Alcohol and drug problems put severe stress on a relationship. Many times, the drinking or drug use is the problem causing tension between them. Substance abuse problems frequently strain financial resources, give rise to alcohol or drug-related legal problems, cause problems at work, impair physical health, and place stress on a relationship in ways that are too numerous to count. The increased stress of a drug or alcohol problem results in more conflict between the partners, and increases the risk of the conflict turning violent.

To return to Bob, his alcohol abuse may have been the problem about which he and his partner were fighting. Perhaps his wife objected to his spending more on Budweiser than bills, and tried to take his car keys to avoid another DUI. Perhaps she complained that Bob could more easily find his way to the liquor store than a job interview, and reminded him what his doctor said about his liver. Drug and alcohol abuse creates its own stress on a relationship.

As an example of the stress that substance abuse can create, consider John's story. John, a former client, did not have a job and relied totally on his girlfriend for financial support. To be honest, John was not much of a worker. He was, however, an all-star drinker. One Sunday, John asked his girlfriend for money to buy a "40-ouncer." She gave him the money and John took the short walk to the liquor store to buy his beer.

A little later, John asked her for another "40-ouncer," and she gave John more money. When John asked for a third bottle a couple of hours later, his girlfriend refused. She angrily told John that he had had enough, and besides, she had better things to spend her money on than beer. By this time, John was intoxicated and his behavior showed it. He demanded more beer money and belligerently grabbed her purse. In the ensuing struggle over her purse, John punched her.

It is hard to see how partner abuse counseling would have been helpful to John in the absence of an alcohol abuse component in his treatment plan. To his credit, John agreed to get alcohol abuse counseling in addition to partner abuse counseling. By addressing both of these problems, John made good progress.

Does Substance Abuse Cause Partner Abuse?

Most researchers agree that there is a correlation between substance abuse and partner abuse. In other words, people with substance abuse problems may have higher rates of partner violence than people who do not have substance abuse problems. While the abuse of drugs and alcohol may make violence more likely, it does not necessarily cause the violence.

Correlations do not indicate causality. The distinction between correlation and causality becomes clinically important when clients assert, for example, that the alcohol made them abusive." Personally, I am uncomfortable with a paradigm that attributes abusive behavior solely to alcohol or substance abuse. While the body of research may generally support a correlation between the two, the body of research is not supportive of a CAUSAL relationship between substance abuse and partner violence.

In the study by Straus & Gelles (1990), for example, binge drinkers engaged in more violence than moderate drinkers did, and binge drinkers were three times more violent than non-drinkers were. Nevertheless, only about 20% of the binge drinkers engaged in any form of domestic violence during the year of the study. This means that 80% of binge drinkers did not engage in any form of violence against their partners. The chart also shows that 6.8% of people who were violent toward their partners do not drink at all. Clearly, alcohol did not cause the violence among couples who never use alcohol.

Substance abuse is an important contributing factor in many incidents of domestic violence, but I believe that the ways people think during partner conflict – their belief systems about responsibility, aggression, and control – are still the most important factor in abusive behavior. A person who thinks like an abuser acts like one. It may be that the abuse of alcohol or drugs can facilitate this thought process, or that similar belief systems are involved with both substance abuse and partner abuse. The research described earlier seems to suggest that a person is more likely to think and act like an abuser when he or she is intoxicated than when he or she is sober.

It is my clinical experience that clients who think (and subsequently behave) like an abuser while they are sober AND abuse alcohol or drugs are especially dangerous to their partners. This dangerous combination was supported in a 1990 study, which found that men who rarely drink but think it is OK to hit your partner had higher rates of partner abuse than heavy drinkers who think it's wrong to hit your partner (Kaufman, Kantor, & Straus, 1990). This finding suggests that thoughts and beliefs may be a more salient factor than substance abuse alone when it comes to partner violence. As one might intuitively predict, the highest rates of violence in the study were among heavy drinkers who ALSO believe it is OK to hit your partner.

To summarize, the body of research as of this writing generally supports the following assumptions about the relationship between substance abuse and partner violence:

- The more one drinks, the greater the likelihood that he will be involved in a domestic violence incident against his or her partner. Studies report that heavy or binge drinkers appear to have a greater rate of assaulting their partners than people who do not drink. The same assumptions also apply to many forms of drug abuse.

- Alcohol and substance abuse alone do not appear to cause a person to hit his or her partner. Most heavy drinkers in the studies discussed did not hit their partners at all, despite their frequent drunkenness.

- Getting control of a drinking problem may do a lot to lower the risk of further violence, but it is no guarantee that the violence will stop. Many people who stop drinking, or who have never had a drinking problem, nevertheless abuse their partners. In the Straus and Gelles (1990) study, about 7% of the people who abstain from alcohol entirely had engaged in at least one episode of domestic violence against their spouse during the year of the study.

The best conclusion the practitioner can draw from knowledge gained from clinical experience and the body of literature may be this: if your client has a drug or alcohol problem, encourage him or her to get help, and formalize that goal as a component in your treatment plan. In so doing, you may greatly lower the odds of future partner assaults. However, it is probably a mistake to assume that substance abuse counseling alone will stop abusive behavior. The client must also change destructive beliefs and attitudes, gain important skills, and accept full responsibility for his or her behavior towards the partner. Positive and meaningful changes are likely to come from addressing the drinking or drug problem, and by applying the concepts and skills learned in partner abuse counseling.

I make the following recommendations to abusive clients. "First," I advise them, "if you are having a lot of marital problems, I recommend that you stop drinking until things are on a more stable footing at home. Drinking will only compound your problems and increase the risk of violence during an argument. Second, if you have engaged in any abusive or violent behavior in the past while under the influence, you should stop drinking or using altogether. Ask clients to honestly answer the following questions:

1) *Have you been arrested or had legal problems (DUI) due to alcohol or drug use?*
2) *Has drinking or drug use caused problems in your relationships?*
3) *Have you ever gotten into trouble at work due to your drug or alcohol use, or has substance abuse caused financial problems?*
4) *Has drug or alcohol use threatened your physical health or mental well-being?*
5) *Have you ever verbally, sexually, or physically abused your partner while under the influence of alcohol or drugs?*

If your client answered "yes" to any of these questions, recommend that he or she get help, or refer them to a resource that can evaluate the situation in more detail. Being willing to acknowledge a problem and get help for it is a big first step in reducing the risk of further violence.

The *Alcohol Use Disorders Identification Test (AUDIT)* is another tool in evaluating alcohol problems. The AUDIT is a widely used method of identifying alcohol problems. Have your client answer the questions and add up the score. In a study of treatment matching with persons who had a wide range of alcohol problem severity, it was found that AUDIT scores in the range of 8-15 represented a medium level of alcohol problems whereas scores of 16 and above represented a high level of alcohol problems.

If stopping your drinking seems like too hard a thing to do, your client needs to re-examine priorities. Nothing should be more important than stopping the violence in his or her relationships. Clients should be willing to make any changes that will help attain that goal. If a client is unwilling to make those changes, it is time to evaluate the level of commitment to a violence-free lifestyle. Now is the time to get help.

Don's Marijuana Time-Out

In closing, let me warn you about clients who use alcohol or drugs to self-medicate, or "cope" with partner conflict. Don, a member of my group several years ago, raised his hand during a session. "Dr. Adams," he said, "I agree with everything you say about alcohol and other drugs, but you're wrong about marijuana. Whenever my wife and I get into it, I go to the garage and smoke a joint. My anger goes right away, and no more problem. I've done this for years and it works great!"

Don was describing a "marijuana time-out," and he highly recommended it. Over the years, other clients have made similar comments about their drug (or drink) of choice. One client said cocaine reduced his anger, but alcohol increased it. Another claimed that wine was a good conflict-reducer, while tequila was deadly and should be avoided at all cost.

I asked Don, "If marijuana works so great, what are you doing in a counseling program for partner abuse? Did you score bad weed or something?" Don blinked a couple of times and thought it over. I reminded Don of the concepts in The Box, how getting high never solves the problems that cause tension between partners, and unsolved problems lead to lingering tension that grows and festers. Over time, the average tension level rises. Eventually, tensions may explode in an episode of physical violence.

"Drugs and alcohol can't get you back to the OK Zone of The Box." I continued. "You may not feel the tension when you're stoned or inebriated, but it's there, and it will be waiting for you when your sobriety returns. When you are high, you feel a drug-induced OK Zone, but things are not OK. You just don't feel the tension because of the drug. Tensions are not gone, really. You are just using the marijuana to help you pretend that things are OK. Tension lingers and builds strength over time, and running away from your problems only makes things worse. The only effective way to deal with conflict is to solve the problems that cause it, and that requires knowledge, skill, and commitment. You can't find that in a drug or a bottle, Don."

Choices Chains

Some clients readily accept responsibility for their abusive behavior; others do not. Difficult clients have a hard time understanding how they go from "Point A" (the pre-conflict OK Zone) to "Point B" (out of The Box abusive behavior). Specifically, they find it hard to see the crucial importance of their own choices in the sequence of events that took place between Point A and Point B. Very often, they see themselves as victims of the abused partners, who "keep pushing me until I lose it." They attribute their abusive conduct to provocative choices made by their partners, and either minimize or deny the importance of their own choices. "She is the one who needs the counseling," they assert, "not me."

The counselor should not minimize the problems that exist between the client and his or her partner; the problems and frustrations are often legitimate and reality-based. However, abusive clients must understand that the problems are not destroying their relationships. Rather, their own abusive responses – the aggressive choices they make in the heat of conflict – raze their relationships to the ground. Relational problems alone do not have the power to destroy homes. In contrast, the choice to abuse destroys lives, and abusive behavior is always a choice. After clients assume responsibility for their abusive choices, and the destruction their choices have inflicted on their relationships, meaningful change is possible. The challenge for the counselor is getting clients to attend to their destructive responses to relational problems, rather than to the problems themselves.

An important philosophical position lies at the heart of the client's argument that his or her partner "drives him to abuse." Are people wholly responsible for their choices? Is there a point, after sufficient provocation, when clients cease to be wholly responsible for their behavior, when their partners must assume some responsibility for our clients' abusive behavior? How you answer these questions assumes great importance among this population of clients. How your clients answer this question is crucial. In this field of counseling, there is no single issue of greater importance.

I work with a wide variety of clients. There are times when I try to lessen the responsibility that some clients assume for the events in lives. There is the depressed client who feels excessive guilt, the victim of sexual assault who believes she somehow invited the rape, or the father who lost a daughter in an auto accident and blames himself for lending her the family car. In contrast, I hold abusive clients fully responsible for the choices they make. I ask them to assume full responsibility for their every choice, every time, without exception. "The only person responsible for the violence," I tell them, "is the one doing the hitting."

As discussed earlier, clients typically attribute their abusive behavior to their emotional state (anger). They attribute their emotional state to their partners' behaviors. The choices made by the client are conspicuously absent. Ask clients why they abused, and they will tell you why they were angry. Ask them why they were angry, and they will tell you what their partners said and did. They attribute their abusive conduct to their partners' choices, rather than their own choices. Their paradigm suggests that the partners cause their abuse. To stop the abuse, you (the therapist) must help the client change their partners' behavior. This is the basis of the client's assertion, "She needs counseling more than I do."

One way of responding to this assertion is to point out its impracticality. "When I started working in this field many years ago," I say, "I explained to my clients that there are two ways to approach the problem of partner abuse. The first approach is to try to get everyone to be nice to us. We can try to get everyone to treat us fairly, respectfully, and considerately. We can try to get everyone to express anger responsibly, never provoke us, and never give us a reason to abuse them. The problem with that approach is that it will take a long, long time.

The second approach is to assume from the start that other people will sometimes say and do things that we do not like. Assume that people will sometimes disrespect us, hurt us, express anger childishly, provoke us, and do all manner of things that vex us. We can just accept the fact that people are not as good and responsible as we wish they were, and talk about how we will react to it. We can accept that we do not get to control how others act, nor choose the situation with which we have to deal, but take heart in the knowledge that we always choose our response to the situation. We can try to eliminate difficult and trying interpersonal situations from our lives, or learn to make wise and skillful choices in the face of such situations. The second approach seemed a lot more practical."

Another response is to challenge the client's notion that he or she is a victim. "Your life and your relationships are pretty much what you have chosen for yourself," I often say. "Your choices are more important, as far as your own life is concerned, than anyone else's choices. Victims lack choices. You make choices every hour of your life. Your life and relationships are the sum of all of the choices you have made, day by day and month by month, as the years went by. You chose your partner.

180

You chose your strategy for handling problems. You chose your reaction to the choices of others. You chose your reaction to emotional upset and relational conflict. You chose to stay in the relationship or leave it. You chose to respond to conflict with love, support, and understanding, or with anger, insult, and aggression. You chose to assert leadership in the face of marital conflict or to think and behave like an angry child.

"Challenges of life and the choices of others certainly influence your life, but they do not define it. Nor do they have the power to define your relationships. Your choices, the way you choose to respond to challenges, are far more powerful in defining your life and your relations. If you do not like your life, make different choices. If you do not like your relationship, make better choices for yourself and your family. Your partner's choices have never diminished your ability to choose not to abuse. As far as your life is concerned, your choices matter more than the choices of others. More than any other factor, your life today is what you chose it to be yesterday. More than anything else, your life tomorrow will be a reflection of the choices you make today."

Newer clients hate it when I say this stuff. They feel irresponsible and guilty. Good – appropriate guilt has its place. More advanced clients love it when I talk this way. They feel stronger and more optimistic, and that is how I want them to feel. By taking responsibility for choosing their past, they open the door to choosing their future. They can choose better for themselves and their families, regardless of the challenges ahead. They can choose not to abuse.

"Choices chains" help clients identify poor choices from the past and identify better choices for the future. They help clients understand the true power of their own choices, and improve the choices they make in times of conflict. This treatment approach asks abusive clients to accept the following concepts:

- *Every day of your life you face situations in which you have to make choices. Your life today is, more than anything else, the result of the choices you have made.*

- *Do not blame others. Keep your focus on yourself, because only you can solve your problems.*

- *You are 100% responsible for how you choose to respond to every situation and person in your life. Everyone else is 0% responsible.*

- *Your choices are the most important factor in how you feel. Happiness occurs when you make wise and responsible choices, while unhappiness is the frequent companion of irresponsible choices. If you choose better for yourself and your family, you will experience the good feelings that accompany responsible choices.*

- *In the words of psychiatrist William Glasser, "Happiness occurs most often when we are willing to take responsibility for our behavior."*

- *Never make excuses, feel sorry for yourself, or blame others for your irresponsible choices. Irresponsible and childish behavior is never justified, no matter how much you may have suffered at the hands of others.*

- *To be successful as an adult, you must be willing to judge your own behavior and make changes when your behavior falls below your standards. If you fail to judge your own behavior you will not grow as a person and nothing will get better.*

- *If you get angry it is because you choose to anger yourself. If you remain calm, it is because you choose to stay calm and balanced. Your thoughts cause your anger. If you abuse, it is because you choose to abuse. If you do not abuse, it is because you choose to behave responsibly.*

- *You alone are responsible for your behavior. Right or wrong, you must accept full responsibility for your choices.*

- *Your choices are the single most important reason why your life (and your relationship) is what it is. In fact, your life at this moment is an accumulation of the thousands of choices you've made over the years. You chose your partner. You chose to stay in the relationship or leave it. When problems came up, as they always do, you chose to respond to them the way you did. You chose to say and do certain things, and you chose to not say and do other things. Every choice you made along the way had a positive or negative effect on your relationships and your life.*

- *Today and in the future, you have more choices to make. You will choose to apply the concepts and skills you have learned, or choose to ignore them. Either way, you will be the person you choose to be, and your relationship will be what you make it. You alone must decide whether you will take the responsible path.*

Clients may say, "Wait a minute, Dr. Adams, what about my partner's choices? What about all the hurtful things my partner does? Why do I always have to focus on my choices?"

"Human nature being as it is," I reply, "it is easier to identify your partner's poor choices than your own. But you can't change your partner – you can only change yourself – and by changing yourself, you can often change your relationship. Change has to start somewhere and with someone. You might as well step up to the plate and take a leadership role by starting the change process in yourself. Further, it only takes one person to stop your abuse and your poor choices – you. It's easier to ask your partner to change than for you to change. As I said, it's easier to see your partner's shortcomings than your own. Most people I work with can go on and on about their partners' wicked behavior, but they find it harder to talk about the changes they need to make.

"If you examine past incidents of abuse openly and honestly, you will always find that, regardless of the behavior of your partner, there were choices that you could have made that would have led to a more positive outcome. Understand the choices you made that resulted in abuse, and identify the choices, which, had you made them, would have led to a more positive outcome for everyone. It is important to understand how your past choices led to abuse, and to identify better choices. With this understanding, it will be easier for you to make different choices the next time you are in a similar situation."

Before going further with the chaining exercise, remind your clients of the pitfalls of blaming, minimizing, and denying. While they may be tempted to make themselves out as a powerless victims, they are neither powerless nor victims, and should not think of themselves in that way. At this stage of counseling, they have the power to choose a violence-free relationship. They have the power to choose not to abuse again in the future. They can choose to solve problems with their heads rather than with their hands, to communicate rather than shout, and to understand rather than demand. They can choose to remain calm, even when others are not. They can choose better for themselves and their partners, but only if they let go of their views of themselves as helpless victims. If they are to take control of their futures, there can be no room for blaming, minimizing, or denying.

Making Choices Chains

As discussed above, behavior chains help clients identify their poor choices, and identify opportunities to make constructive choices during relational conflict. Choices chains help clients focus on themselves and their choices, rather than on their partner and their partners' choices. There is another way in which choices chains help clients. Frequently, their first attempts to apply the concepts and skills in this program do not turn out as well as they might have hoped. It is relatively easy to learn these concepts and skills, but it is more difficult to apply them in the heat of conflict. When clients fail to apply a concept or skill successfully, a choices chain can help evaluate what went wrong.

When a problem comes up between clients and their partners, the goal is to get from Point A (a state of Tension) to Point B (back to the OK Zone of The Box) as shown in the illustration below.

Suppose they try to use the concepts and skills in this program such as recognizing warning signs, self-talk, problem solving, time-out, the Big Picture, avoiding blame and control, and so forth, but instead of getting from Point A to Point B, they wind up at Point C (out of The Box). What happened? Clients should ask themselves, "How did I get from Point A to Point C? I tried to stay in The Box and use my skills, but everything went wrong." This is when choices chains help clients out. They show each of the choices made one-by-one. A thoughtfully prepared choices chain will tell clients what went wrong – how they got from Point A to Point C, instead of Pont A to Point B, and how to avoid making the same mistake the next time.

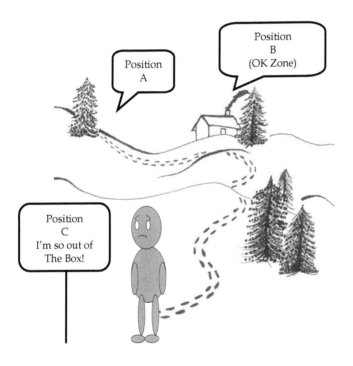

Choices chains show clients they ended up out of The Box one step at a time. Every choice brings a client closer to the goal (the OK Zone of The Box), or takes him further from it. Choices chains are like looking at footprints in the snow; they tell the steps the client took toward or away from the OK Zone.

The examples that follow illustrate how choices chains are used: Louis, a former client, provides the first example. Louis was married, but he still liked to have fun with the guys, especially if the guys planned to go to a club. It is not too surprising that Louis' wife had a problem with his club fun. As I recall, Louis worked a swing shift at his job, so his hours were irregular.

On the night described in Louis' choices chain, he got off work early and headed to a club with his cousin, where his fun lasted all night. Scheduled to work the morning shift at his job the following day, he did not make it home that night and headed back to work directly from the club. To Louis' surprise, his wife was waiting for him at work in the morning. The tension between them was high and there was some verbal abuse between them. The problem was not resolved that morning, and the tension followed Louis home after work, where the problem came up again. Louis made a series of choices that eventually led to abuse, as he described below:

Louis' Actual Choices

I got off work early and my wife thought I was going to be working overnight, so me and my cousin went to a club and I didn't tell my wife. When I got to work the next morning, my wife was outside my job.

↓

When she saw me, we started to argue and I played the macho role and told her that I'm a grown man and I don't have to ask her permission to do anything.

↓

When I got home, the arguing continued and I told her that I don't want to hear her mouth and that she needs to grow up and stop acting like a big kid.

↓

The fighting continued and I got frustrated and pushed her down on the living room floor. Someone called the police and I went to jail!

Notice that when Louis made his choices chain, he only wrote down his own choices. He kept the focus on himself rather than on his partner. This is an important part of a choices chain: Clients only write down the choices that they made. Clients cannot change their partners' choices. They can only change their own. Keep the focus on the things that clients have control over – their own choices. After Louis described the choices he made, he wrote down the choices that he could have made that would have led him to a better outcome. In other words, he wrote down the choices that would have led him from Point A to Point B (the OK Zone of the Box).

Louis' Actual Choices	Louis' Better Choices
I got off work early and my wife thought I was going to be working overnight, so me and my cousin went to a club and I didn't tell my wife. When I got to work the next morning, my wife was outside my job.	I should have talked with my wife and let her know I was getting off early and that I wanted to go out with my cousin.
↓	↓
When she saw me, we started to argue and I played the macho role and told her that I'm a grown man and I don't have to ask her permission to do anything.	I should have listened to what she had to say and understood where she was coming from, and I should have been more considerate toward her feelings.
↓	↓
When I got home, the arguing continued and I told her that I don't want to hear her mouth and that she needs to grow up and stop acting like a big kid.	I should have called a time-out and let the situation calm down, and kept my comments to myself and not put her down when she did nothing wrong.
↓	↓
The fighting continued and I got frustrated and pushed her down on the living room floor. Someone called the police and I went to jail!	I should have been a man and taken everything she had to say to me because we are supposed to be partners in this relationship.

Any of Louis' "Better Choices" would probably have prevented the violence that led to his arrest. When Louis started his counseling, he blamed his wife for the whole incident. After doing a choices chain, he understood the power of his own choices. He understood clearly that he had several chances to make choices that would have led to a different outcome. Unfortunately, he did not make those "Better" choices. He chose to abuse his wife, and by making that choice, he chose to get himself arrested that night. He had the power to choose better for himself and his partner, and he has only himself to blame that things turned out the way they did.

Holly, another client, wrote the choices chain below. Holly had been married for several years, and the first years of her marriage were good. Unfortunately, her husband started drinking heavily. Holly's attempts to reason with him did not help, and one night he came home in the small hours of the morning, reeking of alcohol and very intoxicated. Holly met him at the door. Her choices chain tells the rest of the story.

Holly's Actual Choices	Holly's Better Choices
I reacted to the situation without thinking first.	I should not have tried to reason with someone who had been drinking. I should have removed myself from the situation.
↓	↓
I proceeded to yell and start name-calling.	I should have stayed inside The Box; I should have recognized my warning signs.
↓	↓
I stayed outside The Box, continued my name-calling and demanded he get out of my house.	I should have known that demanding would only make things worse and wouldn't accomplish anything.
↓	↓
I became more frustrated and angry when he wouldn't leave because I didn't feel in control. I continued my yelling and demanding that he leave.	I should have taken a time-out and realized that I couldn't reason with him at that time. I should have left since obviously he wasn't going to.
↓	↓
I became more frustrated and angry and unfortunately then I kicked him.	I should have not allowed myself to be "pulled" into continuing to argue. I should have just left myself instead of being controlling and demanding HE leave.

Like Louis, Holly initially blamed her partner for the incident. As she completed her choices chain, however, she came to understand that she had been in control of her own destiny all along. If she had made any of the "Better Choices" available to her, there would have been no violence, and she would not have gone to jail that night.

Perhaps you sympathize with Holly. Certainly, everyone in her group understood the problem and Holly's anger, and everyone agreed that Holly had to do something about her husband's drinking problem. She could not just ignore it. However, Holly understood that her choice to deal with the problem by becoming verbally abusive and physically violent was a poor choice.

In her own words, those choices did not accomplish anything and it only made things worse. It was her responsibility to stay in The Box and express her anger in a non-violent manner. She chose not to.

The only thing her choices got her was a night in jail. Like Louis, she chose abuse and violence for her partner and for herself.

Any of her "Better Choices" would have led to a very different outcome. To her credit, she took responsibility for her poor choices that day, as did Louis. Holly did not choose the situation she had to deal with, but she did choose the way she reacted to it. We all do. Even when faced with blatant wrongdoing from our partner, we have the choice to stay in The Box and act like a leader, or to leave The Box and behave abusively.

Richard, a divorcee who shared custody of his son, Brandon, with his ex-spouse Linda, provides the next example. Because of Richard's past abusive behavior, the court issued a protective order that required him to stay away from Linda, but Richard sometimes ignored the order. Richard blamed Linda for their failed marriage, and objected to her new boyfriend.

On the day in question, Richard picked up his son at school to take him to lunch. Richard knew that Linda worked at Brandon's school and that he might see her there. That is, of course, just what occurred. As Richard was leaving the school with Brandon, he saw Linda. Richard's refusal to comply with the protective order – and his controlling behavior towards Linda – are about to cause new problems for him. Look at his choices one-by-one, as Richard later described them to his counseling group.

Richard's Actual Choices	Richard's Better Choices
I stopped at Brandon's school to see him for lunch. I saw Linda while I was walking out.	I should have waited until after work to see Brandon.

Richard's first choice was to ignore the court order by going to Linda's workplace. It was a poor choice. As Richard later acknowledged, he was angry with Linda and was looking for a chance to confront her. Picking up Brandon for lunch was an excuse to see Linda "by accident." Had he chosen to abide by the protective order, he would have spared everyone the entire incident. Instead, he chose to ignore the order.

Richard's Actual Choices	Richard's Better Choices
I talked to Linda outside of Brandon's school about her boyfriend.	I should not have talked to her and proceeded to lunch with Brandon.

Richard still had time recover from his first choice. He could have chosen to avoid talking to Linda and simply gone to lunch with his son.

Instead, he chose to violate the protective order by approaching Linda and bringing up an emotionally charged topic. Linda's relationship with her boyfriend was none of Richard's business, but he still wanted to control things.

Richard's Actual Choices	Richard's Better Choices
I told her she should stop taking drugs and start taking care of Brandon. I told her she was very immature and not responsible enough to take care of children.	I should not have said anything. I can't change her. I should have kept my opinions to myself and worried about Brandon with me.

If Richard believed that Linda was endangering Brandon by abusing drugs with her boyfriend, there are appropriate ways to address the problem (raise his concerns in family court, report them to the Department of Children and Family Services, etc.). His choice to confront Linda in public on the steps of a school building, at Linda's workplace and in front of his son, and in a manner that violated a protective order was foolish and unhelpful. Richard's belligerent attitude and claim that Linda was unfit to care for Brandon was provocative and sent the tension level sky high.

Richard's Actual Choices	Richard's Better Choices
I called her a junkie and yelled at her in front of Brandon. I accused her of things she may not have done. Then she slapped me.	I should have kept the name-calling out of it and expressed concern for her and Brandon. I should never have accused her because it only made her more defensive and made things worse.

Nothing good happens when clients get out of The Box, and Richard was definitely out of The Box. He wanted to hurt Linda by verbally abusing her, and he selfishly ignored the effect of his behavior on his son, who had to witness his father's humiliating tirade against his mother. Richard's concerns about Linda's behavior may or may not have been legitimate, but even if his concerns about her were entirely valid, they did not justify his choice to abuse her. The school authorities called the police, and they arrested Richard (for violating a protective order) in front of Brandon and the other people at the school. Any of Richard's "Better Choices" would have led to a different outcome for himself, his son, and Linda.

When Richard started counseling, he was indignant about his arrest. He saw himself as a victim and railed against the police and the court system. Richard created a victim role for himself by limiting his attention to his first choice (I stopped at Brandon's school to see him for lunch), and the result (she slapped me). As so many people do, he chose to narrow his attention to the last few seconds of the incident, and to ignore the choices that he made along the way.

He refused to look at his own "footprints in the snow." He found himself at Point C (slapped and arrested), did not like it there at all, and blamed others for it. Initially, he ignored his choice to use verbal hostility. I am not suggesting that Richard is responsible for Linda's behavior. She made her own choices, as did Richard. I am suggesting that Richard's assertion that he was an innocent victim in this situation was nonsense. He chose to go to Point C, step-by-step and choice-by-choice.

A choices chain forced Richard to stop thinking of himself as a helpless victim. As he worked on his choices chain, his footprints were unavoidable. They provided undeniable evidence that he had walked to Point C all by himself. He understood that, as far as his life went on that day, his own choices mattered more than Linda's choices. In fact, his own choices mattered more than the choices of the police, the district attorney, or the court because any one of his Better Choices would have led to a very different outcome for him. Had he chosen to use one of his Better Choices, Linda would not have hit him, the police would not have been called, and he would not have faced jail and the ire of the judge. Richard eventually acknowledged that his own choices were more powerful than any other person's choices in determining what happened to him on that day.

Choices chains are valuable because they show clients the power of their choices. "When you see yourself as a victim," I advise my clients, "you are pretending that your own choices aren't powerful. They are! All you have to do to show yourself how powerful your choices are is to complete a choices chain."

To their credit, Louis, Holly, and Richard were willing to look honestly at their choices and learn from their mistakes. Over the course of their counseling, each of them provided many examples of their ability to make Better Choices, and thereby choose a better life for themselves and the people who love them.

Character and Trust

Maintaining an abuse-free relationship requires character, the strength of will to choose to do the right thing when you want to do the wrong thing, and behaving in a manner that fosters trust. In the closing sessions of counseling, I often relate the following children's story as a way of explaining the task that lies ahead of every client. Over the years, I have been surprised at the powerful reaction of many clients to this simple story.

The Chicken and the Eagle

Years ago when I was a boy, someone told me this tale about chickens and eagles. It is an old story, and I have heard several versions of it over the years. The details changed depending upon who was telling the story, but the moral of the story was always the same. Here is the story as I remember it:

There was once a beautiful and majestic eagle. The eagle built a nest in the top of the tallest tree on the highest mountain in the region. In the nest, she laid a single egg. A wise and noble mother, the eagle kept constant watch over her egg and protected it. She spread her wings by day to shade her egg from the heat of the sun, and she kept it close to her body at night to fend off the frosty air. She rarely slept or left the nest to hunt because she knew there were other creatures living on the mountain that would eat her egg if they got the chance.

One day a hunter saw her soaring high in the sky. He saw how beautiful she was and made up his mind to kill the eagle for her fine feathers; such feathers were much prized by the people in the valley below. He followed her to her nest, and when he found her in the tree, he shot her. The next day the egg shook and cracked, and a baby eagle was born. The young eagle called and called, but his mother did not come. Struggling to the edge of the nest to call for her again, he fell from the nest to the ground below.

This should have been the last of the baby eagle. By chance, however, a farmer looking for one of his sheep happened to wander by. When he got near the tree, he heard the young eagle calling for his mother. Looking first at the nest above, and then at a few feathers on the ground left by the hunter, the farmer guessed what had happened. "You're alone now, young eagle, and your mother is no more," said the farmer. "I'll take you to my home where you'll be safe." The farmer put the infant eagle in his coat pocket. He carried the eagle to his farm in the valley below, and put the baby eagle in a pen with his chickens.

A couple of summers passed. One day, a man whom the people in the valley considered very wise happened to walk by the farmer's house, and there he saw something remarkable. Among the farmer's chickens was a beautiful eagle. The eagle pecked at the ground just like the chickens, and he walked and clucked just as the chickens did.

Walking over to the eagle he asked, "Eagle, why are you here among the chickens?" "Sir, I don't know what you mean," replied the eagle, "this is my family." "No," said the wise man, "this is not your family. You are an eagle! You belong to the sky, not to the earth." The wise man tried to teach the eagle, but the eagle did not understand. The eagle had never flown because no one had ever taught him to fly. He believed he was a chicken because he had always lived the life of a chicken.

The wise man thought for a long while. Then an idea came to him. He said, "Come with me and I'll show you who you really are." With that, the wise man picked up the eagle and put him on his shoulder. At first, it frightened the eagle greatly to be on the wise man's shoulder as he had never been so high above the ground, but at the same time, he felt something familiar stir deep inside him. "Where are we going?" asked the eagle. "We're going to the top of that mountain where the sun is setting," answered the wise man. "Why?" asked the eagle. "You'll see in time," said the man. The eagle asked many more questions, but all the wise man said was, "You'll see in time."

The sun set as they reached the place where the mountain meets the valley, and all night they climbed toward the summit. The eagle could not remember ever being so far from the other chickens and the security of the farm. As they climbed he heard the voices of other animals, both the howl of the hunters and the cries of the hunted, and it all seemed strange but somehow familiar to him. On they walked through the night. The sky was just starting to lighten when the wise man stopped. "This is where you belong," he said to the eagle.

The eagle was bewildered. The sky was getting lighter, but it was still too dark to see clearly. "I don't understand," said the eagle. "You will soon understand," said the wise man, as they stood facing the growing light in the east. Slowly, the sun rose, casting a golden light in the face of the eagle. The morning wind rustled his feathers. The sun rose higher revealing a valley far below, and the eagle felt his heart race in his chest. "You are an eagle!" shouted the wise man. "Fly!" With that, he threw the eagle off the mountaintop!

Terrified, the eagle tumbled over and over, falling to the valley below. The air rushed through his wings, and he fell faster and faster towards what seemed certain death on the valley floor. To his astonishment, something stirred in the eagle's heart. He heard himself cry out, and the sound he made surprised him. It was not a cry of fear,

but the screech of an eagle that the chickens heard in the valley below.
The eagle spread his wings and he flew. He soared higher and higher in
the morning sky. He understood. He was an eagle!

I ask clients to think of themselves as the eagle in the story.
What sort of ending would they write for the eagle? They could write an
ending that goes like this: The eagle no longer lived the life of a chicken.
He saw himself as an eagle and grew the heart of an eagle. He soared
high over the valley and became the noble creature he was meant to be.

Unfortunately, some people write a different ending for
themselves: The eagle returned to the life of a chicken. Learning to fly
was a lot of work, and his chicken friends thought all this flying and
soaring was silly. They laughed at him, and told him to knock it off and
act more like the other chickens. The eagle had thought and acted like a
chicken for so long that he had grown a chicken's heart. Soon, the eagle
was back to pecking the dirt and clucking with his chicken friends, trying
to forget his scary experience on the mountaintop.

"Do you see yourself as an eagle or a chicken?" I ask my clients.
"I admit there are a lot more chickens than eagles in this world, and in
some ways a chicken's life is easier. Chickens do not take responsibility
for their mistakes or try to figure out what is wrong. They just blame
others for their problems. They do not take responsibility for their anger,
and they are unwilling to learn or change. No one expects much from
them; they are only chickens, after all. They just go on living their
chicken lives."

There are relatively few eagles among us. Eagles have the
courage to acknowledge their weaknesses and the wisdom to correct
them. They have the strength to become a respected leader, rather than
a feared tyrant. Eagles have no fear of the criticism of chickens; an
eagle's commitment to growth is unshaken by the ridicule of the
chickens around them. Courage, wisdom, strength, respect,
fearlessness, commitment – that is what matters to an eagle. Most
important of all, eagles have strength of character; chickens have none.
The presence or absence of character is the easiest way to tell a chicken
from an eagle. Eagles have it; chickens do not.

Character

"Character," I explain, "means choosing to do the right thing
long after the desire to do the right thing is gone. In other words,
character is doing the right thing even when you are sorely tempted to
do the wrong thing. It is easy to avoid abuse and violence when
everything around you is the way you like it. Even chickens can do that.
But when you're really angry and those around you are treating you
unfairly or disrespectfully, it's hard to do the right thing, to be a leader,
use your skills, and stay in The Box.

Sometimes a partner may deliberately try to provoke you. Now is when you find out whether you are a chicken or an eagle. Do you have the strength of character to do the right thing? There have been people in my counseling program who talked like an eagle in their group. When the going at home was easy, they acted like an eagle. But when things at home got tough and they were really challenged, they returned to their old chicken behavior. They got out of The Box, ignored the skills and concepts they learned over months of counseling, and abused their partners again. It is easy to talk like an eagle. It is a lot harder to live like one. Living the life of an eagle takes real character."

Let me tell you about Joe, a former client of mine. Joe had as much character as any person I have ever met. Before I met Joe, he had lived a chicken's life. In fact, Joe was the head chicken in his neighborhood. Active in gangs since childhood, violence was all he had ever known. He was not just violent and abusive – Joe was a killer, and even the other gang members feared him. His life was a revolving door of crime, violence, and prison terms. As one would expect, Joe was also abusive to his wife and children. He was a chicken's chicken.

Joe came to counseling as a condition of his parole after serving several years of a prison sentence. He was not a youngster any more. Joe was in his thirties, and he was tired of his chicken life. Joe talked about his wife and children in his sessions. He said he wanted to be part of their lives, and that he was determined to do whatever it took to be a good husband and a real father to his kids. Joe wanted to be an eagle. Privately, I doubted that he had the character to change, to live an eagle's life. After all, like the eagle in the story, all Joe knew was the life of a chicken.

Joe surprised me. As the weeks and months went by, he participated constructively in his group and took his counseling very seriously. Joe took responsibility for his choices and set a positive example for others in the program. His crudely written homework assignments were almost illegible, but there was sound understanding and application of the concepts and skills that he was learning. I had to admit that Joe seemed to be transforming himself into an eagle, but the story he told us one week astonished everyone, including me. Joe related the following story in his group, which I have written as best as I recall it.

Joe's Test of Character

"I took my family to see a movie that my kids wanted to see," said Joe. "There were four or five teenage guys – "wannabe gangsters" – sitting a few rows behind us, and they were talking loudly, swearing, and cracking jokes during the previews. I tried to ignore them, but I felt myself getting mad. My wife and kids were really looking forward to seeing the movie, and I wanted them to have a good time. Besides, it cost a lot of money to see it. I used self-talk to calm down, but these guys kept talking. I felt my wife squeeze my hand. I think she knew I was getting mad and she was afraid what I might do. She didn't want me to get in any trouble."

"The movie started and these guys just got louder. I knew my kids couldn't hear the movie. I think the other people there were afraid to say anything, so I stood up and told them to knock it off. I didn't yell at them; I just told them to be quiet so my kids could hear the movie.

They quieted down after that, but then they started throwing popcorn and stuff and some of it hit my kids. I saw my warning signs. Mainly, I started to think about ways to hurt these guys, and I knew I had to get myself out of there or I was going to get out of The Box. I had to think about what to do. I got my family up and we went to the very back of the theatre where we could be alone. That seemed to solve the problem and we watched the rest of the movie in peace.

"When the movie was over I told my wife and kids to stay in their seats until everyone left. I didn't want any more trouble or to have another confrontation with those guys. But those guys didn't leave with the other people. They waited until everyone left and then came up the stairs to where we were sitting. I thought, *well, here we go.* Part of me said a real man doesn't take this shit! I've had enough. These punks asked for it and now I'm going to 'f' them up like I used to do. But another part of me said *no, stay calm*. Think of my wife and kids. They need me, and I want to be with them. These guys aren't worth my time. (Joe meant the time he would have to do if he violated his parole by getting in a fight.) The guys came up to me and stood in front of my chair, and one of them threatened me by flashing gang signs. They did this right in front of my wife and kids! I wanted to kill them!"

This was a true test of Joe's character. Part of him did not want to do the right thing anymore. His prior life as a chicken told him to go one way; his recent life as an eagle told him to go another. He had to choose to continue living like an eagle, or to return to the life of a chicken. Conflicting thoughts ran through his head. He alone had to choose.

I had underestimated Joe. When the going got tough, he spread his wings and flew. He stayed in The Box. He was an eagle, and he proved that he had the character to live an eagle's life. He thought about this as he walked to the car with his family. He really had changed. In the past, he would have been walking to a police car while his wife and kids looked on. Now things were different. He had the skills and the character to choose a better life, both for himself and for his family. Joe's group members were amazed that he had been able to keep his head in the face of such provocation, and they congratulated him. One of the newer group members said, "Hell, I wouldn't have taken that shit.

I would have kicked their ass then tried to get away!" Joe just looked him in the eye without saying a word. Some chickens will never understand why eagles want to fly.

Your Partner's Trust

"Dr. Adams, I haven't hit my wife in three months and she still doesn't trust me! How long is this going to take?" The client who asked this question was obviously frustrated. He had abused his wife for years, but seemed to think that after three months of semi-responsible behavior he should get a prize or something. Clients must understand that regaining trust is not easy. It is easier to lose trust than to get it back. Once lost, trust returns slowly, if it returns at all.

"You lose trust," I explain, "by getting out of The Box. Every 'out of The Box' incident erodes the trust that your partner has in you. How do you get trust back? Well, sometimes you can't. If there have been a lot of out of The Box incidents, or if the incidents have been severe, your partner and children may never trust you again. Your partner may leave you. If that is what has happened to you, don't blame them. That is the price for acting like a child. All you can do is take responsibility for your actions, and master the skills and concepts you learn so that you do not make the same mistakes in your next relationship. If you are still with your partner, getting back the trust you have lost should be foremost on your mind. The only way to get trust back is to stay in The Box and let the clock run."

Words and promises are not enough to win trust. Words are cheap; promises are easy to make and easy to break. Only by choosing to stay in The Box will clients regain their partners' trust. Someone once said, "What you do speaks so loud I can't hear a word you're saying." Advise clients that they will have to prove themselves trustworthy repeatedly, and that winning trust back is a gradual process that takes time. For clients who want something more concrete, here's a two-step process that's almost guaranteed to get results:

Step One: Do something to show your partner that you are trustworthy.

Step Two: Now do it again a thousand times.

"You didn't expect it to be easy, did you?" I ask. "If you start to doubt that getting back trust is worth the effort, pull out your Big Picture and read it. It should become clear that your efforts are worthwhile. Be warned, however, about the dangers of claiming to be an eagle and then returning to roost with the chickens. In other words, if you claim to have changed and then get out of The Box, trust will be harder than ever to win. Getting out of The Box, even if it is only once every hundred times you get angry, will generate mistrust. If you are going to win your family's trust and maintain an abuse-free relationship, you have to commit yourself to staying in The Box from now on, and from now on means forever."

Closing Comments

In this book I have tried to provide the reader with the concepts and treatment strategies that have demonstrated their effectiveness in a clinical setting with the majority of clients the majority of the time. The issues addressed here provide a solid foundation for clinicians faced with the problem of partner abuse. In closing, I would like to speak to the widely held perception among mental health professionals that abusive clients are unresponsive to treatment. Many of my colleagues avoid such clients in the belief that they simply do not change.

A few days ago, for example, I met with Larry and Rachel. Larry started counseling several weeks ago to address his abusive behavior toward Rachel. Larry presented with an extensive history of explosive outbursts of anger that included episodes of verbal and physical assaults upon Rachel; the assaults were increasing in frequency and severity. Rachel's history included treatment for bipolar disorder by her psychiatrist, psychiatric hospitalizations (largely due to medical non-compliance), impulsive and irresponsible behavior in a variety of areas, anger outbursts of her own, and substance abuse. Rachel's substance abuse was a significant issue and source of conflict in the marriage; a medical professional, she had lost her employment due to abuse of prescription drugs.

Despite the daunting problems in their relationship, Larry and Rachel loved each other. Both adamantly declared their desire to stay together and work through their issues rather than separate. Rachel is currently receiving appropriate treatment for her issues. She actively participates in a substance abuse program, attends individual counseling, and cooperates with her psychiatrist to manage her medication. Larry participates in individual counseling and actively participates in a specialized group for partner abuse. He expresses a firm commitment to do whatever he has to do in order to stop his abusive behavior.

Larry's prognosis is very optimistic. Over the weeks, all physical abuse has stopped. He still gets out of The Box and verbally abuses Rachel, although the frequency and intensity of these incidents are declining. Larry acknowledges the incidents, and more importantly, assumes full responsibility for them. He makes no effort to blame Rachel for his abusive conduct. Larry learns from his mistakes, and demonstrates increasing skill in evaluating his behavior to identify areas that need correction. Though sometimes discouraged, he continues to participate constructively in his individual and group sessions.

In short, Larry is exactly where I would expect him to be at this stage of counseling. He is increasingly knowledgeable, but he is not yet proficient. He is making his first fumbling attempts to apply the skills and concepts that he will eventually master and rely upon for the rest of his life. Larry is following the learning curve that I have seen thousands of others follow over the years.

Recently, Rachel asked to see me privately. Tearful and distraught as she spoke, Rachel said her psychiatrist had advised her to get out of her marriage now. "It is only a matter of time," he told her, before Larry hits her again. The counselors at her substance abuse program also encouraged her to divorce her husband, and suggested that her sobriety depended on it. She had to choose, they suggested, between sobriety and her marriage. Through some mystic clairvoyance that I have never been party to, her counselors were unanimous in their opinion that Rachel's goal of an abuse-free relationship with her husband is idealistic and hopeless. "Wake up and smell the roses," they implied. Abusive behavior is not amenable to treatment. Your hope is ill founded. Larry will never change. Give up. It is only a matter of time. Get out now.

Unfortunately, there is more asserted about partner abuse than has ever been demonstrated. Myths abound. There exists a pervasive notion in our profession that abusive conduct is unresponsive to any form of intervention – that abusive clients are different from other people. The prognosis for abusive men and women is not guarded; it is decidedly pessimistic. As a clinician who has worked in this field for many years, I am not surprised when abusive clients stop abusing. To the contrary, I am surprised when they do not stop abusing. Given a treatment protocol that provides clients with sound concepts and needed skills, I assure you that reasonably motivated people can and do stop abusing.

This is not to say that treatment is successful for every abusive client. Some people simply refuse to change, and they will make their position abundantly clear in the first six weeks of counseling. Among such clients, out of The Box incidents will continue unabated, and when discussing them they doggedly insist upon critiquing their partners' mistakes rather than their own. They deny responsibility for their choices, and flash with anger at the counselor's suggestion that they alone are responsible for their abusive conduct. They understand the concepts behind the strategy; they just decline to apply them. It is my experience, however, that such clients are the exception rather than the rule. A modicum of motivation warrants optimism.

Most clients follow a relatively predictable course in treatment. I have found, for example, that physical violence typically stops long before verbal abuse. The typical course of treatment is six to twelve months. Six months into treatment, the majority of clients have achieved important objectives. New incidents of physical assault are unlikely. Incidents of verbal abuse are few, and when they do occur, they are of less intensity and of shorter duration. The client acknowledges these setbacks when they occur, and shows genuine remorse. They are usually surprised by their conduct and disappointed in themselves; they thought they were beyond such outbursts. They assume responsibility for their behavior, and they demonstrate increasing competence in evaluating the incidents and taking corrective action quickly and efficiently. The process is slow, arduous, and time-consuming. Set-backs are common, but the goal is worthy of the effort.

David is a client approximately six months into his counseling program. His grandmother is terminally ill, and he spends a lot of time comforting her in the hospital. Recently, he stayed with his grandmother until the early hours of the morning. Upon leaving the hospital, he felt depressed and lonely, and although it was late, he drove to his girlfriend's apartment to talk. Arriving at her apartment, David heard sounds of a party inside. Looking through her window, David saw his girlfriend and several other people in various stages of undress. He watched as they took turns doing lines of cocaine on the coffee table.

"I was pissed," he said. "I wanted to bust the door in and beat the hell out of everybody." Beating the hell out of everybody was more than idle thought; David is a professional boxer. "Then I thought about The Box," he continued, "and how nothing good ever happens when I get out of The Box. I just got back in my car and drove home." David made a choice consistent with his goal of a non-violent lifestyle (at least as far as his personal relationships are concerned). Consistently choosing to stay in The Box will allow him to maintain it, as so many have done in the past.

And what of Larry and Rachel? Their future is still undecided. Will events prove Rachel's counselors right, or will they justify her hope for an abuse-free life with Larry? I don't have a crystal ball, but if I were a betting man, I would place my money on Larry and Rachel's marriage. Knowing them as I do, I think the odds are on their side.

References and Suggested Reading

Adams, W. E. (2003). *The Choices Program: How to Stop Hurting the People Who Love You.* W. E. Adams, copyright 2003. (Ordering information available on this website.)

Adamson, J. L., & Thompson, R. A. (1998). Coping with interparental verbal conflict by children exposed to spouse abuse and children from non-violent homes. *Journal of Family Violence, 13,* 213-232.

Brookoff, D. (1997). Drugs, alcohol, and domestic violence in Memphis. *National Institute of Justice Research Preview.* Washington, DC: U.S. Department of Justice.

Buzawa, E. S., & Buzawa, C. G. (2003). *Domestic violence: The criminal justice response (3rd Ed.).* Thousand Oaks, CA: Sage.

Carlson, B. E. (1984). Children's observations of interpersonal violence. In A. Roberts (Ed.), *Battered women and their families: Intervention strategies and treatment programs.* New York: Springer.

Giles-Sims, J. (1985). *Wife battering: A systems theory approach.* New York: Guilford.

Greenfeld, L. A., Rand, M. R., Craven, D., Flaus, P. A., Perkins, C. A., Ringel, C., Warhol, G., Matson, C., & Fox, J. (1998). *Violence by intimates: Analysis of data on crimes by current or former spouses, boyfriends and girlfriends (NCJ-167237).* Washington, DC: U.S. Department of Justice, Bureau of Justice Statistics.

Jacobson, N. S. & Gottman, J. M. (1998). *When men batter women: New insights into ending abusive relationships.* New York: Simon & Schuster.

Kadushin, A. & Martin, J. A. (1981). *Child abuse: An interactive event.* New York: Columbia University Press.

Kalmuss, D. (1984). The intergenerational transmission of marital aggression. *Journal of Marriage and the Family, 46,* 11-19.

Kaufman Kantor, G. K. & Straus, M. A. (1990). Response of victims and the police to assaults on wives. In M. A. Straus & R. J. Gelles (Eds.), *Physical violence in American families: Risk Factors and adaptations in 8,145 families (pp. 473-486).* New Brunswick, NJ: Transaction.

Kosky, R. (1983). Childhood suicidal behavior. *Journal of Child Psychology and Psychiatry and Allied Disciplines, 24,* 457-468.

Roberts, A. R. (1987). Psychosocial characteristics of batterers: A study of 234 men charged with domestic violence offenses. *Journal of Family Violence, 2,* 81-93.

Roberts, A. R. (1988). Substance abuse among men who batter their mates. *Journal of Substance Abuse Treatment, 5,* 83-87.

Spaccarelli, S., Coatworth, J. D., & Bowden, B. S. (1995). Exposure to serious family violence among incarcerated boys: Its association with violent offending and potential mediating variables. *Violence and Victims, 10,* 163-182.

Straus, M. A., & Gelles, R. J. (1990). *Physical violence in American families: Risk factors and adaptations to violence in 8,145 families.* New Brunswick, NJ: Transaction.

Straus, M. A. (1980). Wife beating: How common and why. In M. A. Straus & G. T. Hotaling (Eds.), *Social causes of husband wife violence.* Minneapolis: University of Minnesota Press.

Straus, M. A., Gelles, R. J., & Steinmetz, S. K. (1980). *Behind closed doors: Violence in the American family.* Garden City, NY: Anchor.

Tjaden, P. & Thoennes, N. (1998). *Prevalence, incidence, and consequences of violence against women: Findings from the National Violence Against Women Survey.* Washington, DC: National Institute of Justice.

Tjaden, P. & Thoennes, N. (2000). *Extent, nature, and consequences of intimate violence: Findings from the National Violence Against Women Survey.* Washington, DC: National Institute of Justice.

Willson, P., McFarlane, J., Malecha, A., Watson, K., Lemmey, D., Schultz, P., Gist, J., & Fredland, N. (2000). Severity of violence against women by intimate partners and associated use of alcohol and/or illicit drugs by the perpetrator. *Journal of Interpersonal Violence, 15,* 996-1008.

Contacting Dr. William E. Adams:

I am happy to respond to questions or comments about the treatment strategies presented in this book. You may purchase additional copies of this book or purchase the companion treatment manual, ***The Choices Program: How to Stop Hurting the People Who Love You*** online at Amazon.com. I can be contacted at:

William Adams, Ph.D.
1945 Palo Verde Avenue, Suite 204
Long Beach, CA 90815
Phone: (562) 799-1226
Website: drwilliamadams.com
Email: dv.doc@verizon.net

Made in the USA
Charleston, SC
17 August 2016